JEWISH IDENTITY AND CIVIL RIGHTS IN AMERICA

What does it mean to be Jewish? This ancient question has become a pressing civil rights controversy. Despite a recent resurgence of anti-Semitic incidents on American college campuses, the U.S. Department of Education's powerful Office for Civil Rights (OCR) has been unable to protect Jewish students. This failure has been a problem not of execution but of conceptualization. The OCR has been unable to address anti-Jewish harassment because it lacks a coherent conception of either Jewish identity or anti-Jewish hatred. Given jurisdiction over race and national origin but not religion, federal agents have had to determine whether Jewish Americans constitute a race or national origin group. They have been unable to do so. This has led to enforcement paralysis, as well as explosive internal confrontations and recriminations within the federal government. This book examines the legal and policy issues behind the ambiguity involved with civil rights protections for Jewish students. Written by a former senior government official, this book reveals the extent of this problem and presents a workable legal solution.

Kenneth L. Marcus holds the Lillie and Nathan Ackerman Chair in Equality and Justice in America at the City University of New York's Bernard M. Baruch College School of Public Affairs. He is also Director of the Initiative on Anti-Semitism and Anti-Israelism at the Institute for Jewish and Community Research. Previously, Marcus was the Staff Director at the U.S. Commission on Civil Rights.

T0370780

Jewish Identity and Civil Rights in America

Kenneth L. Marcus

CUNY Baruch College, School of Public Affairs
Institute for Jewish & Community Research

CAMBRIDGE
UNIVERSITY PRESS

CAMBRIDGE UNIVERSITY PRESS
Cambridge, New York, Melbourne, Madrid, Cape Town, Singapore,
São Paulo, Delhi, Dubai, Tokyo, Mexico City

Cambridge University Press
32 Avenue of the Americas, New York, NY 10013-2473, USA

www.cambridge.org
Information on this title: www.cambridge.org/9780521127455

First published 2010
Reprinted 2010

A catalog record for this publication is available from the British Library.

Library of Congress Cataloging in Publication Data

Marcus, Kenneth L.
  Jewish identity and civil rights in America / Kenneth L. Marcus.
    p.   cm.
  Includes index.
  ISBN 978-0-521-76673-9 (hardback) – ISBN 978-0-521-12745-5 (paperback)
  1. Jews – United States – Identity.   2. Jews – Civil rights – United States.
  3. Antisemitism – United States.   4. United States – Ethnic relations.   I. Title.
  E184.36.E84M37   2010
  973'.04924–dc22   2010022340

ISBN 978-0-521-76673-9 Hardback
ISBN 978-0-521-12745-5 Paperback

*For my sweet Stephanie, partner in all I do, and for my beloved
Shoshana, in the hope that she will never
know the problems described here.*

Contents

Acknowledgments

This book would not exist without Gary A. Tobin. He was the visionary who saw the need to write it, the entrepreneur who found the resources to support it, and the mentor who provided the encouragement to complete it. His wisdom, courage, strength, intellect, wit, and friendship were an inspiration and blessing throughout our collaboration. Since his untimely passing, this book has become a first feeble effort to fulfill his request that I continue the work that he began. Collaborations with institute colleagues Diane Tobin, Aryeh Weinberg, and Dennis Ybarra have been indispensable, as has been the support of the Kauffman, Koret, Marcus, Samueli, and Viterbi foundations.

The City University of New York's Bernard M. Baruch College School of Public Affairs provided a most congenial academic base for the writing of this book. Dean David Birdsell generously provided summer research support, Associate Dean Jonathan Engel graciously reviewed drafts, and faculty research workshop participants energetically discussed key sections. The graduate students in my fall 2009 seminar on "Anti-Semitism and Civil Rights Policy" proved to be excellent interlocutors, joining me as I wrestled with some of the vexing problems presented here. In funding the Lillie and Nathan Ackerman Chair in Equality and Justice in America, Irwin and Rosalyn Engelman generously supported not only my position at Baruch but also the excellent research assistance that I have received. For this last blessing, Amita Dahiya and Avital Eliason deserve especial thanks.

Three governmental institutions played important roles. The U.S. Department of Education's Office for Civil Rights and the U.S. Commission on Civil Rights provided the initial vehicles for my exploration of these issues, and my research was enriched from the outset by learned, passionate, and committed colleagues at both agencies. The records of the Office for Civil Rights and the files of Arthur Zeidman provided important documentation. The U.S. Holocaust Memorial Museum fostered this research further through a two-week workshop at its Center for Advanced Holocaust Studies. The participants in this workshop, including Chairs Alvin Rosenfeld and Bernard Harrison, were enormously helpful both during and after the session, and the museum's staff and library have been an excellent resource.

This research was further advanced by feedback received at the numerous venues at which portions or iterations were presented, including Berkeley, Boston College, Columbia, Irvine, Michigan, San Jose State, Santa Cruz, Southern California, Stanford, Wayne State, and Yale; the U.S. Congress and the Canadian Parliament; the Annual National Conference on Race and Ethnicity in Higher Education (NCORE); the Be'chol Lashon think tank; the Zionist Organization of America; and various chapters of the Anti-Defamation League. Some of these presentations were facilitated by other important organizations: Chabad-Lubavitch, the David Project, Hillel: the Foundation for Jewish Life, Scholars for Peace in the Middle East, and StandWithUs.

Among the many readers who commented on chapters, drafts, or interim papers, Richard Delgado, Gordon Hull, Kenneth Karst, Frederic Schauer, Peter Schuck, Rosemarie Tong, and Eugene Volokh were especially helpful. Various governmental officials and nongovernmental participants, including Susan Tuchman and Arthur Zeidman, provided important information and documentation. William E. Forbath and Susan Martha Kahn generously shared advance copies of their then-unpublished work. The usual disclaimers apply. This book reflects my own views rather than those of the various agencies with which I have been associated. The flaws remaining in the end remain mine alone.

Some of this material was published previously in a series of law review articles and benefited from the editorial assistance of their respective law review editors: *Jurisprudence of the New Anti-Semitism*, 44 WAKE FOREST LAW REV. (Summer 2009) 371; *Higher Education, Harassment, and First Amendment Opportunism*, 16 WM. & MARY B. RTS. J. (April 2008) 1025; and *Anti-Zionism as Racism: Campus Anti-Semitism and the Civil Rights Act of 1964*, 15 WM. & MARY B. RTS. J. (February 2007) 837. The former two articles were presented as symposium papers at Wake Forest University and the College of William & Mary, where organizers and participants provided great stimulation.

Above all, Stephanie Marcus provided the love and support without which nothing else would be possible. Shoshana Marcus, meanwhile, provided inspiration, distraction, and happy interruptions. To Stephanie and Shoshana, this book is lovingly dedicated.

Introduction

During the waning days of 2009, the Jewish world was torn over the case of a 12-year-old English boy whose application for admission to the prestigious North London Jewish School had been declined.[1] Identified in court documents only as "M," the boy was rejected because the school (confusingly known as "JFS") did not recognize the validity of his mother's non-Orthodox conversion. M's parents sued the school, taking his case all the way to the United Kingdom's highest court. Sitting on this case, Lord Kerr observed that the "basic question" on appeal could be stated simply: "Was M treated less favourably on racial grounds?"[2] Yet this simple question turns out to be exceedingly difficult. In the *New York Times'* assessment, "The questions before the judges in Courtroom No. 1 of Britain's Supreme Court were as ancient and as complex as Judaism itself. Who is a Jew? And who gets to decide?"[3] True enough.

But of all the ways in which this "ancient" and "complex" question could be raised, why did M's lawyers frame his complaint in terms of race? To the modern mind, the idea of a "Jewish race" recalls nothing so forcefully as the catastrophic experience of twentieth-century Nazi racial science and its antecedent forms of nineteenth-century pseudoscience. Under English law, however, even state-funded religious schools may give admissions preferences, when oversubscribed, to students who share their faith. What they may not do is discriminate on the basis of

---

[1] *R (on the application of E) v. Governing Body of JFS and the Admissions Appeal Panel of JFS*, UKSC 15 (2009). The school is also known as "JFS," which stands for the "Jewish Free School."

[2] *Id.* at 43.

[3] Sarah Lyall, *Who Is a Jew? Court Ruling in Britain Raises Question*, New York Times, November 7, 2009; available at www.nytimes.com/2009/11/08/world/europe/08britain.html.

race. Hence M claimed racial discrimination based on his mother's gentile ancestry. But are Jews a "race?" And is discrimination against Jews
(or gentiles) "racial?" "The difficulty of the present case," Lord Mance
observed, "is that the word 'Jewish' may refer to a people, race, or ethnic
group and/or to membership of a religion."[4]

This difficulty must have been felt in a peculiarly personal way by
the president of the United Kingdom's Supreme Court, Baron Phillips
of Worth Matravers. Lord Phillips had surprised the English legal community the year before when he announced that his own mother was of
Sephardic descent. This had led the local Jewish press to inquire, "How
Jewish is Lord Chief Justice Phillips?"[5] Before his dramatic announcement, Lord Phillips had no known ties to England's Jewish community.
Moreover, as the *Jewish Chronicle* wryly observed, Nicholas Addison
Phillips is "not a Yiddische moniker," and Lord Phillips' Royal Navy
background does not fit with the ostensible Jewish preference for wan-
dering on dry land.[6] Nevertheless, in light of Phillips' announcement,
his bushy eyebrows, and his legal training, the *Chronicle* was moved to
judge Phillips "guilty as charged": "88% Jewish!"[7]

As the *Chronicle*'s tongue-in-cheek treatment of this distinguished
jurist suggests, the question of Jewish identity is a live one not only in the
courts but also throughout the worldwide Jewish community. While this
question occasionally has been a source of humor, it also has been quite
serious. Some 30 years ago, one Mr. Seide, a toolmaker, complained
to England's administrative tribunals that he had been ill treated by a
co-worker.[8] When he tried to enlist another co-worker to support him,
management transferred him to a less desirable shift. Seide sued his
employer under the United Kingdom's Race Relations Act, which bans
racial but not religious discrimination. Here again, the question arose
as to whether anti-Jewish discrimination could properly be described as
"racial."

[4] *JFS*, UKSC 15 (2009), slip op., at 26.
[5] *How Jewish Is Lord Chief Justice Phillips?* THE JEWISH CHRONICLE, July 10, 2008;
available at www.thejc.com/lifestyle/how-jewish-is/how-jewish-lord-chief-justice-
phillips.
[6] *Id.*
[7] Phillips might find consolation in the fact that even Rahm Emanuel was adjudged
to be only 93% Jewish. *See How Jewish Is Rahm Emanuel? The Jewish Chronicle*,
November 13, 2008; available at www.thejc.com/lifestyle/how-jewish-is/how-jewish-
rahm-emanuel. Apparently, Emanuel's "Rahm-bo"-like behavior, his pungent linguistic tendencies, and his marriage to a convert precluded a perfect score.
[8] *Seide v. Gillette Industries, Ltd.*, IRLR 427 (1980).

In the United States, courts wrestled with this same question in the wake of the 1991 Crown Heights riot. An angry mob, believing that a Hasidic community ambulance had wrongly failed to treat an African-American car accident victim, marched to the Jewish neighborhood to exact vengeance. Yelling "there's a Jew, get the Jew," the mob randomly seized a young Australian Hasid named Yankel Rosenbaum, beat him up, and stabbed him to death.[9] The perpetrators, African-Americans, were convicted under a statute enacted to enforce the Thirteenth Amendment by criminalizing certain injuries inflicted because of a victim's race or religion.[10] In their appeal, the perpetrators argued that Congress lacked power to protect Jewish victims under this antislavery amendment because Jews are not among the "races" that it was intended to protect.

A few years before the Crown Heights riot, neo-Nazis had spray-painted the Shaare Tefila Congregation of Silver Spring, Maryland, with a number of anti-Semitic messages: "Death to the Jude," "In, Take a Shower Jew," "Dead Jew," "Arian [*sic*] Brotherhood," "White Power," and so forth. Congregants sued the vandals under 42 U.S.C.S. §1982, the successor to an 1866 statute that bans certain forms of discrimination on the basis of race.[11] Again, the perpetrators argued that Jews cannot avail themselves of an antiracism provision because Jews are not a race. Here, though, the irony was even more palpable because the perpetrators themselves were the ones who viewed Jews as racially distinct. One defendant testified that the point of the desecration was to give Jews "an insult to your race."[12] But are Jews really a race, and should the courts treat them so, when theories of racial distinctness are so frequently interwoven with perceptions of racial inferiority?

In such cases, Anglo-American courts generally have acknowledged both the complexity of Jewish identity and the variousness of anti-Jewish discrimination. Lord Denning once observed that a "'Jew' may mean a dozen different things."[13] For example, Judaism is a religion. Thus a convert from Christianity is considered to be a Jew. Jewishness is also an ethnic category: A man of Jewish parentage is sometimes described as Jewish, even though he may be a convert to Christianity. To some people, it may even suffice if his grandfather was a Jew and his grandmother was not. Indeed, Denning added, with a somewhat

---

[9] *United States v. Nelson*, 68 F.3d 583, 585–586 (2d Cir. 1995).
[10] 18 U.S.C. §245(b)(2)(B).
[11] *Shaare Tefila Congregation v. Cobb*, 481 U.S. 615 (1987).
[12] *Shaare Tefila v. Cobb*, 785 F. 2d 523, 529 (Wilkinson, J., dissenting).
[13] *Mandla v. Dowell Lee*, 3 ALL E.R., 1108, 1112 (CA) (1982) (Denning, J., opposing).

jarring flourish, Jewishness may be a racial category even in the biological sense: "The Jewish blood may have become very thin by intermarriage with Christians, but still many would call him a 'Jew.'"[14] In all four cases, the courts recognized a racial character inherent in either Jewish identity or anti-Jewish animus. Their reasoning, however, varied widely. No court was as bold, as blunt, or as controversial, for example, as Lord Denning in his anachronistic-sounding reference to "Jewish blood."

The U.K. Supreme Court, in a 5–4 decision against JFS, adopted what has been called a "categorical" approach. That is to say, the court held that Jews *as a category* constitute a distinct race within the meaning of the pertinent civil rights law.[15] "It is ... a fundamental tenet of the Jewish religion derived from ... Deuteronomy]," Lord Phillips intoned (as if in response to the *Jewish Chronicle*), "that the child of a Jewish mother is automatically and inalienably Jewish."[16] The court thus affirmed an appellate opinion that had announced: "It appears to us clear (a) that Jews constitute a racial group defined principally by ethnic origin and additionally by conversion, and (b) that to discriminate against a person on the ground that he or someone else either is or is not Jewish is therefore to discriminate against him on racial grounds."[17] In other words, anti-Semitic conduct may constitute racial discrimination because Jews are a distinct race. While the English law lords divided over whether JFS had discriminated racially in M's case, they were unanimous in their view that Jews are covered under the Race Relations Act as "a group with common ethnic origins."[18] Indeed, one dissenting law lord insisted that "*[t]here can be no doubt* that Jews, including those who have converted to Judaism, are an ethnic group" and that this proposition had long been "*indisputable.*"[19]

The U.S. Supreme Court, in the *Shaare Tefila* case, adopted a variation on this categorical approach. Like the English appeals court, the U.S. Supreme Court held that Jews may be considered to form a distinct

---

[14] *Lord Denning, Mandla v. Dowell Lee*, 3 ALL E.R., 1108, 1112 (CA) (1982).
[15] The "categorical approach" is described in Lisa Tudisco Evren, Note, *When Is a Race Not a Race? Contemporary Issues under the Civil Rights Act of 1866*, 61 NY UNIVERSITY LAW REVIEW (November 1986) 976, 998.
[16] *JFS*, UKSC 15 (2009), slip op., at 2.
[17] *R (E) v Governing Body of JFS*, EWCA Civ. 626 (2009); WLR (D) 209 (2009).
[18] *JFS*, UKSC 15 (2009), slip op., at 67 (Lord Hope, J., dissenting). Lord Rodger went so far as to say that the decision "produces such manifest discrimination against Jewish schools in comparison with other faith schools that one can't help feeling that something has gone wrong."
[19] *Id.*, slip op., at 87 (Brown, J., dissenting) (emphasis added).

"race" within the meaning of at least one civil rights statute. In *Shaare Tefila*, it was the Civil Rights Act of 1866. The *Shaare Tefila* Court did not, however, find that Jews constitute a racial group under either prevailing scientific norms or current popular understandings. Rather, the Court determined only that the 1866 Congress intended to include Jews within its broad prohibition on racial discrimination because Jews were thought to be a race at that time. In other words, the Court held not that Jews *are* a distinct race but that rather that they should be *deemed to be* for the limited purpose of interpreting a particular statute.

The United Kingdom's Employment Appeal Tribunal based the *Seide* case on a different, noncategorical rationale. That is, it did not hold that Jews *are* a "race" (or *should be deemed such*) under scientific standards, popular usage, original intent, or any other analysis. Instead, it used what might be called a "subjective approach," focusing on the character of the discriminatory conduct rather than the category of the victimized group. Under this approach, the tribunal announced that the question of civil rights protection turned on "whether what happened here was on the ground of [Mr. Seide's] religion" rather than on whether Jews are categorically protected.[20] If the perpetrators were motivated by religious bias, their conduct would not be covered under the United Kingdom's Race Relations Act. "On the other hand," the tribunal continued, "if it was on the ground of his race or ethnic origin, then it would be within the ambit of the Act."[21] In this way, the court established that anti-Jewish discrimination can violate a prohibition on racial discrimination, but only if it is motivated by a racial animus.

While U.S. and U.K. courts both generally have found that Jews are protected from racial discrimination, the American bureaucracy has not. This issue is also now playing out, repeatedly and badly, in the U.S. system of administrative civil rights enforcement, particularly in the corner of the federal bureaucracy where discrimination in the American university system is addressed. The U.S. Department of Education's Office for Civil Rights (OCR), responsible for ensuring equal opportunity in colleges and universities, has been forced to confront this question of Jewish identity in order to address the resurgent problem of contemporary anti-Semitism in American higher education.

In 2006, the independent, bipartisan U.S. Commission on Civil Rights charged that anti-Semitism had become a "serious" problem on

[20] *Seide v. Gillette Industries, Ltd.*, IRLR 427 (1980).
[21] *Id.*, at §§[22]–[23].

many American college campuses and directed OCR to aggressively enforce federal civil rights laws to address the situation.[22] OCR, however, has not prosecuted a single allegation of anti-Semitism, either before or after receiving the Civil Rights Commission's pointed admonition. Indeed, OCR dropped even its most notorious anti-Semitism case – *In re University of California at Irvine* – in a manner that has drawn considerable congressional and public criticism.[23] Those criticisms undoubtedly would have been more intense if the public had been aware of the extraordinary dissension, accusations, and recriminations that took place *within* OCR as *Irvine* was investigated.

What does it mean to be a Jew? What does it mean to be an anti-Semite? What does it mean to be the subject of Jew hatred? Like the great Sphinx, the elephantine federal bureaucracy has posed these three riddles to the Jewish community. In Greek mythology, the Sphinx strangled or devoured those who were unable to solve its riddles. In the United States, the price of failure is the loss of fundamental rights. If these riddles are not answered correctly, Jewish students at publicly funded colleges, universities, and public schools will be denied the protections of the most significant civil rights statute governing educational institutions. The federal bureaucracy has struggled with these riddles for decades. Its inability to solve them has paralyzed civil rights enforcement in cases of campus anti-Semitism. So far no one has stepped forward to provide the solution. This book answers the Sphinx.

The *Irvine* case was perhaps the most extraordinary of the many cases that have drawn public attention to the problem of anti-Semitism on twenty-first-century American college campuses. Over the course of several years, Irvine students alleged a pattern of harassment, intimidation, stalking, rock throwing, vandalism, and other disturbing behavior directed against Jewish students and supporters of Israel. Significant

---

[22] U.S. Commission on Civil Rights, FINDINGS AND RECOMMENDATIONS OF THE UNITED STATES COMMISSION ON CIVIL RIGHTS REGARDING CAMPUS ANTI-SEMITISM 1 (2006) (hereinafter U.S.C.C.R., FINDINGS AND RECOMMENDATIONS).

[23] See Letter from Charles R. Love, Program Manager, Office for Civil Rights, Region IX, U.S. Department of Education, to Dr. Michael V. Drake, Chancellor, University of California, Irvine, *In re UC-Irvine*, November 30, 2007; available at www.ocregister.com/newsimages/news/2007/12/OCR_Report_120507-Z05145157-0001.pdf (hereinafter *Irvine* or "Love Letter to Irvine"]; Letter of Senators Arlen Specter, Sam Brownback, and Jon Kyl to Secretary of Education Margaret Spellings, February 27, 2008; Letter of Representatives Brad Sherman, Steven Rothman, Linda Sanchez, Allyson Schwartz, and Robert Wexler, April 30, 2008; available at www.zoa.org/media/user/documents/publ/ushousetoedsecyretitlevi.pdf.

problems also had been identified at Berkeley, Columbia, San Francisco State, and elsewhere. These cases typically involved a mix of old-fashioned and more contemporary anti-Semitic discourse, often combined with intimidating or destructive behavior. Typically, the anti-Jewish rhetoric is complicated by at least some form of criticism of the State of Israel, raising claims of free speech or academic freedom. In its first major higher-education anti-Semitism case, OCR conducted a lengthy, extensive investigation to determine whether this activity violated Title VI of the Civil Rights Act of 1964, which prohibits discrimination "on the ground of race" in federally assisted programs and activities.[24]

Although OCR's career staff determined that a hostile environment had formed at Irvine, they were overruled by political appointees within the second George W. Bush administration.[25] This political reversal was ironic in that the first George W. Bush administration had adopted landmark legal guidance prohibiting precisely the activities that the second George W. Bush administration allowed. At a conceptual level, the reversal reflected a legal disagreement over whether anti-Semitism can be described, for purposes of affording civil rights protections, as discrimination "on the ground of race." On a broader societal level, it reflected disagreement about the extent to which anti-Jewish harassment should be addressed by the federal government.

The basic problem is that Congress has given OCR jurisdiction over race and national origin discrimination but not over discrimination on the basis of religion. Despite several more recent, helpful lower court rulings, the Supreme Court has narrowed the definition of "national origin" discrimination to describe only the "nation" from which one's family has emigrated.[26] Such narrow conceptions of nationhood clearly exclude Jews, who have lacked a common governing or political authority for most of their history. These two constraints force questions of educational anti-Semitism into the domain of "race." In order to receive full civil rights protections, victims of anti-Semitic harassment must argue that they have faced "discrimination on the basis of ... race." With this jurisdictional limitation in mind, OCR routinely rejects anti-Semitism allegations on the grounds that Judaism is only a religion.

This has created various anomalies. African American, Arab, Hispanic, female, disabled, Boy Scout, or older students who charge

---

[24] 42 U.S.C. §2000(d) (2000).

[25] This important fact has not been reported previously.

[26] The controlling Supreme Court authority is *Espinoza v. Farah Manufacturing Co.*, 414 U.S. 86 (1973).

their schools with discrimination can have their cases investigated by the federal government. On the other hand, if a Jewish student submitted the same complaint, it would be rejected on the grounds that Judaism is not a racial or national origin category. OCR officials might sympathize with the complaining student and might recommend that she try to hire a private attorney if she could afford one, but OCR would not open an official file, send a team of investigators, provide its own civil rights lawyers, or deploy its formidable federal law enforcement apparatus to protect the Jewish student in the same way it would for students of other ethnicity.

This is an extraordinary gap in American civil rights law.[27] Virtually all major civil rights laws enacted during the heyday of the civil rights movement covered religion as well as race, color, and national origin. This had been true of executive orders throughout the 1940s and 1950s, as well as statutes passed during the 1950s and 1960s. The landmark Civil Rights Act of 1964, which was the principal statutory tool used to end state-sanctioned racial segregation, covered race, color, and national origin in virtually all of its provisions – except for the critically important Title VI, which prohibited discrimination in federally assisted programs and activities, including most public and private colleges. The reason for this unusual omission was that Congress did not want to risk interfering in parochial schools and religiously oriented universities. As we now know, it would have been eminently feasible for Congress to prohibit religious discrimination in education while still carving out an exception for religious institutions. But it did not do so.

In the heat of the moment, however, when questions remained as to whether Congress would have the fortitude to enact the landmark legislation protecting African Americans, key congressmen decided that it would be more "expedient" simply to remove any reference to religion from the applicable statutory provision. The result, nearly a half-century after the fact, is that Congress still has never passed legislation to prohibit religious discrimination in American education. This is not to say, of course, that it is lawful for public elementary and secondary schools or public universities to discriminate against religious minorities. The First

---

[27] This lacuna is explored at greater length in two of my earlier articles, *Privileging and Protecting Schoolhouse Religion*, 37 J. LAW & EDUC. (October 2008) 505, and *The Most Important Right We Think We Have But Don't: Freedom from Religious Discrimination in Education*, 7 NEV. LAW J. (Fall 2006) 171.

Amendment to the United States Constitution guarantees all Americans the right to freely exercise their religion. The Fourteenth Amendment, which renders the First Amendment applicable to the states, also guarantees the equal protection of the laws. The lesson of the civil rights movement, however, was that constitutional rights have little worth if they are not backed by effective enforcement schemes. This is why the basic civil rights laws passed during the 1960s so-called second reconstruction period were concerned primarily with developing systems to enforce rights that had already been established by the Constitution.

Since 1964, Congress has passed more legislation protecting the civil rights of American students. Successive statutes protected the rights of women and girls, students with disabilities, students of nontraditional age, and even students who are members of certain patriotic youth organizations such as the Boys Scouts of America. Congress has not, however, added "religion" to the list of protected classifications. At the margins, some legislation has been helpful. For example, the Equal Access Act ensures that religious groups will, under many circumstances, have equal rights to enjoy the use of school facilities during noninstructional time (mainly after school). This does not, however, provide much protection to religious minority students who face discrimination or harassment, such as the creation of hostile environments within public and private universities. Some support may be found in other places, such as state law provisions or accrediting agencies' standards. The problem is that none of these authorities provide the protective apparatus of federal civil rights enforcement.

Ultimately, the fault for this governmental failure lies as much with the federal bureaucracy as with Congress. For Jewish students, the long-standing statutory omission should have been easily solvable. After all, it is well established that anti-Semitism may take several forms, including not only religious but also ethnic and racial animus.[28] The U.S. State Department, for example, uses Merriam-Webster's long-standing, influential definition of anti-Semitism as "hostility toward or discrimination against Jews as a religious, ethnic or racial group."[29] Moreover, the U.S.

[28] This observation is commonplace within the historical literature, but it also has been recognized within the U.S. federal courts, for example, by Judge Richard Posner in *Bachman v. St. Monica's Congregation*, 902 F. 2d 1259, 1260–1261 (7th Cir. 1990).

[29] U.S. Department of State, CONTEMPORARY GLOBAL ANTI-SEMITISM: A REPORT PROVIDED TO THE UNITED STATES CONGRESS (2008), 6 (quoting WEBSTER'S THIRD NEW INTERNATIONAL DICTIONARY (Philip Babcock Grove, ed.) (Springfield, MA, 2002), 96.

Supreme Court had defined the concept of "race" fairly broadly, at least as that term is used in the 1866 statute, to refer to shared "ethnic and ancestral" characteristics.[30] The problem is that OCR uses rather formalistic approaches to determining, within the meaning of the statute that provides the source of its authority, whether anti-Semitism is "discrimination on the basis of ... race." Since at least the Carter administration, OCR has concluded that it is not.

In 2004, OCR pledged for the first time to enforce federal civil rights law against those forms of anti-Semitism which are based on Jewish ethnic or ancestral heritage. Drawing on Supreme Court precedents, OCR issued policy statements announcing that anti-Semitic harassment is prohibited by Title VI's antiracism provisions. Naturally, OCR conceded that purely religious or theological discrimination is not prohibited. The agency announced, however, that discrimination on the basis of ethnic or ancestral characteristics is no less permissible against groups that also have religious attributes than against groups that do not. In an important guidance letter, OCR announced that it "recognizes that anti-Semitic harassment may include adverse action taken against individuals based on a victim's ethnic background or ancestry, notwithstanding the prospect that such harassment may constitute religious discrimination as well."[31]

Since 2004, unfortunately, OCR has not enforced this policy despite prodding from the Civil Rights Commission and from various members of Congress. Aside from the usual bureaucratic inertia – the tendency of government officials to be risk averse – OCR officials have had significant substantive misgivings. As a jurisdictional matter, OCR has been reticent to address discrimination against religious groups after Congress chose to exclude "religion" from within the scope of Title VI protection. More important, OCR has been reluctant to suggest that Jews are members of a biologically distinct racial group, given the genocidal ramifications that that theory had had during the last century. It was, after all, Adolf Hitler who had most eventfully insisted that "Jewry is without question a race and not a religious community."[32]

[30] See *Shaare Tefila Congregation v. Cobb*; *Saint Francis College v. Al-Khazraji*.
[31] OCR Guidance Letter from Kenneth L. Marcus Delegated the Authority of Assistant Secretary of Education for Civil Rights to Sid Groeneman, Senior Research Associate, Institute for Jewish & Community Research, October 22, 2004; available at www.eusccr.com/letterforcampus.pdf ("OCR Guidance Letter to IJCR")
[32] Alan E. Steinweis, STUDYING THE JEW: SCHOLARLY ANTISEMITISM IN NAZI GERMANY (2006), 7, quoting Letter of Adolf Hitler to Adolf Gemlich, September 16, 1919.

This subject is laden with irony. In the Crown Heights riot case, Judge Guido Calabresi observed that the constitutional provision banning slavery was being used against black people who, the jury found, were motivated by a belief that they had faced discrimination.[33] The greater irony may be that Jews have been denied protection based on a concern that inclusion could be more offensive or damaging than exclusion. In the Crown Heights riot case, prosecutors were forced, in seeking justice for a Jewish victim, to argue that Jews are among the "races" that the antislavery amendment was intended to protect. To protect Jews, in other words, it was necessary to resort to a racial discourse that proved so lethal only a few decades before. This is a pill that some would rather not swallow.

Additionally, although not explicitly articulated, some officials may be reluctant to extend civil rights protections to the socially and economically successful Jewish community. After all, many people view civil rights as compensation for disadvantages that other American groups have experienced to a far greater degree. Finally, efforts to combat anti-Semitism (like antiracism generally) have become victims of their own success. Since World War II, as one wag put it, Adolf Hitler gave anti-Semitism a bad name. As a result, much contemporary anti-Semitism (like other forms of racism) has become covert, systemic, and in some cases unconscious. This has made enforcement more difficult, particularly when perpetrators engage in speech protected under the First Amendment or the doctrine of academic freedom.

Ultimately, the resolution of OCR's problem may turn on whether policymakers can develop a coherent conception of what it means to be Jewish: whether, that is to say, Jews are a racial or an ethnic or religious group. This long and hotly debated question is hardly easy, safe, or politically uncontested territory for a governmental agency. In 1958, Israeli Prime Minister David Ben Gurion asked this question of the most prominent Jewish thinkers of his time in order to develop citizenship policies for children born to mixed marriages. They gave him scores of contradictory answers.[34]

---

[33] *United States v. Nelson*, 277 F. 3d 164, 191 n. 27. Judge Calabrese allowed that he would "make no effort to dissolve this irony, noting only that the post–Civil War amendments 'specific historical focus on black Americans and the amendments' generally egalitarian language are all too often in tension." *Id.*

[34] Eliezer Ben-Rafael, Jewish Identities: Fifty Intellectuals Answer Ben Gurion (Boston: Brill Academic Publishers, 2002). I am indebted to Susan Martha Kahn for this anecdote. See Kahn, *Are Genes Jewish: Conceptual Ambiguities in The New*

In a most uncharitable formulation of this conflict, philosopher Michael Neumann has identified what he calls "the venerable shell-game of Jewish identity: 'Look! We're a religion! No! a race! No! a cultural entity! Sorry – a religion!'"[35] Neumann's implication is that Jews, at any given time, advance whatever self-definition best serves their interests. This ignores the extent to which non-Jews also equivocate in the same manner, the conflicting perspectives within the Jewish community; the likelihood that Jews sometimes adopt self-conceptions contrary to collective interest; and the possibility that it may be perfectly appropriate for a community to define itself in a manner that best serves its members' well-being. It has been said that the question of identity is more problematic for Jewish Americans than for any other American group.[36] If so, it reflects what historian Edward S. Shapiro has called "the perplexing nature of what it means to be Jewish."[37]

One of the most emotional issues that the Jewish community faced during the last quarter of the twentieth century was the decision of the Reform movement in the 1980s to replace the traditional definition of what it meant to be a Jew. According to Jewish tradition, a Jew is a person who is born to a Jewish mother or who has converted to Judaism under Jewish law. The Reform movement broadened the definition to include persons born to a Jewish father and a gentile mother if the parents involved their children in Jewish communal activities. This change in religious doctrine may have been necessitated by the high incidence of intermarriage, but it triggered a public fury among many Jews who held other conceptions of what it means to be Jewish. In light of such controversies, public officials now understand that one must trod gently when issues of Jewish identity are raised.

The question is as difficult academically as it is politically. In one important essay, Canadian scholar Sara R. Horowitz asks, "[F]undamentally, what is meant by the adjective 'Jewish'?" Specifically, she inquires, is it a "system of beliefs? Race? Ethnicity?" Each category has some resonance, yet none of them seems completely satisfactory. This has led some scholars to conclude that Jews are "a religious community,

Genetic Age in *The Boundaries of Jewish Identity* (Susan Glenn and Naomi Sokoloff, eds.) (Seattle: University of Washington Press, 2010).

[35] Michael Neumann, *What Is Anti-Semitism?* in *The Politics of Anti-Semitism* (2003), 1.

[36] Edward S. Shapiro, *American Jews and the Problem of Identity*, 14 SOCIETY 14 (September-October 1997).

[37] *Id.*

a nation, an ethnic group, [and] a race."[38] Others, however, would take issue with this formulation as well because it is not at all clear that Jews are all of those things. With some chagrin, Horowitz ultimately exclaims that "none of these terms suffice, suggesting that the categories we use to sort knowledge may be off the mark, not only for things Jewish, but in general."[39] From an academic perspective, Horowitz may be right about this. Unfortunately, judges and government officials do not have the luxury of rejecting all the categories. They must choose. Under the reigning practices, if Jewish students cannot be pigeonholed into a protected legal category, they are excluded from the protections of antidiscrimination law.

It is for this reason that we ask the historically and emotionally fraught question as to whether Jews are members of a "race" within the meaning of Title VI. As we have seen, there are three primary ways of approaching this question. We can ask what Congress intended the term to mean when it passed the 1964 act. We can ask whether Jews truly are a "race" according to modern scientific notions. Or we can ask whether Jews are a "race" as that term is popularly understood and used in common parlance. Interestingly, as we will see later on, all three of these questions yield the same simple and immediate response, and it is incorrect. To address these questions in a serious fashion requires us to put aside facile characterizations and commonly held assumptions. We must plumb deeply into several fields of scholarship, including legislative history, anthropology, race theory, and cultural theory. Indeed, to address the question fully, we must explore the most recent scholarship in the one field that many readers (and this author) might most want to avoid: biology, including population genetic demography.

The *Shaare Tefila* case used an "originalist" approach to determine how broadly terms such as "race" should be construed. This approach requires historical investigation of the original public meaning that the term "race" had at the time that the applicable statute was enacted. Under this approach, one might ask whether Jews were considered to be members of a protected "race" when that legislation was passed during the summer of 1964. When the answer is phrased in this manner, it has a quick, easy, and intuitive answer, and that answer is wrong.

---

[38] W. Petersen, ETHNICITY COUNTS (New Brunswick, NJ: Transaction, 1997) 241.

[39] Sara R. Horowitz, *The Paradox of Jewish Studies in the New Academy*, IN INSIDER/ OUTSIDER: AMERICAN JEWS AND MULTICULTURALISM (D. Biale, M. Galchinsky, S. Heschel, eds.) (1998) 116, 124.

Many lawyers have assumed that the answer is "No" because the racial conception of Jews was widely rejected after World War II. As we will see, however, this intuitive response misreads the legislative history of the 1964 act. In fact, it has long been widely understood that the intent of the Civil Rights Act's sponsors was not to develop a new set of civil rights but to establish an enforcement system to guarantee rights that had been enunciated a century before – at a time when Congress and the public certainly *did* consider Jews to be included within civil rights legislation. The originalist approach to civil rights has been criticized, in part, on the ground that it ignores advances made by scientific theory. There is something unseemly, after all, about an approach that uses out-moded and discredited nineteenth-century racial theories to determine which American groups are entitled to civil rights protection.

The most obvious alternative is to determine whether Jews are a "race" as that term is understood by modern science. Here again, there is a quick, easy, and intuitive response to this reframed question, and once again, that answer is incorrect. A chorus of voices can be heard to proclaim that Jews are not a race because they are not a biologically distinct population group. In fact, this answer proves too much because the same logic could be use to demonstrate that no human group quali-fies as a "race" in this sense. As the American Association of Physical Anthropologists has proclaimed, "Pure races, in the sense of genetically homogeneous populations, do not exist in the human species today, nor is there any evidence that they have ever existed in the past."[40] But con-temporary anthropology does not deny that racial groups exist; it merely shows that racial categories are socially constructed. The question as to whether Jews are socially constructed as a racial group is rather com-plex, but it is addressed by recent scholarly advances in such fields as race theory and critical Jewish studies. Moreover, the death of biological conceptions of race may have been overstated or premature. New studies in population genetics provide interesting, if controversial insight into the question of Jewish identity. At the end of the day, however, scientific approaches are unsatisfactory because social scientists and geneticists neither can nor will provide a theory that gives sufficiently specific and concrete guidance to courts and enforcers.

It is for this reason that some jurists will turn to the public under-standing of race as the default position in light of inadequacies that are

---

[40] *AAPA Statement on Biological Aspects of Race*, 101 AMERICAN JOURNAL OF PHYSICAL ANTHROPOLOGIST (1996) 569, 569.

perceived to limit the theories of original intent and the prospect of a scientific resolution. Here again, as with the former two approaches to Jewish identity, the apparent nature of the public understanding is in fact illusory. In the twenty-first century, there is virtually no one – with the possible exception of certain white supremacists and other reactionary bigots – who would say that Jews belong to a separate race. The postwar ideology of racial homogeneity is simply too deeply ingrained in social orthodoxy even to permit the contrary response. Yet, when cultural practices are carefully examined, it turns out that public attitudes are entirely incomprehensible under any theory that does not acknowledge that notions of racial distinctiveness are profoundly held by both Jews and non-Jews. This can be seen in the social practices of "Jew-hooing," as well as in the intense public interest in the results of DNA tests used to confirm the "bloodlines" of marginal or emerging Jewish communities such as the sub-Saharan Lemba people.[41]

This focus on Jewish identity has significant limitations, however. Historical, scientific, and public meaning approaches to civil rights statutory interpretation all require bias victims to prove that they are members of groups that Congress intended to protect rather than placing the material burden on the defendant. This creates a host of equitable and analytical problems. Another course, although thus far rejected by the Supreme Court, would be to focus not on the victims but on the perpetrators of hate and bias acts. Under such a subjective standard, agencies such as OCR (as well as courts of law) would ask whether civil rights antagonists are racially motivated rather than asking whether the victims are members of a distinct racial group. This sort of approach has powerful advantages, but it also has generates its own set of very significant problems. Here again, the racial character of anti-Semitic conduct is often not apparent at first blush, but further analysis shows its depth and importance.

There is one final, subtle, and important, if previously unconsidered way of looking at whether anti-Semitism is "discrimination on the basis of ... race." We can ask whether anti-Semites inflict a distinctly racial *harm*. Instead of asking whether Jews are a race or whether anti-Semitism's perpetrators are racists, this third way asks whether the injuries caused by anti-Semitism are racial in nature. In other words, the third way is to ask whether Jewish college students suffer a distinctly "racial"

---

[41] The concept of "Jewhooing" is explained *infra* at note 22 of Chapter 10 and accompanying text.

injury as a result of the climate of anti-Semitism that exists on some college campuses. This might include, for example, injurious aspects of "racial formation" or "reracialization" that occur when groups are subjected to racial stereotypes, group defamations, and resulting forms of racial misperception. This complex question, in turn, requires us to consider recent work in cultural studies, race theory, and critical Jewish studies.

One of the fundamental findings of this book is that a major civil rights agency has been essentially paralyzed in its ability to enforce equal opportunity by its inability to resolve a problem that is entirely conceptual: that is, the meaning of the phrase discrimination "on the ground of race" as that term is used in a particular statutory context and as it is applied in a particular social context. This books aims to provide not only a clear and comprehensive answer to that question but also, and perhaps equally important, a wide range of analytical tools and apparatus for resolving similar problems of civil rights enforcement. As we will see, all reasonable approaches lead to the same ineluctable conclusion: Jewish students are entitled to the same equal opportunity as all other students, and OCR must conform its policies to recognize this principle. Along the way, we will explore a number of facts and theories that readers may find surprising.

I

The Dilemma of Jewish Difference

Late in the election year of 2004, a soft-spoken but determined civil rights lawyer named Susan Tuchman filed a complaint with the San Francisco regional office of the U.S. Department of Education's Office for Civil Rights (OCR). Tuchman, little known then even within the organized Jewish world, was the new director of the Center for Law and Justice at the Zionist Organization of America. Already an experienced litigator, Tuchman had been the first woman litigation partner at her Boston law firm before moving to New York the previous year. Tuchman's complaint described an extraordinary pattern of anti-Semitic intimidation, harassment, threats, and vandalism at the prestigious Irvine campus of the University of California. Within two years, this OCR case would catapult Tuchman to the *Jewish Daily Forward*'s prestigious "*Forward* 50" list of the people who are "making a difference in the way American Jews, for better or worse, view the world and themselves."[1] At the same time, it would demonstrate deep ambivalence, discomfort, and confusion in the way that the federal government perceives American Jews.

In her complaint, Tuchman Irvine with fostering a hostile environment for Jewish students in violation of the prohibition on racial and national origin discrimination contained in Title VI of the federal Civil Rights Act of 1964. With extraordinary specificity, Tuchman detailed that Jewish students had been physically and verbally harassed, threatened, shoved, and targeted by rock throwing; that Jewish property had been defaced with swastikas; and that a Jewish holocaust memorial was vandalized. Signs were posted on campus showing a Star of David dripping with blood. Jews were chastised for arrogance by public speakers;

---

[1] THE JEWISH DAILY FORWARD, *Forward 50*, 2006; available at www.forward.com/forward-50-2006/.

called "dirty Jew" and "fucking Jew"; told to "go back to Russia" and "burn in hell"; and heard people urge one another to "slaughter the Jews."[2] One Jewish student who wore a pin bearing the flags of the United States and Israel was told to "take off that pin or we'll beat your ass." Another was told, "Jewish students are the plague of mankind" and "Jews should be finished off in the ovens."

As Tuchman demonstrated, campus speakers were providing lectures that some Jewish students considered to be anti-Israeli, anti-Jewish, or both. OCR would later observe that many of these speakers were known for using "strong rhetoric" when criticizing the State of Israel and, in some cases, denying Israel's right to exist. In fact, this "strong rhetoric" included virtually the entire arsenal of traditional anti-Semitic propaganda: Holocaust inversion, racial hatred, ethnic stereotypes, conspiracy theory, physical intimidation, and even the medieval blood libel. In May 2004, one Irvine speaker had argued that "[t]his ideology of Zionism is so racist, so arrogant, based on so much ignorance." Two years later, another announced: "They are the new Nazis…. they're saying when you see an Israeli flag next to an American flag, they're saying we're with imperialism. We are down with colonialism. We are down with white supremacy." Jewish students were warned that "you settle on stolen land, you got to deal with the consequences." More bluntly, they were told that "now it's time for you to live in some fear because you were so good at dispensing fear. You were so good at making people think that y'all was all that and the Islamic tide started coming up."

Amir Abdul Malik Ali used Irvine's podiums to advance many of the most potent anti-Semitic stereotypes, calling Jews "Liars. Straight up liars, Rupert Murdoch, Zionist Jews…. " Malik Ali used the conspiracy stereotype to anticipate and defuse the inevitable anti-Semitism charge: "They say it's anti-Semitic if you say Jews control the media." He argued that "anti-Semitism" charges reflect Jewish arrogance and racism: "They have taken the concept of the chosen people and fused it with the concept of white supremacy." Malik Ali explained, "Once you take the concept of chosen people with white supremacy and fuse them together, you will get a people who are so arrogant that that will actually make a statement and imply that [they] are the only Semites. That's arrogance and it's the same arrogance they display every day and that's the same type of arrogance that's getting them into trouble today." Malik

---

[2] Except where otherwise indicated, this description of the *Irvine* case is based on OCR's official findings. See *Love Letter to Irvine*, at 2.

Ali culminated his remarks by reiterating the classic "blood libel," which Christians used from the Middle Ages onward to justify the indiscriminate killing of Jews: "You all definitely don't love children and you know why? Because you kill them."

Irvine's administration was, Tuchman argued, "silent and passive" in the face of these various incidents.[3] This, for example, was her view of the administration's response to a Jewish student who expressed her fears to several Irvine administrators, including its chancellor at the time. The student wrote, "Not only do I feel scared to walk around proudly as a Jewish person on the Irvine campus, I am terrified for anyone to find out. Today I felt threatened that if students knew that I am Jewish and that I support a Jewish state, I would be attacked physically."[4] Tuchman reports that the chancellor never responded to the student's letter.[5] One administrator who did respond recommended that the student seek professional counseling from the university's counseling center.[6] Irvine's administration, which has controversially squelched free speech and academic freedom in other situations, has vigorously defended not only the right but also the value of anti-Semitic hate speech. Vice Chancellor Miguel Gomez, for example, allegedly insisted that "one person's hate speech is another person's education."[7]

Tuchman's decision to file with OCR was neither casual nor accidental. The Civil Rights Act of 1964 establishes a remedial system to enforce the promise of equal protection. The system relies on three pillars: private-party litigation in the federal courts, U.S. Department of Justice (DOJ) enforcement in the federal courts, and administrative enforcement in executive agencies such as OCR. Private-party litigation is important because Congress never provides agencies with enough money to pursue all the antidiscrimination cases within their jurisdiction. Also,

---

3   Zionist Organization of America, Memo in Support of Its Title VI Claims Against the University of California, Irvine (Case No. 09–05-2013) (on file with the WILLIAM & MARY BILL OF RIGHTS JOURNAL). As one might imagine, Irvine's administration disagrees, claiming that it has taken several actions to respond to anti-Semitism on its campus.

4   Susan B. Tuchman, *Statement Submitted to the U.S. Commission on Civil Rights Briefing on Campus Anti-Semitism, in U.S. Commission on Civil Rights, Campus Anti-Semitism: Briefing Report* (2005) 15.

5   *Id.*, 14.

6   *Id.*

7   See Reut Cohen, *Jewish Students Discuss Vandalism with Chancellor*, CAMPUS J. (October 24, 2006); available at www.campusj.com/2006/10/24/jewish-students-discuss-vandalism-with-chancellor/. Gomez subsequently denied making this statement.

federal agencies, by their nature, seldom push the boundaries of the law as aggressively as private parties and public-interest advocacy groups are free to do. DOJ enforcement is also important because actions undertaken by the DOJ have an impact vastly disproportionate to the limited number of "pattern or practice" or public-interest cases actually prosecuted. Even the possibility of a DOJ investigation can have *in terrorem* effects.

In the education world, however, OCR is more important than either DOJ or private-party litigation. DOJ handles few education cases apart from aging desegregation matters and intervention in pending civil rights litigation brought by other parties. By contrast, OCR has jurisdiction over virtually all other federal civil rights cases involving education. For this reason, OCR processes approximately 5,000 cases per year, an extraordinary share of the total national civil rights caseload involving educational institutions.[8] Given the discretionary nature of DOJ's jurisdiction in this area and the costs of private-party litigation, a determination by OCR to decline jurisdiction frequently constitutes a death sentence for potential civil rights claims. If OCR does open an investigation, it is taken very seriously. OCR's leverage is that it can block the flow of federal funds to a college or school that violates civil rights laws. In light of the dependency of both higher education and the public schools on federal largesse, the power to control the federal financial spigot makes OCR a powerful player in education. When ethnic and racial minorities are harassed at schools and universities, OCR is the go-to federal agency. For example, over the last few years, several racial minority students have complained that they faced name-calling at their schools. OCR has investigated these cases and, where it finds the allegations credible, has required the schools to rectify the problem.[9]

When Tuchman filed her case in San Francisco, OCR's California regional director, Arthur Zeidman, was initially skeptical. The problem was not that Zeidman was insensitive to the problem of anti-Semitism.

8   U.S. Department of Education, Annual Report to Congress of the Office for Civil Rights, Fiscal Year 2007–2008 (2008) 4; available at www.ed.gov/about/reports/annual/ocr/annrpt2007–08/annrpt2007–08.pdf.
9   U.S. Department of Education, 2007–2008 Annual Report (2008) 18; U.S. Department of Education, Annual Report to Congress of the Office for Civil Rights, Fiscal Year 2006 (2006) 14; available at www.ed.gov/about/reports/annual/ocr/annrpt2006/report_pg13.html#resolutions-2; U.S. Department of Education, Annual Report to Congress of the Office for Civil Rights, Fiscal Year 2005 (2005) 14; available at www.ed.gov/about/reports/annual/ocr/annrpt2005/report_pg13.html.

A deeply religious man, Zeidman is an adherent to the *Lubavitcher* school of ultra-Orthodox Judaism. At the time, Zeidman had just left military service to accept his appointment to OCR, and he maintained the clean-shaven appearance that military discipline had required. Only a black *kippah* and *tzitzit* (inconspicuous under a suit jacket) revealed Zeidman's religious inclinations. Over time, Zeidman would return to the traditional *Lubavitcher* appearance, growing his beard out to considerable lengths and donning *tallit* as a regular part of his business attire. Zeidman also was, however, a lawyer of conservative predispositions, and he was uncertain as to whether Tuchman had sufficiently alleged facts that would bring her complaint within OCR's jurisdiction. There also was the question of timing: Had Tuchman filed her case soon enough, or was her case barred by OCR's timeliness requirements?[10]

Zeidman knew that this case would be hot and that it should be reviewed at the agency's highest levels. He could not, however, have known how hot it would get. His top lawyer, Regional Counsel Paul Grossman, cautioned him not to open the complaint until they could get guidance from headquarters.[11] Grossman, also Jewish, had been at the agency and its predecessor since 1972 but had made his reputation in the very different area of disability law. Like Zeidman, Grossman was inclined to dismiss the case for lack of jurisdiction and timeliness.[12] "It was a departure from OCR policy as I knew it," he said, "to address the issue of anti-Semitism on campus."[13] Grossman understood, however, that the case would be resolved under the agency's new policy on this topic.

Zeidman quickly faxed the complaint to me and my top staff in Washington, D.C. At the time, I was the highest-ranking official at OCR, and Zeidman knew that I was on the lookout for cases of this nature. This was not standard protocol. OCR resolves most cases within its 12 regional offices. These grievances expressed an extraordinary range of pleas by people who claim injustice in America's educational system: parents who believe that their children's disabilities are not properly accommodated, athletes who claim that women's collegiate or high school

---

[10] Zeidman describes his initial impression of Tuchman's complaint in *Deposition of Arthur C. Zeidman, Zeidman v. Spellings,* EEOC No. 550–2008–00363X, Vol. 2, February 25, 2009, 9–10. Unless otherwise indicated, subsequent citations to court papers, such as affidavits, declarations, and depositions, refer to this case.

[11] *Affidavit of Paul D. Grossman,* February 20, 2008, at 8.

[12] *Id.,* at 65.

[13] *Id.*

programs are inequitably treated, immigrants who want programs that will better facilitate their children's English language acquisition, minorities who argue that their children are denied educational resources that white children receive, advocacy groups that challenge various forms of affirmative action, and many others. Some of the complaints are quite specific and persuasive, whereas others are sketchy and weak.

KARST'S CONUNDRUM

This one, however, was different. To start, few complaints were as luridly detailed or as compelling as Tuchman's, which painted an appalling portrait of both anti-Jewish harassment and administrative indifference. The number of incidents, the detail with which they were presented, and the extent to which they formed a pattern of malfeasance were extraordinary for an OCR complaint. Of all the complaints that I had reviewed at OCR, only one or two remotely approached the power, complexity, and lawyerly craftsmanship that Tuchman had put into hers. More important, hers was the first to apply OCR's new policy on mixed ethnic/religious discrimination, which I had issued just months before, to a systemic case of hostile anti-Jewish environment in higher education.[14]

Before that summer, OCR's standard response in anti-Semitism cases was denial. This practice was based on a long-standing OCR determination, inconsistently communicated and applied, that no statute within OCR's jurisdiction prohibits discrimination against Jewish students. In Title VI of the Civil Rights Act of 1964, as we have seen, Congress gave OCR jurisdiction over race, color, and national origin discrimination but not religion. In part, OCR did not want to contravene the intent of Congress to exclude religious discrimination from Title VI. Like many federal agencies, OCR was anxious to avoid any appearance that its activities were *ultra vires* (that is to say, that they exceeded the jurisdiction granted by Congress and the president). This was not, however, the whole reason for OCR's position. After all, scholars have long recognized that anti-Semitism has not only religious but also racial and ethnic overtones. OCR could have investigated anti-Semitism under its racial and national origin responsibilities, which were well established under Title VI.

---

[14] Initially, Tuchman's intent was not to apply the new policy but to challenge the old one. When she filed her complaint, Tuchman was unaware that the OCR had recently adopted a new approach to anti-Semitism claims.

The main impediment was that OCR did not want to say that Jews are a "race." OCR officials understood that the weight of anthropologic and other social science scholarship precluded any such characterization. Aside from the science, OCR officials understood that the very notion that Jews might be a "race" has a long and ugly pedigree, resonant of Nazi racial dogma. The broader problem is that the concept of a Jewish race was frequently combined with ideas of racial inequality throughout the Western world. Even in English-speaking countries, the notion of Jewish racial separateness tended to carry with it, prior to World War II, the belief that races were hierarchically organized and that Jews were members of an inferior race, characterized by peculiar mental and physical pathologies.[15]

Nazi racial science, which was developed to provide an intellectual justification for the forced segregation of the Jewish people, ultimately rationalized the reduction of Jews to the status of an expendable subhuman species.[16] The relationship between racial conception and genocidal result in Nazi Germany was likely more than historical happenstance. Some sociologists have argued that anti-Semitism is most dangerous when it is rooted in racial conceptions of Jewish identity.[17] Their explanation is that the attribution of supposed Jewish transgressions to an intrinsic or biological quality is more likely to justify elimination of the Jews because such qualities cannot be changed in any other way.[18] For these reasons, among others, the whole idea of biological "races" has been highly suspect since World War II. While even some notable Jewish scholars, writers, and intellectuals embraced the notion of Jewish racial distinctiveness prior to the Holocaust, they largely suppressed or abandoned those views afterwards.[19] Since then, scholars have tended to emphasize that the idea of genetically distinct "races" is largely a myth,

---

[15] *See* Todd M. Endelman, *Anglo-Jewish Scientists and the Science of Race*, 11 JEWISH SOCIAL STUDIES (Fall 2004) 52, 53.

[16] ALAN E. STEINWEIS, STUDYING THE JEW: SCHOLARLY ANTISEMITISM IN NAZI GERMANY (2006) 63.

[17] Gunther Jikeli has recently contributed important insights to the development of criteria for evaluating the extent of anti-Semitism dangers. *See* Gunter Jikeli, *Assessing Manifestations of Antisemitism – Reflections on Criteria*, conference paper delivered at European Sociological Association, September 2009.

[18] Helen Fein, *Dimensions of Antisemitism: Attitudes, Collective Accusations, and Actions, in The Persisting Question: Sociological Perspectives and Social Contexts of Modern Antisemitism* (Helen Fein, ed.) (1987) 73–74.

[19] *See* Endelman, at 52–92.

concealing the broad commonalities among people and accentuating the social perception of difference.

OCR was caught in what legal scholar Kenneth Karst has called the "dilemma of difference." When the government (or anyone else) uses social categories such as "race" to protect individual rights, it tends to reinforce socially constructed differences either by ignoring them or by observing them.[20] That is to say, agencies such as OCR, which ensure equal opportunity by enforcing social concepts such as "race," often will have an unpalatable choice. When they use racial categories, they may sustain or "reify" the way in which people are socially perceived through these categories. In some cases, this "misplaced concreteness" bears potentially catastrophic consequences, as we have seen. On the other hand, when they fail to use these categories, they leave affected people without basic constitutional and statutory protections. Ironically, this allows bigots to reinforce, through blunter means, the very differences that the agencies may be unwilling to invoke.[21] As Martha Minow explained, "[d]enying the presence of those traits ... and their significance in society, deprives individuals of protection against discrimination due to outmoded or unsubstantiated conceptions of group difference."[22]

To understand this paradox, consider the tension that arises from the opening of anthropologist Raphael Patai and geneticist Jennifer P. Wing's classic (and pointedly titled) treatise *The Myth of the Jewish Race*. Describing the catastrophic effects of such categories, Patai and Wing begin their work by stating that the "systematic extermination of 6 million Jews by Nazi Germany and its satellites was the culmination of the notion that Jewish people form a race, with distinct inherited physical and mental characteristics, alien to the Gentile population in whose midst they lived, and overtly or secretly inimical to it."[23] In other words, it was the conceptualization of Jews as racially distinct that ultimately brought on the devastating consequences of the Holocaust.

In the very next sentence of their book, however, Patai and Wing characterize this same problem as "racial": "Modern European racial

[20] Kenneth L. Karst, *Myths of Identity: Individual and Group Portraits of Race and Sexual Orientation*, 43 UCLA L. REV. 263, 324–25 (December 1995).
[21] Martha Minow develops a similar argument about the dilemma of difference in *The Supreme Court, 1986 Term: Foreword: Justice Engendered*, 101 HARV. L. REV. 10, 21–12 (November 1987).
[22] *Id.*
[23] RAPHAEL PATAI AND JENNIFER P. WING, THE MYTH OF THE JEWISH RACE (1975) 5 (emphasis added).

anti-Semitism, which in the years of World War II led to the largest genocide ever perpetrated is a special sub-variety of a generic phenomenon
known as *'racism'*...."[24] The irony in this juxtaposition is palpable: Patai
and Wing first demolish the notion of Jewish "race" and then attribute
the destruction of Jewry to "racism." Having ascribed genocidal results
to the racial conceptualization of Jews, Patai and Wing appear to resort
to the very same error in characterizing Nazi anti-Semitism as an example of that concept. After all, "racism" is a bias or animus on the basis
of "race." In order to address this problem of group identity, Patai and
Wing appear to embrace the very concept from which they maintain that
the problem is constructed.

Historian Gavin Langmuir explained this problem in his well-known
book, *Toward a Definition of Antisemitism*. "Since the best present
knowledge so obviously invalidates the Aryan theory," he wrote, "it follows that we cannot use 'racism', the central and false concept of that
myth, to explain the hostility toward Jews ... displayed by the propagators of the myth."[25] In other words, since we do not share the Nazi
ideology, we cannot explain Nazi animus on the basis of that ideology.
In a sense, it is this very conundrum that prevented OCR from pursuing
cases involving anti-Semitism until 2004 – and which paralyzes federal
civil rights enforcement efforts to this day.

[24] *Id.*
[25] GAVIN I. LANGMUIR, TOWARD A DEFINITION OF ANTISEMITISM (Berkeley: University
of California Press, 1990) 313.

2

The Jewish Question in Civil Rights Enforcement

What happened in 2004 was that a Sikh man complained to the Department of Education's Office for Civil Rights' (OCR's) New York office that his son, a New Jersey junior high school student, had been beaten up and called "Osama." The father said that his son had been beaten up because of his "faith." Instead of simply dismissing the case, as they might earlier have done, the New York regional staff immediately forwarded the case to OCR's national headquarters. They knew that I was concerned about mistreatment of religious minorities as well as other vulnerable groups. In this case, I instructed regional staff that the father's statement of the nature of discrimination (*i.e.*, that it was based on his son's "faith") should be taken with a grain of salt. After all, the legal categorization of the assault is a question for OCR to assess independently.

Sikhism is one of the world's great religions. For purposes of enjoying civil rights protection, however, I emphasized that Sikhs also shared numerous ethnic characteristics, such as distinctive dress, music, and culture and common geographic origins. While Sikhism is neither a race nor a national origin when those terms are defined narrowly, Sikhism's adherents generally share the ethnic or ancestral characteristics that should suffice to bring them within the law's broad protections. When the New Jersey child was taunted as "Osama," it was not because his classmates disagreed with the tenets of the Sikh faith. Rather, the bullies were taunting him because of his (actual or perceived) ethnicity and geographic origins. To be sure, their taunts showed ethnic ignorance. This is neither unusual nor surprising in bias cases. Either the bullies confused Sikhs with Arabs, or they misunderstood Bin Laden's ethnic heritage, or they did not care. Ethnic and racial ignorance is common, and such ignorance should not become a defense for the discriminator. "Go ahead and investigate," I directed my enforcement staff. "This looks like a case of ethnic or racial harassment."

In deciding this case, I relied on two landmark U.S. Supreme Court cases that had established in 1987 that anti-Jewish discrimination and anti-Arabic discrimination, respectively, are barred by the Civil Rights Act of 1866 prohibition on racial discrimination in the formation of contracts and enjoyment of property. In the first case, *Saint Francis College v. Al-Khazraji*, an Iraqi-born Arab-American professor sued the college that had denied him tenure, arguing that the college had discriminated against him on racial grounds in violation of § 1981.[1] In the second, *Shaare Tefila Congregation v. Cobb*, a Jewish congregation sued vandals under § 1982 for racial discrimination after the defendants spray-painted anti-Semitic messages on the walls of their synagogue.[2] Deciding both cases on the same day, the Court reasoned that the term "race" (ironically not contained in the original statute) was understood broadly in 1866 to encompass many ethnic and ancestral groups, including Jews and Arabs, who are not understood today to constitute distinct racial categories. The Court had not addressed the question of whether the Sikhs are members of a distinct "race," nor had it applied its reasoning to Title VI or any twentieth-century legislation. Both opinions were quite short and relatively cursory on the central issues, perhaps because the decisions were unanimous. I concluded, nevertheless, that the Court's basic principles were entirely applicable to the civil rights of Sikhs under modern civil rights law.

Although I was unaware at the time, the United Kingdom's House of Lords had examined these questions at much greater length two decades earlier in the influential case of *Mandla v. Dowell Lee*.[3] In the early 1980s, a Sikh father sued an English private school under Britain's Race Relations Act of 1976 when the headmaster refused to admit the man's son unless he cut his hair and ceased wearing a turban. The trial court dismissed the case, and the Court of Appeals affirmed, on the ground that Sikhism is a religion and not a race. Like Title VI, the British Race Relations Act does not bar religious discrimination. Interestingly, the lower British courts interpreted this omission similarly to the way in which OCR had interpreted the analogous Title VI omission prior to my tenure.

---

[1]   481 U.S. 604 (1987).
[2]   Id. at 615.
[3]   [1983] 2 AC 548 24.

The House of Lords reversed the lower courts' decision, holding that Sikhs are members of a "racial group" as that term is defined within the Race Relations Act of 1976. As Lord Fraser of Tullybelton observed, "Sikhs are a group defined by reference to ethnic origins for the purpose of the Act of 1976, although they are not biologically distinguishable from the other peoples living in the Punjab." The Lords granted the Sikh plaintiff's appeal, ruling that the school had committed unlawful discrimination by refusing to admit his son. The Lords' reasoning was based on the language of the Race Relations Act, which defined "racial group" as a "group of person defined by reference to colour, race, nationality or ethnic or national origins...."[4] As the *Mandla* case instructs, Parliament added the terms "ethnic origins" and "national origins" to the definition of "racial group" in order to "include groups whose racial characteristics were different from other groups, but who did not conform clearly to the main biological racial groups, in order to avoid difficulty of definition and proof." What groups could Parliament or the House of Lords have had in mind? The "most obvious case of a group falling into this category," the *Mandla* court observed, is Jews.

The reason, in the court's view, is that Jews are "regarded by themselves as a religion, but regarded by many others as a race." In light of the "centuries of discrimination and hatred" that Jews have endured, the Lords explained, it was "unthinkable that Parliament would have passed a Race Relations Act which did not afford protection for the Jews." More recently, in her majority opinion in the *JFS* case, Lady Hale reiterated this point, insisting that "No Parliament, passing legislation to protect against racial discrimination in the second half of the twentieth century, could possibly have failed to protect the Jewish people, who had suffered so unspeakably before, during and after the Holocaust."[5] Parliament resolved Karst's conundrum by including Jews as a "racial group" for purposes of assigning protection while

---

4   The Act's operative language was taken from the International Convention on the Elimination of All Forms of Racial Discrimination (CERD). The CERD is binding on member nations such as the United Kingdom and the United States. This raises some interesting questions. For imply OCR's current interpretation example, does that Congress' failure to protect Jewish and certain other minority groups in educational institutions is a violation of U.S. international treaty obligations. Alternatively, should Title VI be interpreted in a manner which avoids violation of U.S. international commitments?

5   [2009] UKSC 15, slip op., at 24.

defining the relevant terms in such a way that Jews were not necessarily defined as a "race." It was something of a fudge, but it seems
to have worked. The British courts now view Jews as a "race" for
purposes of extending civil rights protections. For that matter, the
broad definition devised to encompass Jews also has brought Sikhs
within its sphere.

From the perspective of international law, it is also "unthinkable"
that Jews could be denied the protections of antiracism provisions. For
example, it is well established that Jews are the paradigmatic example of
a "racial group" that the international Convention Relating to the Status
of Refugees is intended to protect.[6] The convention's drafters did not
define the category of refugees who are at risk for reasons of "race," but
the scholarly consensus is that their intent was to protect Jewish victims
of the Holocaust.[7] For this reason, the persecution of Jews because of
their "religion, perceived 'race,' and 'nationality'" presented the archetypical situation that the convention's framers intended to encompass.[8]
The theory underlying the post-Holocaust asylum regime was that persecuted Jews could avail themselves under several, and perhaps even all,
of the five enumerated grounds: religion, race, social group, nationality,
and political opinion.[9]

In the United States, the question is whether it is any less "unthinkable" that Congress would exclude Jews from one of its most important
civil rights acts. After all, American law had long recognized that the
Jewish people have been "the most vilified and persecuted minority in
history."[10] In the wake of the New Jersey Sikh case, I decided to issue
nationwide guidance to OCR's attorneys and investigators, as well as to
colleges, universities, and public schools. Despite resistance from some
career bureaucrats, Secretary of Education Rod Paige, to his credit,
backed me up on this, as did Under Secretary Ted McPherson, General

[6] 189 U.N.T.S. 2545, entered into force on April 22, 1954.

[7] *See, e.g.,* James C. Hathaway, THE LAW OF REFUGEE STATUS (Toronto,
Canada: Buttersworth, 1991), Section 5.1, p. 141; Sale v. Haitian Ctrs. Council, Inc.,
509 U.S. 155, 207 (1993) (Blackmun, J., dissenting) (observing that the convention
was enacted largely in response to the experience of Jewish Holocaust survivors).

[8] Daniel J. Steinbock, *Interpreting the Refugee Definition,* 45 UCLA L. REV. (February
1998) 733, 766.

[9] Tuan N. Samahon, Note, *The Religion Clauses and Political Asylum: Religious
Persecution Claims and the Religious Membership-Conversion Imposter Problem,*
88 GEO. L. J. (July 2000) 2211, 2214–15.

[10] W. Va. State Bd. of Educ. v. Barnette, 319 U.S. 624, 646–47 (1943) (Frankfurter, J.,
dissenting).

Counsel Brian Jones, and the senior leadership of the Department of Education. Educators needed to know that anti-Semitism cases were within OCR's jurisdiction and that anti-Semitism allegations would no longer be dismissed out of hand. Over the summer and early fall, I issued a series of policy statements announcing that OCR would assert, for the first time, jurisdiction to pursue claims alleging harassment of Jewish students, Sikhs, and others. These statements were issued, in somewhat bureaucratic legal jargon, as guidance on "complaints of race or national origin harassment commingled with aspects of religious discrimination against Arab Muslim, Sikh, and Jewish students."

Occasionally I am asked why, as a political matter, the George W. Bush administration chose to tackle this issue, in this way, and at this time. After all, the Bush administration had not seized a great number of civil rights issues. For example, the administration did not issue guidance on affirmative action or racially exclusive scholarships in the wake of the Michigan affirmative action cases *Grutter v. Bollinger* and *Gratz v. Bollinger.* Indeed, the administration issued no guidance on those cases until the end of the second Bush term, five years after these landmark cases were decided. Instead, the administration focused primarily on a few carefully chosen civil rights priorities, such as No Child Left Behind, religious freedom, and human trafficking.

The new policy was not adopted for political reasons. Rather, it genuinely appeared to be both legally correct and morally appropriate in light of the Sikh case and the resurgence of campus anti-Semitism. At the same time, the new anti-Semitism policy was consistent with principles that President Bush had personally endorsed. The president had spoken frequently about the importance of religious freedom and had developed a signature initiative relating to faith-based institutions. Moreover, while counteracting anti-Semitism is neither a liberal nor a conservative issue, contemporary anti-Semitism had been associated even more with extreme left-wing movements than with the extreme right. This made opposition to campus anti-Semitism a potentially appealing prospect for a conservative administration. These considerations were not a significant factor in the development of the new policy, but they were not unhelpful.

On June 24, 2004, I sent my top staff a guidance memorandum explaining the agency's new approach to such cases.[11] At the beginning,

[11] Kenneth L. Marcus, Delegated the Authority of Assistant Secretary, *Memorandum to Enforcement Directors and All OCR Office Directors re OCR Jurisdiction Over*

I acknowledged that "OCR's jurisdiction does not extend to religious discrimination."[12] However, I emphasized, "the existence of facts indicative of religious discrimination would not divest OCR of its jurisdiction to investigate and remedy allegations of race or national origin discrimination arising from the same general set of facts."[13] Concerned about the sensitivities that people have about the term "race," I focused on "national origin." In a salient example, I explained that "OCR would have jurisdiction under certain circumstances to investigate whether discrimination against an Arab Muslim or Jewish student [is] in fact prohibited by the Title VI ban on national origin discrimination."[14]

In retrospect, the position that I took on anti-Semitic discrimination, which some considered to be overly aggressive, was in fact deliberately quite moderate. In particular, each of my policy guidance documents emphasized that OCR did not have jurisdiction over claims that Jewish students had faced discrimination based exclusively on the tenets of their religious faith. In this respect, I felt I was bending over backwards to acknowledge the limits of OCR's jurisdiction in anti-Semitism cases. In view of the existing case law, I might have been able to defend a more sweeping policy that admitted no exceptions for purely religious discrimination. I did not, however, believe that such an aggressive move was warranted in light of the text, history, and context of Title VI and of the policy ramifications that would follow.

At least two federal district courts had taken a broader view of the extent to which anti-Semitic discrimination can be considered "racial" under other civil rights laws. The first case, *LeBlanc-Sternberg v. Fletcher*, involved a Hasidic group's challenge to the incorporation of their Ramapo, New York, community as a village. The Hasidim believed that incorporation was intended to facilitate zoning laws that would prevent them from conducting services in the home of their leader, Rabbi Yitzchok LeBlanc-Sternberg. They had been disparaged, allegedly, as "foreigners and interlopers," "ignorant and uneducated," "an insult to the community," and as "a bunch of people who insist on living in the past."[15] The Hasidic worshipers sued under §§ 1981 and 1982, claiming that they faced racial discrimination and citing *Shaare Tefila*

Race and National Origin Discrimination, Where Such Discrimination May Be Factually Interrelated with Religious Discrimination, June 24, 2004.
[12] *Id.*, at 1.
[13] *Id.*
[14] *Id.*
[15] LeBlanc-Sternberg v. Fletcher, 67 F. 3d 412, 418, 430 (2d Cir. 1995).

Congregation v. Cobb. Village officials defended themselves on the ground that any discrimination was based not on race but on Orthodox Jewish religious tenets and lifestyle. Nevertheless, the court held that since Jews are protected as a "racial group" under *Shaare Tefila,* the court "need not inquire any further" as to whether the discrimination that Jews faced there was racial in character.[16]

Similarly, in *Singer v. Denver School District No. 1,* the court tried to distinguish religious from racial anti-Semitism but concluded that this distinction is irrelevant to Jewish discrimination claims. In that case, a Denver public school teacher named Yishai Singer alleged discrimination on the basis of his Hasidic religious beliefs, dietary observances, grooming habits, and traditional garb. Singer was a Hispanic convert to Hasidic Judaism (birth name Jesse Hernandez), so his claim to Jewish racial (or "ancestral") distinctness was rather attenuated. Nevertheless, the Colorado Federal District Court ruled in Singer's favor, reasoning that "since Singer is claiming he was discriminated against as a Jew, a distinct racial group for the purposes of § 1981, Defendants are not entitled to judgment on the basis that he is claiming religious discrimination."[17]

These cases do have a certain attraction. As the *LeBlanc-Sternberg* court observed, "racial and religious discrimination against Jews cannot be ... easily distinguished" because "Jewish culture, ancestry, and ethnic identity are intricately bound up with Judaic religious beliefs."[18] To the extent that racial discrimination is barred but religious discrimination is not, fact-finders must make the very difficult determination as to the precise nature of the animus. This can present very difficult enforcement challenges. On the other hand, while there are certainly many cases in which religious anti-Semitism is difficult to distinguish from its racial variants, *LeBlanc-Sternberg* was not one of them. Nor was *Singer.* Both cases provide clear examples of religious discrimination if clear examples can be found.[19] Moreover, the rule that these cases suggested – and which other courts generally have eschewed – is rather troubling. It amounts to the theory that some groups, because of certain shared characteristics, are entitled to a level of protection denied to other groups, even against discrimination that is unrelated to those characteristics. Concluding that

---

[16]   *Id.,* at 268.
[17]   Singer v. Denver Sch. Dist. No. 1, 959 F. Supp. 1325, 1331 (D. Colo. 1997).
[18]   LeBlanc-Sternberg, 781 F. Supp. at 267.
[19]   William Kaplowitz makes this point in his student note, *We Need Inquire Further: Normative Stereotypes, Hasidic Jews, and the Civil Rights Act of 1866,* 12 Mich. J. Race & L. (Spring 2007) 537, 553.

the *LeBlanc-Sternberg-Singer* line of cases was not good law or policy, I maintained that Title VI's bar on anti-Jewish discrimination did not extend to purely religious animus.

Although U.S. courts had not observed the religious discrimination exemption that I described, the distinction could be found in foreign law. For example, English courts following *Sandla* similarly have distinguished between religious and ethnic or racial anti-Semitism. In a 1980 case concerning offensive anti-Semitic remarks in the workplace, the United Kingdom's Employment Appeal Tribunal had observed that the plaintiff's case turns on "whether what happened here was on the ground of [the plaintiff's] religion."[20] If it was, the court held, then it would not be covered under the United Kingdom's Race Relations Act. "On the other hand," the tribunal continued, "if it was on the ground of his race or ethnic origin, then it would be within the ambit of the Act."[21] In that case, the English court affirmed the tribunal's ruling in favor of the Jewish plaintiff because the anti-Semitism at issue was not merely because of the plaintiff's faith but also because of his "Jewish race or of Jewish ethnic origin."[22] This case has been influential for two separate reasons, as another English court recently observed. "In the first place," the court explained "it is clear authority, *if indeed authority were required for such an obvious position*, that Jews are an ethnic group."[23] This was also the main point of OCR's 2004 policy. "Secondly, however, there is the clear proposition that anti-Semitic behavior may be based on the victim's Jewish ethnic origin – in which case the … Act applies – but may, on the other hand, be based simply on the victim's Jewish religion or faith – in which case the 1976 Act does not apply."[24] This is precisely the exception that OCR's 2004 policy recognized. "And whether in any particular case it is one or the other is a matter of fact, to be determined on the facts of the particular case."[25]

On September 13, 2004, I sent over 20,000 "Dear Colleague" letters to university presidents, state education chiefs, and school superintendents telling them what OCR's policy now was.[26] This guidance letter

---

[20] Seide v. Gillette Industries, Ltd. [1980] IRLR 427.
[21] *Id.*, at paragraphs [22]–[23].
[22] *Id.*
[23] [2008] EWHC 1535/1536, paragraph [148] (emphasis added); reversed on other grounds in [2009] EWCA Civ 626.
[24] *Id.*
[25] *Id.*
[26] OCR Dear Colleague Letter from Kenneth L. Marcus, Deputy Assistant Secretary for Enforcement, Delegated the Authority of Assistant Secretary of Education

announced OCR's decision to "exercise its jurisdiction to enforce the
Title VI prohibition against national origin discrimination, regardless
of whether the groups targeted for discrimination also exhibit religious
characteristics" and thus "aggressively investigate alleged race or ethnic
harassment against Arab Muslim, Sikh and Jewish students." This letter
was OCR's first public commitment to enforce Title VI to protect Jewish
students (and, of course, Sikh students) against harassment.

In meetings on Capitol Hill, my guidance was warmly received by
congressional staff and policy advocates. Then-Senator Rick Santorum,
who held a senior position in the Senate Republican leadership, helpfully
set up a series of briefings in which I explained OCR's new policy to representatives of Jewish and non-Jewish religious and human rights organizations. These meetings, I felt, would be important both to educate
key stakeholders and to create a constituency for the new policy in the
event that it should later be attacked. Some of the groups thought that
more guidance would be helpful. They wanted an even clearer, stronger
statement of OCR's commitment to using Title VI even in cases in which
the Jewish student asserted no racial or ethnic discrimination other than
discrimination on the basis of the student's status as a Jew.

I addressed these requests in a policy letter addressed to a San
Francisco–based think tank called the Institute for Jewish and
CommunityResearch in late 2004. The institute had asked whether,
for purposes of extending civil rights protections, "'Jewish' may be
interpreted as an ethnic [or] ... racial category ... even if the alleged
victims are Caucasian and American born." Although I had not been
familiar with the institute previously, I was impressed with its quick
grasp of the issues involved. Years later, after leaving the government,
I would join the institute as the director of their Initiative on Anti-
Semitism and Anti-Israelism in American Education while also serving
on the School of Public Affairs faculty at the City University of New
York's Baruch College.

On behalf of OCR, I answered the institute's question in the affir-
mative in a formal policy letter.[27] With the *Shaare Tefila* and *Saint
Francis College* decisions in mind, I responded that the U.S. Supreme
Court had already answered the question in the affirmative in analogous

for Civil Rights, U.S. Department of Education, *Title VI and Title IX Religious
Discrimination in Schools and Colleges* (September 13, 2004) ("OCR 2004 Dear
Colleague Letter").
[27] OCR Guidance Letter to IJCR, *supra* note 31.

statutory contexts. In order to deflect the socially uncomfortable question of Jewish "racial" identity, I told the institute that the appropriate question "is not whether 'Jewish' is a racial or national-origin category per se, but whether anti-Jewish incidents may be covered within Title VI's broad protections against racial or ethnic discrimination." I insisted that OCR would prosecute anti-Semitism cases, explaining that "anti-Semitic harassment may include adverse action taken against individuals based on a victim's ethnic background or ancestry, notwithstanding the prospect that such harassment may constitute religious discrimination as well." The question of whether Jews are Caucasian was, I believed, a red herring. "In short," I concluded, "OCR recognizes that Title VI covers harassment of students of Jewish heritage regardless of whether the students may be Caucasian and American born."

Attempting a rhetorical flourish to conclude the letter, I wrote that "OCR cannot turn its back on victims of anti-Semitism on the grounds that Jewish heritage may include both religious and ethnic characteristics." This statement was a kind of "poison pill." It was intended to make my successors think twice before reneging on this new agency commitment. Would any subsequent OCR chief want to bring on himself or herself the charge that, in OCR's own terms, he or she had caused OCR to "turn its back on victims of anti-Semitism"? In retrospect, it was realistic to foresee that OCR's new anti-Semitism policy could be challenged but optimistic to believe that my successors would worry about whether they were turning their backs on anti-Jewish harassment.

No sooner had I issued this guidance than Susan Tuchman filed the Center for Law and Justice's complaint against the University of California at Irvine. Ironically, Tuchman was not aware of the new policy at the time. Rather, she thought that her complaint would challenge OCR's prior policy of nonenforcement. At my direction, OCR's San Francisco regional office opened a full investigation. Shortly afterwards, an independent task force, initially chartered by Hillel, began an investigation of the same events.[28] While the case was pending, the White House recruited me for the directorship of the U.S. Commission on Civil Rights. In my absence, the OCR investigation was handled by civil rights officials who had a very different view of the nature and dangers of anti-Semitism. The ultimate resolution of the OCR investigation, as well as

---

[28] Hillel International, also known as Hillel: The Foundation for Jewish Campus Life, has been described as the largest Jewish campus organization in the world. It maintains centers on or near the campuses of hundreds of colleges and universities. Many of these centers are lodged in buildings known as "Hillel Houses."

its divergence from the task force's simultaneous inquiry, would speak volumes as to the federal government's current ability to comprehend anti-Semitism cases within the existing civil rights policy framework.

THE U.S. COMMISSION ON CIVIL RIGHTS

Shortly after the 2004 election, while the *Irvine* case was pending, President George W. Bush appointed me as staff director of the U.S. Commission on Civil Rights. That independent agency had a 50-year history as the "conscience of the nation on civil rights." Established under President Dwight Eisenhower, the commission had laid the groundwork for the most important federal civil rights laws, including the Civil Rights Act of 1964, the Voting Rights Act, the Fair Housing Act, and the Americans with Disabilities Act. In recent years, the commission had suffered various misfortunes ranging from severe budgetary cutbacks to significant management failures to internal ideological battles. Nevertheless, the commission continued to enjoy the name recognition and, if somewhat tarnished, the reputation and influence that had enabled it to achieve its earlier victories. Although the commission, unlike OCR, had no enforcement powers, it had a powerful force of moral persuasion. Its recent reports on the failings of the Indian health care system, for example, were widely cited and influential. It was this force that I had hoped to marshal on behalf of civil rights concerns.

One of my first substantive priorities at the commission was to address the resurgence of anti-Semitism on college campuses such as Irvine. Some of the commissioners, especially Abigail Thernstrom and Jennifer Braceras, also thought that OCR's new anti-Semitism policy should be more broadly publicized. On November 18, 2005, the commission convened a panel of experts to provide testimony regarding anti-Semitic incidents on college campuses. At my invitation, three of the top national experts provided eye-opening testimony. Susan Tuchman, who was still pursuing the *Irvine* case, testified about the problems at that campus. Gary Tobin, president of the Institute for Jewish & Community Research, presented his research on anti-Semitism and anti-Israelism nationwide. Tobin had just co-authored a study of this subject, *The Uncivil University*, that his institute released to coincide with the commission's hearing.[29] Finally, the American Jewish Congress's then–Governmental

[29] GARY A. TOBIN, ARYEH K. WEINBERG, & JENNA FERER, THE UNCIVIL UNIVERSITY (2005), at 172.

Affairs Director Sarah Stern described the problems at San Francisco State and Columbia. These universities, like Irvine, had become flashpoints for anti-Isaelism and, as Stern argued, anti-Semitism as well. The problems at San Francisco State, Columbia, and Irvine weighted heavily on the commission's deliberations.

SAN FRANCISCO STATE UNIVERSITY

Although *Irvine* was OCR's first major test under its new anti-Semitism policy, it certainly was not the first of the recent spate of anti-Semitism incidents that have emerged around the country since the dawn of this new century. On May 7, 2002, an ugly incident at San Francisco State University awakened public attention to this new emergence of an ancient prejudice. On that campus, which had already developed a reputation in some circles as an unwelcoming place for Jews, "several hundred Jewish students conducted a Sit-in for Peace in the Middle East, trying to engage the pro-Palestinian students in dialogue." As the rally concluded, many other students surrounded the remaining Jewish students yelling death threats.[30] Professor Laurie Zoloff, a witness to the event, reported that "[c]ounter demonstrators poured into the plaza, screaming at the Jews to 'Get out or we will kill you' and 'Hitler did not finish the job.'"[31] Others reported shouts of "Fuck the Jews!" and "Die racist pigs!"[32]

Police allegedly refused to take any action other than to surround the Jewish students and community members, who reportedly were trapped while an angry mob chanted for their death.[33] The San Francisco police then marched the Jewish group to the campus Hillel building and remained on guard.[34] Some rally participants reported feeling "very threatened" and fearing that violence would ensue but for the police presence.[35] The May 7 rally was hardly the only anti-Semitic episode at San Francisco State that year. "In April, a flyer advertising a pro-Palestinian rally ... featured a picture of a dead baby, with the words, 'Canned Palestinian Children Meat – Slaughtered According to Jewish Rites under American License....'"[36] This flyer explicitly revived the

[30] Sarah Stern, *Campus Anti-Semitism*, IN U.S.C.C.R., CAMPUS ANTI-SEMITISM, at 22.
[31] TOBIN, WEINBERG, & FERER, UNCIVIL UNIVERSITY, *supra* note 94, at 172.
[32] Stern, at 22.
[33] *Id.*
[34] *Id.*
[35] *Id.*
[36] *Id.*

centuries-old blood libel that Jews kill gentile children and eat them or
consume their blood for ceremonial purposes.[37] In this way, it served
as a chilling example of how, in the twenty-first century, contemporary
political speech can be used as a cover for the dissemination of medieval
racial hatred.

San Francisco State's president, Robert A. Corrigan, responded firmly
to these incidents. Responding to the "blood libel" flyers, Corrigan
wrote strong letters to the responsible student groups, insisting that the
flyer "is no political statement," that it is "hate speech in words and
image," and that its language "echoes a type of ugly myth that has been
used through the centuries specifically to generate hatred."[38] He further
announced that "[t]he flier was much more than an offense to the Jewish
community; it was an offense to the entire University community and
all that we stand for – most especially our ability to see the humanity
in those with whom we disagree."[39] Then, in a strongly worded letter to
all members of the university community, he condemned the demonstrators who "behaved in a manner that completely violated the values of
this institution and of most of you who are reading this message."[40] The
commission described these actions at length in its report because they
served as such an excellent model of how a strong university leader can
stand up to bigotry. If Irvine's chancellor had issued such statements, for
example, the university likely would have avoided many of the troubles
that it has faced.

COLUMBIA UNIVERSITY

At Columbia University, a number of students have come forward
claiming that they feel intimidated and fearful in courses in Columbia's
Middle East and Asian Languages and Cultures (MEALAC) Program.
The documentary film *Columbia Unbecoming*, produced by the Boston-
based David Project, details a pattern of anti-Semitic activities at
MEALAC.[41] In one famous incident described in the film, a Columbia
student described an encounter that she had with Professor George

[37] *Id.*
[38] U.S.C.C.R., CAMPUS ANTI-SEMITISM, at 61.
[39] *Id.*
[40] *Id.*, at 62.
[41] See ANTI-DEFAMATION LEAGUE, STATEMENT TO U.S. COMMISSION ON CIVIL
RIGHTS: ANTI-SEMITIC INCIDENTS ON COLLEGE CAMPUSES (November 18, 2005)
[hereinafter, "ADL STATEMENT"].

Saliba. "Towards the end of the semester," the young woman recalls, "Professor Saliba showed what I felt was an anti-Israel film, showing the contemporary conflict between Palestinians and Israelis with a very one-sided view."[42] Such "one-sided views" may be regrettable, but they do not in themselves raise civil rights concerns. "The film and Saliba presented a view," she added, "that Arabs have a prior claim to the land of Israel."[43] Although controversial, such views certainly have a place in any discussion of Middle Eastern politics. The student commented that she "felt very differently" about Arab claims and that she "was sure to express [her] ... opinion."[44] For a few minutes, she discussed the issue with Saliba inside the classroom, and then, she says, he "sort of drew me outside the classroom, and told me to walk with him this way out."[45]

> He said, "You have no voice in this debate." So I said, "Of course, I'm allowed to express my opinion." He came really close to me.... [H]e said, "See, you have green eyes." He said, "You're not a Semite." He said, "I'm a Semite. I have brown eyes. You have no claim to the land of Israel."[46]

In another notorious allegation discussed in the film, Professor Joseph Massad "spent a class recounting the 'massacre' by the Israelis in Jenin. When a student raised her hand to ask [whether] Israel often gives warnings ahead of time before striking terrorist strongholds, Professor Massad [allegedly] screamed back at her, 'I will not have you deny Israeli atrocities in my class!'"[47] In a third incident, Professor Hamid Dabashi is said to have written, on September 23, 2004, that Israelis have "a vulgarity of character that is bone-deep and structural to the skeletal vertebrae of [their] culture."[48]

A faculty committee commissioned to investigate the matter found that there were no anti-Semitic activities. The committee was, from the beginning, accused of bias, and Columbia's president was charged with selecting committee members who lacked objectivity. For example, the Anti-Defamation League charged that "two of the five members had

[42] Stern, at 24–5.
[43] *Id.*
[44] *Id.*
[45] *Id.*
[46] *Id.*
[47] ADL STATEMENT, Professor Massad responds to anti-Semitism on the MEALAC website, which can be found here: http://www.columbia.edu/cu/mealac/faculty/massad/
[48] Stern, *supra* at 69. Professor Dabashi has partially denied the accuracy of Stern's translation. See U.S.C.C.R., CAMPUS ANTI-SEMITISM, *supra* at 59.

signed Columbia's divestment petition, and one had been the thesis advisor of Joseph Mossad and was instrumental in ... [hiring him], and one had written a paper blaming Israel" for increasing global anti-Semitism.[49]

Columbia acknowledges identifying "inconsistencies and weaknesses in the avenues available for students to raise concerns about faculty conduct" and maintains that these problems were addressed by clarifying and strengthening the university's "procedures for adjudicating grievances and establish[ing] additional ... [opportunities] for students" to communicate with university administrators."[50] Columbia's provost, Alan Brinkley, also emphasized to me, days before the commission's hearing, the many efforts that it takes to make Jewish students feel welcome.[51] Similarly, Holocaust scholar Deborah Lipstadt argues that "many pundits have spoken about the problems at Columbia University while ignoring, almost willfully, the fact that it is also home to one of the most multifaceted and vibrant Jewish student communities."[52] Nevertheless, the committee report has been criticized as a "white-wash" (or at least "clumsy"), and critics argue that it yielded nothing more than "a very slight slap on the wrist" for one faculty member and recommendations for better grievance procedures.[53] Others argue that a "close reading of the report makes it clear that the committee was using [the one episode it criticized] to send a broader message," namely: "Anything doesn't go anymore."[54]

THE SYSTEMIC CHARACTER OF CAMPUS ANTI-SEMITISM

The problems at San Francisco State, Columbia, Irvine, and a few other places have come to symbolize the status of campus anti-Semitism around the country, but there have been episodes at other campuses as

[49] ADL STATEMENT, *supra*.
[50] Transcript, U.S. Commission on Civil Rights Meeting of November 18, 2005, at 1–2. Letter from Alan Brinkley, Provost, Columbia University, to Kenneth L. Marcus, Staff Director, U.S. Commission on Civil Rights (November 15, 2005); available at www.usccr.gov/calendar/trnscrpt/1118usccrwappx.pdf.
[51] *Id.*
[52] Deborah E. Lipstadt, *Strategic Responses to Anti-Israelism and Anti-Semitism*, IN AMERICAN JEWRY AND THE COLLEGE CAMPUS: BEST OF TIMES OR WORST OF TIMES? (Deborah E. Lipstadt et al., eds.) (2005) [herinafter, "LIPSTADT ET AL., AMERICAN JEWRY AND THE COLLEGE CAMPUS"] 5.
[53] ADL STATEMENT.
[54] Samuel G. Freedman, *Keeping Things in Perspective*, IN LIPSTADT ET AL., AMERICAN JEWRY AND THE COLLEGE CAMPUS 27–8.

well. Some commentators, such as UCLA's Rabbi Chaim Seidler-Feller, assert that the phenomenon of campus anti-Semitism is "actually limited to a few well-publicized events."[55] Others, such as the late Gary Tobin, argue that these incidents are merely some of the most egregious examples of a problem that is "systemic in higher education and can be found on campuses all over the United States."[56] There is also a wide spectrum of opinion between these polar perspectives; moreover, opinions differ on the importance of the distinction. For some people, even episodic manifestations of this ugly prejudice provide reason for concern. Others, however, argue that the seriousness with which this issue should be taken depends on whether recent episodes are best characterized as systemic or incidental.

There are three respects in which biases can be described as "systemic" of (and not merely incidental to) an institution: high volume or severity, cultural pervasiveness, and structural attachment. A case can be made for the systemic character of campus anti-Semitism using any of these criteria. Gary Tobin, Aryeh Weinberg, and Jenna Ferrer demonstrate in *The Uncivil University* that the volume and severity of recent activities on American college campuses are too great to be characterized as merely incidental.[57] They do not quantify that volume, however, arguing that the number of events is misleading because the fundamental problem currently is one of attitudes, myths, ideolgies, and belief systems.[58] The Anti-Defamation League documented nearly 100 anti-Semitic incidents on American college campuses in 2005 alone.[59] While this figure may overstate the problem in one respect, because many of the incidents may be minor, isolated events, it also may understate the problem in a more important respect, because most incidents are probably not reported to the ADL. Given the number of students who have described anti-Semitic incidents to me and the small proportion who have reported these incidents, I believe that the actual figure is several times higher than the Anti-Defamation League's records suggest. The sheer volume of incidents that Tobin and Weinberg describe belies efforts

---

[55] Chaim Seidler-Feller, *Advocacy and Education as Divergent Strategies in the Effort to Support Israel on Campus,* IN LIPSTADT, ET AL., AMERICAN JEWRY AND THE COLLEGE CAMPUS 33.
[56] TOBIN, WEINBERG, & FERER, UNCIVIL UNIVERSITY, at 35.
[57] *Id.*
[58] *Id.,* at 92.
[59] Press release, Anti-Defamation League, *Annual ADL Audit: Anti-Semitic Incidents Decline in 2005 but Levels Still of Concern in U.S.* (April 5, 2006).

to deny anti-Semitism's systemic grip on higher education if "systemic" bias is defined in purely quantitative terms.

The term "systemic bias" is also used to describe biases that inhere in a culture or institution. In some ways, the bias that universities have toward Jews appears to be philo-Semitic. One recent survey by the Institute for Jewish & Community Research shows that American college professors view Jews more favorably than any other religious group, with 73 percent claiming favorable attitudes and only 3 percent admitting unfavorable attitudes.[60] At first blush, this finding seems difficult to square with the resurgence of anti-Semitic incidents. One explanation that the institute's ongoing research suggests is that the sociopolitical culture of many university campuses is disproportionately influenced by the extreme views of a majority of the university's members. Another explanation is that voluntary reporting of conscious attitudes must be taken with a grain of salt during a period in which prejudices increasingly have become covert or unconscious. English philosopher Bernard Harrison has argued that the new anti-Semitism is characterized largely by an intangible climate of opinion in which conformists espouse positions and express views that are inflected with anti-Semitism even when they do not acknowledge negative attitudes toward Jews.[61]

Finally, systemic anti-Semitism can describe forms of anti-Jewish prejudice that inhere in the basic structures of postsecondary institutions. Examples may include overt discrimination in academic admissions, undergraduate housing, faculty selection, and club membership. Jews faced such institutionalized, structural discrimination during a significant part of the twentieth century.[62] Such barriers are now, as the Anti-Defamation League reported to the Civil Rights Commission in 2005, "largely a thing of the past."[63] There is, however, one caveat. Sociologist Jerome Karabel's painstaking research on "the hidden history of admission and exclusion at Harvard, Yale, and Princeton" has demonstrated that the current admissions systems at highly selective institutions continue to bear the vestigial remains of early-twentieth-century

---

[60] See *Gary A. Tobin & Aryeh K. Weinberg, Profiles of the American University*, v. II, RELIGIOUS BELIEFS AND BEHAVIOR OF COLLEGE FACULTY (2007) 11.

[61] BERNARD HARRISON, THE RESURGENCE OF ANTI-SEMITISM: JEWS, ISRAEL, AND LIBERAL OPINION (2006) 8–9.

[62] See LEONARD DINNERSTEIN, ANTI-SEMITISM IN AMERICA (1994) 84–8.

[63] Anti-Defamation League, *Statement to U.S. Commission on Civil Rights, Anti-Semitic Incidents on College Campuses* (November 18, 2005); available at www.adl.org/main_Anti_Semitism_Domestic/incidents_on_college_campuses. htm?Multi_page_sections=sHeading_4.

anti-Semitism. Karabel has shown that in order to reduce the Jewish student population at these schools from levels that had reached 40 percent at Harvard in the 1920s, these institutions developed numerous subjective practices of exclusion.[64] These included considerations of "character," personality, and leadership; geographic diversity; legacy and athletic preferences; and personal interviews.[65] While these admissions criteria were not intended exclusively to limit Jewish enrollments, they had the effect of limiting the number of Jewish students, and some of them were developed with that purpose in mind.[66]

To the extent that these criteria remain in place today, structural barriers to Jewish admissions can be said to remain at many highly selective institutions. These barriers do not limit the enrollment of Jewish students to numbers below their representation in the institutions' catchment areas, and they were not designed to do so. They were designed, rather, to limit the statistical overrepresentation of Jewish students, and they continue to have this affect. This is a form of systemic anti-Semitism, and it is central to the basic admissions structures in many of the most prominent American universities. It is not, however, directly related to the newer forms of anti-Semitism that impair the atmosphere for Jewish students at many institutions today. Nor does any evidence suggest that these structural barriers are maintained as a result of any present animus against Jewish students. They are, rather, relics of long-forgotten prejudices that are maintained by well-intentioned stewards who likely are oblivious to their unfortunate origins.

It should be noted that many recent campus activities, although arguably anti-Semitic, do not rise to the level of harassment and therefore are outside the scope of this book: divestment movements, anti-Israeli or anti-Zionist academic literature, Holocaust denial, intimidation of pro-Israeli speakers, anti-Zionist bias in programs of Middle East studies, anti-Israel boycotts, and refusal to provide religious accommodations to Jewish students. These phenomena raise serious questions that must be addressed in the broader context of resolving the conflicts that currently confront higher-education institutions. Unlike some of the other incidents that I have seen, however, they do not primarily implicate civil rights law.

---

[64] JEROME KARABEL, THE CHOSEN: THE HIDDEN HISTORY OF ADMISSION AND EXCLUSION AT HARVARD, YALE, AND PRINCETON (2005) 109.
[65] *Id.*, at 89, 99, 108, 111–7, 124–7.
[66] *Id.*, at 132, 136.

In my experience as a civil rights official the truth lies in between the two extreme positions that have been articulated concerning the "systemic" character of American campus anti-Semitism. Few American campuses have witnessed the number and intensity of anti-Semitic incidents reported at such places as Irvine, San Francisco State, and Columbia. On the other hand, dozens of campuses every year experience at least some manifestation of this ugly problem, which is now undoubtedly national in scope. Moreover, these incidents arise from a climate of opinion in which various anti-Semitic attitudes are now more easily accepted than they had been just a few decades ago. These attitudes are not yet incorporated into the basic structures of American higher education, such as student admissions and faculty hiring processes. It cannot, however, be said that such structures are entirely free of the taint of anti-Semitism. The vestiges of older forms of anti-Semitism continue to shape these structures, even as those biases no longer provide the motivation for their continuance.

THE CIVIL RIGHTS COMMISSION'S CAMPUS
ANTI-SEMITISM REPORT

With all these incidents in mind, on April 3, 2006, the U.S. Commission on Civil Rights issued its *Findings and Recommendations Regarding Campus Anti-Semitism*, which strongly reinforced the 2004 OCR policy.[67] The commission's findings were bold. "Many college campuses throughout the United States," we began, "continue to experience incidents of anti-Semitism."[68] Moreover, these incidents had become, once again, "a serious problem" that "warrants further attention."[69] This simple pronouncement would have an important effect. Around the country, college students and even professors would later tell me that this finding gave them a sense of vindication, after college administrators had failed to take their anti-Semitism claims seriously. At Irvine, I am told that some students actually were brought to tears by this acknowledgment by the federal government.

The commission was explicit about the nature of this bigotry. On some campuses, the commission reported, students had been threatened, intimidated, and subjected to derogatory remarks, vandalism, and the

---

[67] U.S.C.C.R., FINDINGS AND RECOMMENDATIONS.
[68] *Id.*, at 1.
[69] *Id.*

use of swastikas and other symbols of hatred. In many cases, this was related to what has been called the "new anti-Semitism." "On many campuses," the commission cautioned, "anti-Israeli and anti-Zionist propaganda has been disseminated that includes traditional anti-Semitic elements, including age-old anti-Jewish stereotypes and defamation."[70] This is different, the commission observed, from run-of-the-mill criticisms of a sovereign state. Rather, it is simply a form of prejudice that may disguise itself as political protest in order to avail itself of legal protections or to evade the calumny that open bigotry otherwise would attract. Fortunately, the commission was able to see through such ruses. "Anti-Semitic bigotry is no less morally deplorable," the commission thundered, "when camouflaged as anti-Israelism or anti-Zionism."

Surprisingly, those bold pronouncements were not the source of controversy within the commission. What made the commission's *Campus Anti-Semitism* report hotly controversial was its affirmation of the anti-Semitism policy that I had established at OCR. In particular, the commission endorsed my conclusion that anti-Semitic incidents, "[w]hen severe, persistent or pervasive ... may constitute a hostile environment for students in violation of Title VI of the Civil Rights Act of 1964."[71] The commission, over the objections of its chairman, called on the Department of Education to "protect college students from anti-Semitic and other discriminatory harassment by vigorously enforcing Title VI against recipients that deny equal educational opportunities to all students."[72]

In the course of deliberations, several fault lines became apparent. First, some commissioners questioned the jurisdictional basis for pursuing anti-Semitism claims under Title VI. Chairman Gerald A. Reynolds, who had preceded me as head of OCR, was reluctant to adopt language that, in his view, appeared to extend that agency's jurisdiction beyond what Congress had permitted. Since Congress had not prohibited religious discrimination in education, the chairman did not want the commission to make any statement that he thought could suggest that religious anti-Semitism (as opposed to ethnic anti-Semitism) was prohibited. Reynolds did not, however, convince any other commissioners to join him in voting against the *Findings and Recommendations*. Led by Vice Chair Abigail Thernstrom and

[70] *Id.*
[71] *Id.*
[72] *Id.*, at 2.

Commissioner Jennifer Braceras, the other commissioners agreed that Title VI does in fact prohibit anti-Semitic harassment. These other commissioners generally understood that my 2004 OCR policy did not prohibit discrimination that was directed exclusively at the tenets of a student's religious faith.

Second, and more ominous, the new OCR chief issued correspondence that pulled back from my 2004 policy. In response to my questions, Assistant Secretary of Education Stephanie Monroe conveyed this position in coded bureaucratic language: "OCR has jurisdiction to investigate complaints raising allegations of religious discrimination or anti-Semitic harassment *if the allegations also include discrimination over which OCR has subject matter jurisdiction*, such as race or national origin (including discrimination based on a person's ancestry or ethnic characteristics)."[73] Thus my successor's position was that OCR will only prosecute anti-Semitism charges "if the allegations *also* include" other matters "over which OCR has subject matter jurisdiction." In other words, OCR will not address anti-Semitism per se.

In order to understand the import of Monroe's statement, one need only observe that one can substitute virtually anything for the term "anti-Semitic harassment" as it appears in her letter, and the meaning of the statement is unchanged. Thus OCR also will unquestionably investigate "complaints raising allegations of," for example, UFO sightings, lost kittens, or gubernatorial philandering "if the allegations also include discrimination over which OCR has subject matter jurisdiction." This is so because OCR is mandated to investigate all complaints that contain allegations of discrimination over which it has jurisdiction, even if the complaints also contain extraneous material. Needless to say, OCR will ignore the portions of the complaint that address only UFOs, kittens, governors, or anti-Semitism, but it will focus diligently on the other, jurisdiction-conferring matters within the complaint.

Monroe's rationale was that anti-Semitism is nothing but a form of religious discrimination, and OCR does not handle religion. This became clear when Monroe was later forced to explain her view of anti-Semitism under oath. Asked about anti-Semitism at Irvine, she sputtered uncomfortably that she did not know how the term "anti-Semitism" was being used: "I am not clear in terms of how – what – how you are using

---

[73] Letter of Stephanie Monroe to Kenneth L. Marcus, Staff Director, U.S. Commission on Civil Rights, dated December 4, 2006; available at www.eusccr.com/lettermonroe.pdf.

that – that term."[74] She explained that she would rather avoid the term entirely because she does not understand "anti-Semitism" as well as other, related concepts. "So I prefer to use the term religious discrimination," she explains, "which I think I have a better understanding of what that is."[75] The problem is that by displacing "anti-Semitism" with the concept of "religious discrimination," Monroe predetermined the outcome of all cases alleging discrimination against Jews. Given that OCR lacks jurisdiction over religious discrimination, it must dismiss any such complaints.

Monroe's public language was sufficiently opaque, however, to enable her to claim that she was not changing the 2004 policy. When Jewish groups questioned her as to whether she was reducing the protections extended to Jewish students, she insisted that she was adhering faithfully to that policy. For example, Monroe told *Inside Higher Education*, that "there has been no change in our policy or our commitment to protect students, including Jewish students, from discrimination."[76] That publication was so convinced by Monroe's representation that it entitled an article about Monroe's letter and the controversy that it provoked, "Much Ado About Nothing."[77] Similarly, the Orthodox Union's Nathan Diament publicly commented that "we've been in touch with her about this issue, and she has expressed that she is as firmly committed to OCR dealing with these issues as her predecessor was."[78] In fact, Monroe's position could not have been further from "her predecessor." Despite her public statements, Monroe privately believed that OCR's 2004 letter, in her words, "took us further away from Congress's intent and our specific statutory quarry than we would be comfortable with."[79] Those who had access only to Monroe's public statements needed to read closely between the lines in order to see that her claims to protecting Jewish students were wholly illusory.

In light of Monroe's position, the commission called on Congress to clarify to the Department of Education that Title VI does indeed protect Jewish students from anti-Semitic harassment. This recommendation (the only one that I did not draft) was a halfway measure to say the least. The correct recommendation would have been to ask Congress to finish what it began in 1964 by prohibiting religious discrimination in federally

74 *Deposition of Stephanie Monroe*, January 14, 2009, p. 16 [hereinafter, "*Monroe Dep.*"].
75 *Id.*
76 *Much Ado About Nothing*, INSIDE HIGHER EDUCATION, April 4, 2006; available at www.insidehighered.com/news/2006/04/04/ocr.
77 *Id.*
78 *Id.*
79 *Monroe Dep.*, at 50.

funded educational programs and activities. The reason that the commission could not do this is that we had not developed a sufficient evidentiary record. The hearing had only addressed campus anti-Semitism. In order to evaluate the case for a Religious Discrimination in Education Act, the commission would have had to examine a much wider range of bias in both higher education and the public schools. Appropriate attention also would have to be given to such issues as the Establishment Clause's separation of church and state and the extent to which religious schools and clubs should be exempted.

After issuing these *Findings and Recommendations*, as well as a commission report on *Campus Anti-Semitism*, the commission commenced a public education campaign to inform Jewish college students about their rights, including their rights under Title VI. The idea was Commissioner Braceras', and it emerged from witness testimony indicating that most Jewish students remain unaware of their rights and remedies under my 2004 OCR policy. Although the commission's preference had been for OCR to conduct this outreach, the new position of OCR's leadership made that impossible. Working with several Jewish organizations, including the Anti-Defamation League, Hillel, the American Jewish Committee, and the Zionist Organization of America's Center for Law and Justice, as well as with many non-Jewish university groups, the commission developed posters, flyers, and a separate public Web site to publicize the problem of campus anti-Semitism. Meanwhile, I traveled the country speaking out against campus anti-Semitism at numerous colleges and universities; in synagogues, community organizations, and policy briefings; and in various interviews.

3

The New Campus Anti-Semitism

Speaking to college audiences, I have been careful to give proper context to the contemporary resurgence of campus anti-Semitism. The troubling incidents that have emerged on many campuses in recent years have been conspicuous not because they reflect a broader atmosphere of hostility toward Jews but rather because they have been ugly exceptions in an environment that has been welcoming in other respects to Jewish students.[1] Indeed, some commentators have described the current moment as a "golden age" for Jewish life on campus.[2] Close observers have noted the paradox that American colleges have emerged as a flashpoint for anti-Semitic incidents a time when they have provided a positive environment in most other respects."[3]

The United States in recent years has enjoyed a period of almost philo-Semitic tolerance for Jews, in contrast to the experience of Jews elsewhere in the world. Research by the Institute for Jewish and Community Research (and others) confirms the general perception that positive attitudes toward Jews have been growing steadily over the last 40 years, whereas negative perceptions have declined precipitously.[4] Similarly,

---

[1] *See, e.g.*, Harold Shapiro and Steven Bayme, *Foreword* to LIPSTADT ET AL., AMERICAN JEWRY AND THE COLLEGE CAMPUS (bemoaning that the "more widespread and sustained narrative of the integration of Jews and Judaism into university culture [has been] dwarfed by the surfacing of anti-Israel invective or anti-Semitic hostility" and suggesting "some level of exaggerated fears and sensitivities").

[2] *See* Chaim Seidler-Feller, *Advocacy and Education* in AMERICAN JEWRY AND THE COLLEGE CAMPUS: BEST OF TIMES OR WORST OF TIMES? (D. Lipstadt, S. Freedman, and C. Seidler-Feller, eds.) (American Jewish Committee 2005) 32.

[3] ANTI-DEFAMATION LEAGUE, STATEMENT TO U.S. COMMISSION ON CIVIL RIGHTS: ANTI-SEMITIC INCIDENTS ON COLLEGE CAMPUSES (Nov. 18, 2005), available at http://www.adl.org/main_Anti_Semitism_Domestic_incidents_on_college campuses.htm.

[4] G. TOBIN A. WEINBERG AND J. FERER, UNCIVIL UNIVERSITY (2005).

many college campuses have provided numerous accommodations to Jewish students, such as excused absence for religious holidays, kosher dining facilities, chaplaincy services, Hillel, and Jewish studies courses. By and large, Jewish students no longer face the forms of institutional discrimination in academic admissions, undergraduate housing, faculty selection, and club membership that they experienced for a significant part of the twentieth century.[5] On the other hand, allegations of anti-Semitic activity appear to have increased on college campuses in recent years and have included physical assaults, stalking, intimidation, vandalism, and various forms of hate speech.

It is curious that college campuses have become prime propagators of anti-Semitism, ironically, at a time when the general public holds entirely different views. Gabriel Schoenfeld argues that the disproportionate rise in campus anti-Semitism reflects an "unexpected twist in the helix of anti-Semitism's DNA" in which "the most vicious ideas about Jews are primarily voiced not by downtrodden and disenfranchised fringe elements of society but by its most successful, educated and 'progressive members.'"[6] Indeed, Schoenfeld argues that one is less likely to find contemporary anti-Semites "in beer halls and trailer parks" than on "college campuses and among the opinion makers of the media elite."[7]

The phenomenon has resulted from a "perfect storm" in which campus anti-Zionism and anti-Semitism have emerged from the confluence of a number of factors. The politics of many American college faculties has become overwhelmingly liberal, and contemporary anti-Israelism has tended to concentrate on the left. In recent years, the media have heightened this concentration by depicting Israel largely as an oppressor. Generally speaking, contemporary anti-Israeli and anti-Zionist ideologies mesh well with anti-Western, anti-American, antiwar, and other ideologies that are also common on college campuses. For this reason, in part, anti-Israel groups have targeted campuses as an arena for expressing an anti-Israel agenda (although, in fairness, pro-Israel groups have

---

[5] An exception could be provided, as discussed above, for systemic admissions discrimination arising from practices previously instituted to limit Jewish admissions but subsequently maintained for other reasons. Historical examples of anti-Semitism in American higher education can be found in LEONARD DINNERSTEIN, ANTI-SEMITISM IN AMERICA (1994) 85–6. For a discussion of historical efforts to exclude Jewish student applicants from admission to highly selective institutions, see Jerome Karabel, The Chosen: The Hidden History of Admission and Exclusion at Harvard, Yale, and Princeton (2005).

[6] Gabriel Schoenfeld, The Return of Anti-Semitism (2004) 3–4.

[7] *Id.*, at 3.

targeted campuses for a pro-Israel agenda). The phenomenon has been magnified because extremist voices are disproportionately influential on college campuses and are frequently able to capture organizational apparatuses even when they do not command majority support. Meanwhile, many universities have failed to take appropriate actions to prevent the spread of anti-Semitism largely as a result of bureaucratic inertia. Those who have the authority to stand up to the perpetrators of anti-Semitic incidents (e.g., administrators, trustees, and faculty) often fail to do so for fear of inviting confrontation, appearing overzealous, or interfering with academic freedom.[8]

DEFINITIONS OF ANTI-SEMITISM

The new anti-Semitism, like anti-Semitism proper, encompasses ideology, attitude, and practice. Many important definitions of anti-Semitism, such as *Merriam-Webster*'s long-standing, influential formulation[9] ("hostility toward or discrimination against Jews as a religious, ethnic, or racial group"[10]) recognize both the attitudinal and practical aspects of the phenomenon.[11] The ideological dimension of anti-Semitism was classically recognized in Theodor Adorno's mid-century definition: "The ideology [of anti-Semitism] consists of ... stereotyped negative opinions describing the Jews as threatening, immoral, and categorically different from non-Jews, and of hostile attitudes urging various forms of restriction, exclusion, and suppression as a means of solving 'the Jewish problem.'"[12]

While the influence of Adorno's early work on prejudice has suffered from the passage of time, this now-antique conception shows disquieting

[8] The "perfect storm" metaphor and the particular factors described here are drawn from both TOBIN ET AL., UNCIVIL UNIVERSITY at 32–3, and Lipstadt, *Strategic Responses*, at 19.

[9] The U.S. Department of State has relied on *Merriam-Webster*'s long-standing definition of anti-Semitism as "hostility toward or discrimination against Jews as a religious, ethnic, or racial group." USDS, CONTEMPORARY GLOBAL ANTI-SEMITISM, at 6.

[10] Significantly, since the term "anti-Semitism" was first coined, it referred only to an animosity directed at Jews rather than to a general antipathy toward the various semitic peoples. See *Walter Laqueur, The Changing Face of Anti-Semitism: From Ancient Times to the Present Day* (2006), at 21–2; BERNARD LEWIS, SEMITES AND ANTI-SEMITES: AN INQUIRY INTO CONFLICT AND PREJUDICE (1986) 117.

[11] The *Merriam-Webster* definition nevertheless is useful in its breadth because it suggests the breadth of prejudices subsumed under this category.

[12] THEODOR W. ADORNO, ELSE FRENKEL-BRUNSWIK, DANIEL J. LEVINSON, AND R. NEVITT SANFORD, THE AUTHORITARIAN PERSONALITY (1950) 71.

freshness as a characterization of the new anti-Semitism, as long as the concept of Israel is substituted for "Jewish" and "the Jews."[13] Thus the ideology of the new anti-Semitism consists of *stereotyped negative opinions describing the Jewish state, its members, supporters, and coreligionists as threatening, immoral, and categorically different from other peoples and of hostile attitudes urging various forms of restriction, exclusion, and suppression as a means of solving the "Israel problem."*

In an influential modern reformulation of the definition of anti-Semitism,[14] the European Monitoring Centre on Racism and Xenophobia (EUMC) established the following working definition: "Anti-[S]emitism is a certain perception of Jews, which may be expressed as hatred toward Jews. Rhetorical and physical manifestations of anti-[S]emitism are directed toward Jewish or non-Jewish individuals and/or their property, toward Jewish community institutions and religious facilities."[15] The U.S. State Department recently determined that "this definition provides an adequate initial guide by which anti-Semitism can eventually both be defined and combated."[16] The EUMC definition is important for its explicit recognition that "such manifestations could also target the state of Israel, conceived as a Jewish collectivity."[17] In particular, the EUMC definition provides several recent examples of anti-Semitism in public life, the media, schools, the workplace, and religious institutions that relate to this collectivity, including the following[18]:

- Making mendacious, dehumanizing, demonizing, or stereotypical allegations about Jews as such or the power of Jews as a collective – such

---

[13] For a discussion of THE AUTHORITARIAN PERSONALITY's waning influence and an example of its continuing vitality, see Clark Freshman, *What Ever Happened to Ant-Semitism? How Social Science Theories Identify Discrimination and Promote Coalitions Between "Different" Minorities*, 85 CORNELL L. REV. (2001) 313, 318–19.

[14] The extent of the EUMC Working Definition's influence may be seen, for example, in its adoption by both USDS, ANTI-SEMITISM, at 6; and ALL-PARTY PARLIAMENTARY GROUP AGAINST ANTISEMITISM, REPORT OF THE ALL-PARTY PARLIAMENTARY INQUIRY INTO ANTISEMITISM (2006).

[15] EUROPEAN MONITORING CENTRE ON RACISM AND XENOPHOBIA (EUMC), WORKING DEFINITION OF ANTISEMITISM (March 16, 2005); available at http://eumc.europa.eu/eumc/material/pub/AS/AS-WorkingDefinition-draft.pdf.

[16] USDS, OFFICE TO MONITOR AND COMBAT ANTI-SEMITISM, FACT SHEET, "WORKING DEFINITION" OF ANTI-SEMITISM (February 8, 2007); available at www.state.gov/g/drl/rls/56589.htm. The State Department also adopted the OSCE Working Definition in its report on CONTEMPORARY GLOBAL ANTI-SEMITISM, at 6.

[17] EUMC 159.

[18] *Id.*

as, especially but not exclusively, the myth about a world Jewish conspiracy or of Jews controlling the media, economy, government, or other societal institutions.

- Accusing Jews as a people of being responsible for real or imagined wrongdoing committed by a single Jewish person or group or even for acts committed by non-Jews.
- Denying the fact, scope, mechanisms (*e.g.*, gas chambers), or intentionality of the genocide of the Jewish people at the hands of National Socialist Germany and its supporters and accomplices during World War II (the Holocaust).
- Accusing the Jews as a people, or Israel as a state, of inventing or exaggerating the Holocaust.
- Accusing Jewish citizens of being more loyal to Israel or to the alleged priorities of Jews worldwide than to the interests of their own nations.[19]

These examples demonstrate the EUMC's insight that the putatively political or anti-Israeli cast of much new anti-Semitism shrouds significant continuities with antecedent forms of the "longest hatred." In addition, the EUMC working definition provides the following examples of "the ways in which anti-Semitism manifests itself with regard to the state of Israel taking into account the overall context":

- Denying the Jewish people their right to self-determination.
- Applying double standards by requiring of it a behavior not expected or demanded of any other democratic nation.
- Using the symbols and images associated with classic anti-Semitism (*e.g.*, claims of Jews killing Jesus or blood libel) to characterize Israel or Israelis.
- Drawing comparisons of contemporary Israeli policy with that of the Nazis.
- Holding Jews collectively responsible for actions of the state of Israel.[20]

The EUMC emphasizes, however, that criticism of Israel similar to that leveled against other countries does not constitute a form of anti-Semitism.[21] Indeed, virtually all commentators agree that criticism of

---

[19] *Id.*
[20] *Id.*
[21] *Id.*

Israel is not a form of anti-Semitism *per se*. The new anti-Semitism is a form of prejudice, not a form of criticism.

SOURCES OF CAMPUS ANTI-SEMITISM

Frequently I am asked where these problems come from. My view is that these episodes are not unrelated to the outbreak of incidents that have been chronicled elsewhere in the world, particularly in Western Europe and the Middle East. The U.S. State Department has provided a helpful analysis of this global outbreak, finding that recent global anti-Semitism has had four major sources.[22] The first is what the State Department calls traditional centuries-old European anti-Jewish prejudice associated with stereotypes of Jewish control of government, the media, international business, and the financial sector. The term "European" in this context may be slightly euphemistic in that the unnamed source of this strain of Jew hatred is Christianity.

The second source is what the State Department calls an aggressive "anti-Israel sentiment that crosses the line between objective [political] criticism of Israeli policies and anti-Semitism." The metaphor of line crossing is frequently employed in this context, but it can be somewhat misleading. In some cases, anti-Israelism may indeed cross a line. The problem, however, is often not one of degree but of fundamental nature. Legitimate or even illegitimate criticisms of Israel typically do not become anti-Semitic simply because they are taken too far. The forms of anti-Israelism that cloak are different in character and motivation from those which do not.

The third form is Muslim anti-Semitism, common among Europe's growing Muslim population, based on age-old hatred of Jews, as well as Muslim opposition to Israel and American policies in Iraq. It is conspicuous that the U.S. State Department does not resort to geographical or ethnic euphemisms in describing Muslim anti-Semitism as it does with Christian anti-Semitism. This may be due in part to the fact that Muslim anti-Semitism can be found in non-Arab countries, and it is espoused domestically by many people who are not of Arab descent. Some people complain that excessive attention to the Muslim origins of domestic anti-Semitism can enflame Islamophobia. In this context, it should be remembered that Christian anti-Semitism

---

[22] U.S. Department of State, Report on Global Anti-Semitism (2004); available at www.state.gov/g/drl/rls/40258.htm.

not only precedes Muslim anti-Semitism historically but was, until recently, the more virulent strain.

The final source identified by the U.S. State Department is Anti-American and antiglobalist anger that spills over to Israel and to Jews who are identified with Israel, globalism, and America. This form is seen in rallies and demonstrations at which Jews and Israel are vilified as part of a broader attack on Western institutions that are seen to be interrelated. To the extent that Jews are seen as the more powerful faction in Middle Eastern conflicts, progressive movements will tend to include the State of Israel in their broader litany of complaints.

The same forms of anti-Semitism also may be found on American college campuses, except that two additional forms also have been found in the American postsecondary context: black anti-Semitism, including incidents associated with the Nation of Islam and fundamentalist intolerance, exemplified by allegations at the U.S. Air Force Academy. By and large, however, the most significant recent episodes of campus anti-Semitism have been associated with anti-Zionism, arising partly in response to the second intifada in 2000 and the continuing Israeli-Palestinian crisis. In other words, the most conspicuous aspect of recent campus disturbances has involved incidents of the "new anti-Semitism."

THE NEW ANTI-SEMITISM

Bernard-Henri Lévy has theorized that the new anti-Semitism rests on three pillars that collectively constitute a new form of anti-Jewish discourse. They may be described loosely as anti-Semitisim-denial, Holocaust-denial, and anti-Zionism.[23] These three pillars correspond, respectively, to what Lévy calls the "triple pillars of the cult of victimhood, the taste for memory, and the punishment of evildoers.... "[24] The newness of this form of an old discourse is, Lévy argues, necessary in the post-Holocaust West for a widespread anti-Semitic movement "to emerge, for people to feel once again the desire and, above all, the *right* to burn all the synagogues they want, to attack boys wearing yarmulkes, to harass large numbers of rabbis, to kill not just one but

---

[23] See BERNARD-HENRI LÉVY, LEFT IN DARK TIMES: A STAND AGAINST THE NEW BARBARISM (2008) (Benjamin Moser, trans.) 155–8.
[24] *Id.*, at 155.

many Ilan Halimis[25] – in order for anti-Semitism to be reborn on a large scale."[26]

The first pillar, anti-Semitism-denial, addresses the "love of victimhood," instantiating the proposition that "[t]he Jews are no longer exploiting the wealth of nations but monopolizing that much rarer good ...human compassion."[27] This putative hoarding of victimhood capital is "the first reason to start resenting them again and, in clear conscience, in the name of the sacred concern due to all the world's dead, to start hating them again."[28]

The second pillar, Holocaust-denial, addresses the "duty of memory,"[29] applying classical anti-Semitic tropes to deflect the history of Jewish persecution. In its strong form, this deflection takes the form of outright denial, accusing Jews of using extraordinary craft and malevolent genius to con the world into "the biggest fraud in the history of mankind."[30] In its weaker form, this deflection takes the form of a Holocaust minimization or revisionism, diminishing the size, scope, and uniqueness of importance of the *Shoah*; accusing Jewish victims of complicity in their own demise; or alleging secret conspiracies between Hitler and the Zionists.[31] Holocaust inversion – by which Jews are alleged to have assumed the role of Nazis – may be construed as a form of Holocaust revisionism because it minimizes the scope of the Nazi crimes.[32] The belief that Nazi crimes were no worse than Israeli conduct has "brought welcome relief to many who had long borne a burden of guilt for the role which they, their families, their nations, or their churches had played in Hitler's crimes against the Jews, whether by participation or complicity, acquiescence or indifference."[33]

---

[25] Halimi is a young French Jew of Moroccan ancestry who was kidnapped, tortured over a period of three weeks, and murdered on January 21, 2006, by a gang of Muslim immigrants known as the "Barbarians." See Nidra Poller, *The Murder of Ilan Halimi: A Jewish Man Is Kidnapped in Paris, Tortured for 24 Days and Then Dies*, WALL STREET JOURNAL, February 26, 2006; available at www.opinionjournal. com/extra/?id=110008006.
[26] LÉVY, LEFT IN DARK TIMES, at 155.
[27] *Id.*
[28] *Id.*, at 156.
[29] *Id.*, at 155.
[30] *Id.*, at 156–7.
[31] *Id.*, at 157.
[32] See LEWIS, SEMITES AND ANTI-SEMITES, at 14 (observing that "[i]f the Israelis were no better than the Nazis, then it follows that the Nazis were no worse than the Israelis").
[33] See *id.*, at 14. Lewis has argued that this notion has "evoked a powerful response" not only among the heirs of the Nazis and their collaborators but "also ... in the

The third pillar, addressing "triumphal antifascism" or the "punishment of evildoers," consists in a particularly toxic form of the ideology of anti-Zionism. This ideology depicts Israel as a "[s]tolen" state, "[p]erpetuated thereafter by crime, occupation, violence, and lies," a "fascist State," a "racist State," the "worst State ... on the face of the earth."[34] The anti-Zionists who adhere to a putatively antiracist ideology deny that they harbor any animus against Jews per se. Rather, what they oppose is "people who traffic in their own memory (Holocaust deniers) and push out the memory of others (competition among victims) for the sole purpose of legitimizing an illegitimate state (third cornerstone of the system – its anti-Zionist stone)."[35]

THE POLITICS OF THE NEW CAMPUS ANTI-SEMITISM

Unlike some prior forms of anti-Semitism, which were associated with right-wing political groups, this burgeoning new form of anti-Semitism has been associated more with certain forms of liberal or progressive activism that have sometimes embraced anti-Semitism together with support for Palestinian causes both in Europe and in the United States.[36] In England, for instance, the All-Party Parliamentary Group Against Anti-Semitism "heard evidence that contemporary anti-Semitism in Britain is now more commonly found on the left of the political spectrum than on the right."[37] Although progressive voices typically have stood for equal rights and social progress, many progressives have found common cause with Arab and Muslim anti-Zionists, however "illiberal" those groups may be, based on shared anti-American and anticapitalist convictions as well as a belief that Palestinian Arabs are the underdog in their conflict with Israel.[38]

The irony here is that this form of bigotry may arise within an ideology that purports to be antiracist. The All-Party Parliamentary Group Against Anti-Semitism points out that "[m]any on the left are firm in their condemnation of racism and would almost certainly not accept

English-speaking countries, where many had chafed under the restraints imposed upon them by the revulsion against anti-Semitism in the immediate post Hitler era." *Id.*

[34] LEWIS, SEMITES AND ANTI-SEMITES, at 158.

[35] *Id.*

[36] See LAQUEUR, THE CHANGING FACE OF ANTI-SEMITISM, at 147–50; SCHOENFELD, THE RETURN OF ANTI-SEMITISM, at 85–100.

[37] ALL-PARTY PARLIAMENTARY GROUP, at 32.

[38] LAQUEUR, THE CHANGING FACE OF ANTI-SEMITISM, at 147–48; TOBIN ET AL., UNCIVIL UNIVERSITY, at 72–8.

that they were guilty of anti-Semitic discourse" and offers, rather generously, that "[i]gnorance of the history of anti-Jewish prejudice means
that some perhaps do not even realize that the language and imagery
they have used has resonances of a long tradition of anti-Jewish discourse and stereotypes."[39] In fact, the phenomenon sometimes may
result from conscious manipulation rather than historical ignorance, as
the All-Party Parliamentary Inquiry concedes: "[W]hen left wing or pro-
Palestinian discourse around the Middle East is manipulated and used
as a vehicle for anti-Jewish language and themes, the anti-Semitism is
harder to recognize and define and Jewish students can find themselves
isolated and unsupported, or in conflict with large groups of their fellow students."[40] As Walter Laqueur has cautioned, however, "[i]t would
be an exaggeration to maintain that contemporary antisemitism is
predominantly left wing in character, just as in previous ages it would
have been an exaggeration to apportion all the responsibility for anti-
semitism to conservatives."[41]

THE RELATIONSHIP BETWEEN ANTI-SEMITISM
AND ANTI-ISRAELISM

This perfect storm has erupted in several high-profile incidents on campuses around the United States over the last few years that generally
fall under the rubric of the "new anti-Semitism." These incidents have
had several ingredients in common. Jewish students have been singled
out, either by other students or by faculty, for adverse treatment. The
perpetrators have been outspoken critics of Israel. And the alleged anti-
Semitic conduct has been intertwined with anti-Israeli or anti-Zionist
rhetoric.

The recent increase in campus anti-Semitism has been closely associated with rising anti-Zionist sentiments and with liberal or left-wing
elements at many American universities. The relationship among these
phenomena has been a source of considerable controversy.[42] In general,
the relationship between anti-Semitism and anti-Zionism is both close

---

[39] ALL-PARTY PARLIAMENTARY GROUP, at 33.
[40] *Id.*
[41] LAQUEUR, THE CHANGING FACE OF ANTI-SEMITISM, at 150.
[42] This has been evident, for example, in the emotional public response to Professor
Alvin Rosenfeld's cogent essay, *"Progressive" Jewish Thought and the New Anti-
Semitism.* See, for example, *Essay Linking Liberal Jews and Anti-Semitism Sparks a
Furor,* NEW YORK TIMES, January 31, 2007, at E1.

and complex, and it has been presented differently in various places and periods. To the extent that liberal or progressive voices have come to adopt anti-Zionist rhetoric, they have taken with it the anti-Semitic attitudes from which much anti-Zionism has been inseparable.

Commentators have articulated the present relationship between these attitudes in several different formulations, each of which appears to contain at least a kernel of truth. Canadian parliamentarian and law professor Irwin Cotler, a former minister of justice, argues that anti-Zionism *is* anti-Semitic in its essence and in *most*, if not all, of its manifestations.[43] Historian Robert Wistrich counters that anti-Zionism and anti-Semitism are both analytically and historically distinct, but the two ideologies *have merged* since 1967.[44] Others, such as historian Deborah Lipstadt, argue that anti-Zionism and anti-Semitism remain distinct but that anti-Zionism *occasionally crosses the line into* outright anti-Semitism.[45] Still others believe that anti-Zionism is analytically distinct from anti-Semitism but that much apparent criticism of Israel or Zionism *is a disguised form of* anti-Semitism. This appears, for instance, to be the import of the 2006 *Report of the United Kingdom's All-Party Parliamentary Inquiry into Anti-Semitism*, which observed that "anti-Zionist discourse ... can be used deliberately as a way to mask or articulate prejudice against Jews."[46] Few serious commentators, if any at all, have taken the more extreme position that all anti-Zionism is anti-Semitism.

Cotler's position has the virtue of clarity and boldness, although other perspectives are more nuanced. Cotler compares "classical" or "traditional anti-Semitism" with the "new anti-Semitism." He defines the former as "discrimination against, or denial of, the right of Jews to live as equal members of a free society."[47] The new anti-Semitism, which he argues has been "correctly or incorrectly" described as "anti-Zionism," is closely analogous because it "involves the discrimination

43 Irwin Cotler, *Human Rights and the New Anti-Jewishness*, FRONTPAGE MAGAZINE, February 16, 2004; available at http://frontpagemag.com/Articles/ReadArticle.asp?ID=12191.

44 Robert Wistrich, *Anti-Zionism and Anti-Semitism*, 16 JEWISH POL. STUD. REV. (2004) 27–8; available at www.jcpa.org/phas/phas-wistrich-f04.htm.

45 Deborah E. Lipstadt, *Strategic Responses to Anti-Israelism*, IN AMERICAN JEWRY AND THE COLLEGE CAMPUS, at 5, 23.

46 See ALL-PARTY PARLIAMENTARY GROUP AGAINST ANTISEMITISM, at 18.

47 Irwin Cotler, *Human Rights and the New Anti-Jewishness*, FRONTPAGE MAGAZINE, February 16, 2004; available at http://frontpagemag.com/Articles/ReadArticle.asp?ID=12191.

against, denial of, or assault upon the right of the Jewish people to live as an equal member of the family of nations."[48] Both, he argues, are forms of discrimination.[49] "All that has happened is that it has moved from discrimination against Jews as individuals – a classical anti-Semitism for which there are indices of measurement – to discrimination against Jews as people – a new anti-Semitism – for which one has yet to develop indices of measurement."[50]

Those who maintain this position must account for the facts that some Jewish individuals and organizations hold views sharply critical of Israeli policy; that a small number of *Haredi* groups, such as the *Neturei Karta*, oppose the existence of a state of Israel (until the arrival of the Messiah) on theological grounds; and that there are also some secular Jews who oppose the State of Israel on antinationalist grounds. This may be addressed in many ways, including through the use of specific criteria (such as those described below) to distinguish between the new anti-Semitism and more innocuous criticisms of the State of Israel. Some commentators also argue that the new anti-Semitism, even when styled as an anti-Zionism, is not so much opposition to any political movement that may be denominated "Zionism" as it is opposition to the Jewish people as a collectivity.

On the other hand, those who deny Cotler's argument must explain the close correlation between anti-Zionist views and anti-Semitic views. Based on a survey of citizens in 10 European countries, recent research has shown that people who hold the former tend to hold the latter as well.[51] This does not necessarily imply that anti-Zionism *is* anti-Semitism. It may, however, shift the burden of persuasion to those who would argue that their animosity to the Jewish state does not reflect a deeper animus against the Jewish people. Statistically speaking, in Europe at least, research now shows that their efforts to do so will fail.

CRITERIA FOR DISTINGUISHING ANTI-SEMITISM FROM NONBIASED CRITICISMS OF ISRAEL

Several government agencies, officials, and other commentators have developed frameworks to distinguish the new anti-Semitism from

---

[48] *Id.*
[49] *Id.*
[50] *Id.*
[51] Edward H. Kaplan and Charles A. Small, *Anti-Israel Sentiment Predicts Anti-Semitism in Europe*, 50 J. CONFLICT RESOLUTION (2006) 548.

nondiscriminatory criticism of Israel. In general, these frameworks boil down to three or four basic criteria, each of which reflects one aspect of a broader standard, which is that anti-Semitic discourse singles out Jews or the Jewish state for adverse treatment in a manner that is neither fair nor justifiable, nor consistent with the treatment of others. The most famous example is Natan Sharansky's "3 D's," which reduce the criteria for identifying discrimination to demonization, double standards, and delegitimation of Israel.[52] Given the extent to which the various frameworks resemble one another, it is not surprising that Sharansky's mnemonically clever schema remains widely cited. It is not, however, the most precise of the various formulations. After all, demonization is but one form of the broader category of long-established anti-Jewish stereotypes, any of which would serve equally well as a criterion. At the same time, the delegitimation of the State of Israel is problematic largely because it exemplifies the use of double standards. The following typology presents what may be a more useful statement of generally accepted criteria for distinguishing the new anti-Semitism from other forms of anti-Israel criticism.

The first criterion is the use of classic anti-Semitic stereotypes to characterize Israel. An excellent example of classic stereotypes is the invocation of blood libel in the San Francisco State flyer described in Chapter 2. That flyer purported to show "Canned Palestinian Children Meat – Slaughtered According to Jewish Rites under American License." This representation is, on the one hand, unquestionably an expression of political sentiments regarding Israeli domestic policy and American foreign policy. On the other hand, it is also a clear and correct application of the medieval blood libel according to which Jews ritually murdered gentile children in order to consume their blood for ritual purposes. It is also somewhat unusual in that it explicitly denigrates "Jewish" people rather than using such terms as "Zionist" in order to conceal the actual target. As Sharansky's "3 D's" suggest, classic stereotypes also may include demonization of Israelis, similar to older characterizations of the Jewish people as the embodiment of evil. For example, flyers are sometimes seen on college campuses in which Israeli leaders are portrayed in diabolical fashion, just as Jews have been portrayed since medieval times as agents or children of the devil.

---

[52] Natan Sharansky, Anti-Semitism in 3D, JERUSALEM POST, February 23, 2004; available at www.ncsj.org/AuxPages/022304JPost_Shar.shtml.

The second criterion is the application of double standards. This may involve requiring behavior of Israel not expected of other countries or denying the Jewish people rights and legitimacy afforded other nations, including the right of self-determination. Those who deny Israel's right to exist do not express anti-Semitic impulses when they also oppose all other forms of nationhood, as some anarchists and globalists, for example, may do. What is salient here is the use of a disparate measure. There are, however, exceptions. Double standards are sometimes appropriate, such as when one holds oneself to a higher standard than others. For example, Israelis who hold their nation to a higher standard than they apply to Arab nations may be entirely free of anti-Semitism (although they may guilty of patronization toward those to whom they direct what has been called the "soft bigotry" of *low* expectations).

The third criterion is holding Jews collectively responsible for Israeli actions and policy regardless of actual complicity.[53] The attribution of collective wrongdoing to particular individuals, regardless of fault, is the defining attribute of prejudice under some conceptions.[54] Gordon Allport, for example, influentially defined prejudice as "[a]n avertive or hostile attitude toward a person who belongs to a group, simply because he belongs to that group, and is therefore presumed to have the objectionable qualities ascribed to the group." In traditional Christian anti-Semitism, this played out in the deicide myth. More recently, it has manifested in assaults on *diasporic* Jews for fabricated complicity in alleged Israeli atrocities.

Discourse exhibiting these characteristics, even if cloaked as criticism of Israel, has been characterized more properly as anti-Semitism.

[53] See, for example, U.S. DEPARTMENT OF STATE, REPORT ON GLOBAL ANTI-SEMITISM (2004); available at www.state.gov/g/drl/rls/40258.htm; and EUROPEAN MONITORING CENTRE ON RACISM AND XENOPHOBIA, WORKING DEFINITION OF ANTI-SEMITISM (March 16, 2005); available at http://eumc.europa.eu/eumc/material/pub/AS/AS-WorkingDefinition-draft.pdf; see also ALL-PARTY PARLIAMENTARY GROUP AGAINST ANTISEMITISM, REPORT OF THE ALL-PARTY PARLIAMENTARY INQUIRY INTO ANTISEMITISM (2006); available at http://thepcaa.org/Report.pdf., at 5; Irwin Cotler, *Human Rights and the New Anti-Jewishness*, FRONTPAGE MAGAZINE, February 16, 2004; available at http://frontpagemag.com/Articles/ReadArticle.asp?ID=12191; Natan Sharansky, *Anti-Semitism in 3D*, JERUSALEM POST, February 23, 2004; available at www.ncsj.org/AuxPages/022304JPost_Shar.shtml; Bernard Lewis, *The New Anti-Semitism: First Religion, then Race, then What?* 75 AM. SCHOLAR (2006) 25, 26–7; Robert Wistrich, *Correspondence from Robert Wistrich, Director, Vidal Sassoon International Centre for the Study of Anti-Semitism, Hebrew University of Jerusalem, to Brian Klug, Senior Research Fellow, Oxford University* (2005); available at http://sicsa.huji.ac.il/klug.html.
[54] See, for example, Gordon Allport, The Nature of Prejudice (1950) 8.

What they have in common is that they all indicate when facially anti-Israeli expressions are in fact an expression of an underlying anti-Jewish animus. They are only indicators, however, and cannot substitute for fact-specific analysis. Whether these forms of anti-Semitism may, in conjunction with other conduct, form the basis for a civil rights claim is of course a separate and exacting inquiry requiring consideration not only of the parameters of Title VI protection but also of First Amendment limitations.

Some commentators also identify a fourth criterion, that is, the use of comparisons between Israel or Jews and Nazi Germany, which is called "Holocaust inversion." This criterion may be viewed more properly as an application of the first two criteria (demonization and double standards), but it appears frequently enough to merit separate discussion. Holocaust inversion is analogous to other forms of what might be called "human rights inversion": the practice of accusing victims of the very wrong that they have suffered. (Other examples include the myth of the black racist and the stereotype of the "Indian giver.") Among its myriad variants, Holocaust inversion includes portraying Jews (especially Israeli Jews) as Nazis, crypto-Nazis, Nazi sympathizers, Holocaust perpetrators, or Holocaust copycats.

Holocaust inversion, like other human rights inversions, has several functions: to shock, silence, threaten, insulate, and legitimize. First and most unmistakably, human rights inversion is *shocking*, even when it is repeated frequently, which is why it is repeated frequently. No one tells Holocaust survivors – or a nation of Holocaust survivors and their children – that they are Nazis without expecting to shock.

Human rights inversion is shocking in a particular manner, a manner that tends to *silence*. Given the sensitivity of many Jews to issues concerning the *Shoah*, Holocaust inversions have the power not only to shock but also to silence expression of Jewish viewpoints, including speech sympathetic to the State of Israel. Moreover, the stereotype of Jewish conspiratorial power, combined with the use of Nazi motifs, has a peculiarly chilling effect. Beyond silencing, human rights inversion is *threatening* because the ascription of guilt carries with it the threat of punishment. This is, after all, the point of the allegation. Consider the warning that Jewish students at the University of California at Irvine received from one recent campus speaker: "[I]t's time for you to live in some fear now, because you were so good at dispensing fear." Nevertheless, human rights inversion is presented in a manner that is frequently immune from criticism because its political guise is *insulating*.

That is to say, it provides a means by which animus can be expressed without provoking the resistance that post–World War II racism tends to precipitate. This masking effect has permitted the growth and dissemination of hate and bias that otherwise would be checked by various social, political, administrative, and legal controls. Finally, it is *legitimizing.* The myth of the black rapist served, in the minds of Southern racists, to legitimize Jim Crow lynchings. The Israelis-as-Nazis analogy serves to justify not only anti-Israeli but also anti-Jewish activity that otherwise is socially or legally repelled. Bernard-Henri Lévy has explained that Holocaust inversion erodes social conventions that have developed as a safeguard against recurrence of genocidal murder, enabling "people to feel once again the desire and, above all, the *right* to burn all the synagogues they want, to attack boys wearing yarmulkes, to harass large numbers of rabbis … in order for anti-Semitism to be reborn on a large scale."

In an early manifestation, German-Jewish linguist Victor Klemperer's 1934 use of Holocaust inversion reveals its inner logic: "To me the Zionists … are just as offensive as the Nazis. With their nosing after blood, their ancient 'cultural roots', their partly canting, partly obtuse winding back of the world, they are altogether a match for the National Socialists." Klemperer could not have intertwined this paleoinversion any more transparently with anti-Jewish stereotypes. This emphasis on Jewish "nosing" would be telling enough, but Klemperer's notion of "nosing after blood" smells strongly of medieval blood libel.

Those hints become explicit in the more recent work of Oxford poet Tom Paulin, who builds on Klemperer's work in his own well-known inversions, especially in his poem, "Crossfire," which speaks of a young Palestinian boy who is "gunned down by the Zionist SS." The blood libel appears more explicitly here in its accusation of child killing. Some commentators also argue that this poem's reference to "dumb goys" is lifted directly from Adolph Hitler's *Mein Kampf.* What is crucial here is that classic stereotypes are combined with Holocaust inversion to portray a murderous crime. The intended impact of the poem could not be clearer: The Jews are guilty of a great crime for which justice must be exacted. As Joseph Goebbals put it, "The Jews are guilty [and] the punishment is coming." For Paulin, the appropriate punishment is clear. Speaking of Brooklyn-born Israeli settlers, Paulin said: "I think they should be shot dead. I think they are Nazis, racists; I feel nothing but hatred for them."

4

Criticism

To the extent that much campus anti-Semitism falls within the rubric of the "new anti-Semitism," its discriminatory status is subject to the same criticism and controversies that have long attended to that term. Critics of the new anti-Semitism argue variously that the new anti-Semitism is not new, that it is not anti-Semitic, that it is not a serious problem, that it rests on an internal contradiction, that it suppresses academic freedom, and that it infringes on the freedom of speech. These critics, in turn, have been charged with turning a blind eye to serious bigotry, developing arguments that insulate wrongdoing from censure, and in extreme cases, succumbing to a pathology of "anti-Semitism denial," analogous to Holocaust denial.[1] While the criticisms vary in degree of persuasiveness, none of them succeeds in refuting the basic reality of contemporary anti-Semitism, whereas all of them provide cover for those who truly mean to render harm. Nevertheless, each criticism also contains an element of truth that must be recognized. The theory and practice of counteracting new anti-Semitism can only be strengthened by a confrontation with these critical perspectives.

THE NEWNESS QUESTION

Some commentators argue that the "new anti-Semitism" is not really new. This argument is sometimes merely technical or academic, but it is often advanced in service of a broader agenda, for example, as evidence that the supposed resurgence is an illusory claim that has resurfaced periodically and never panned out. In 2003, a spate of books was published that announced the arrival of the new anti-Semitism. One prominent

[1] GABRIEL SCHOENFELD, RETURN OF ANTI-SEMITISM (2004) 144–6.

example is *Never Again? The Threat of the New Anti-Semitism*, by Abraham Foxman, the Anti-Defamation League's national director. Critics such as Norman Finkelstein have observed that this supposedly "new" anti-Semitism had been described by Foxman's Anti-Defamation League predecessors Arnold Forster and Benjamin Epstein *not less than 30 years beforehand* in a volume also entitled, *The New Anti-Semitism*.[2] Indeed, it has been argued that Forster and Epstein's volume relies on scholarship published as far back as 1968.[3] Moreover, while some trace the new anti-Semitism to the Six Day War, others trace it back to the end of World War II.

In fact, none of these observations diminishes the fact that new forms of anti-Semitism have emerged since World War II, that these forms became more prevalent after 1968, and that their growth has accelerated since around the turn of the new millennium. From some perspectives, a 40- or 60-year-old phenomenon may seem positively Paleolithic. When considered against the backdrop of the multimillennial history of the Jewish people and their antagonists, however, 60 years is something of a rounding error. In the long run, the contemporary forms of anti-Semitism do have a relative newness, whether of 10 or 40 or 60 years' duration, when compared with the older forms that preceded them. To observe the newness of the garb, however, is not to deny the age of the body it clothes.

The underlying continuity of anti-Semitism, new and old, is important to appreciate. The seriousness with which opponents take the new anti-Semitism is based in no small measure on the concern that it is connected to older forms of the phenomenon that have had catastrophic outcomes. This is explains why even minor incidents give rise to such concerns, at least among some observers. To view the new anti-Semitism as a wholly new phenomenon, without continuities with older forms, is a significant mistake. At the same time, it is also a mistake to ignore discontinuities and to view the new anti-Semitism as entirely unchanged from older manifestations. Hannah Arendt called this mistake the "thesis of eternal anti-Semitism."[4] Arendt explained that this "thesis" carries two dangers: It may justify anti-Semitism by suggesting that Jew hatred is a "normal," unchanging phenomenon, and it may absolve anti-Semites'

[2] See NORMAN G. FINKELSTEIN, BEYOND CHUTZPAH: ON THE MISUSE OF ANTI-SEMITISM AND THE ABUSE OF HISTORY (2005) 21–2.
[3] Jonathan Judaken, *So What's New? Rethinking the "New Antisemitism" in a Global Age*, 42 PATTERNS OF PREJUDICE (September 2008) 531, 532.
[4] HANNAH ARENDT, THE ORIGINS OF TOTALITARIANISM (2004) 17.

"crimes greater than anybody had ever believed possible."[5] For these reasons, it is important to recognize the contingent, malleable nature of anti-Semitism's diverse manifestations. In other words, the qualities and risks of the new anti-Semitism are best appreciated when it is understood in terms of both its newness (*i.e.*, its discontinuities with older forms) and its oldness (*i.e.*, its continuities).

ANTI-SEMITISM DENIAL AND MINIMIZATION

Some critics dispute not only the newness of the "new anti-Semitism" but also its status as anti-Semitism. Most commonly, they charge that the new anti-Semitism is just a label used to suppress legitimate criticisms of Israel. Alan Dershowitz has characterized this common claim as a "straw man argument."[6] Dershowitz has repeatedly offered to pay $1,000 to anyone who can identify any instance in which any Jewish leader has equated anti-Semitism with mere criticism of Israel. His money has been safe because no one really equates the two, although critics constantly refute their purported attempts to do so. The distinctions that Chapter 3 draws between anti-Semitism and nonbiased criticisms of Israel have become largely conventional. In fact, many of the commentators who most vigorously condemn anti-Zionist propaganda as anti-Semitic have hastened to emphasize that much criticism of Israel is neither anti-Semitic nor illegitimate.[7] In some instances, they attempt to demonstrate their progressive bona fides with almost ritual denunciations of the Israeli policies with which they disagree. No other people is expected to offer such self-flagellations as proof of sincerity.

The difficult question is why critics so frequently claim that anti-Semitism studies draw no distinctions between the new anti-Semitism and nonbiased criticisms of Israel, even when the differences are repeatedly articulated in the literature. In fact, the denial of anti-Semitism has both a long history and a stubborn persistence. As we have seen,

[5] *Id.*, at 16–7.
[6] Alan M. Dershowitz, *Making the Case for Israel*, FRONTPAGEMAG.COM, June 1, 2004; available at www.frontpagemag.com/Articles/ReadArticle.asp?ID=13590.
[7] *See, e.g.*, PHYLLIS CHESLER, THE NEW ANTI-SEMITISM: THE CURRENT CRISIS AND WHAT WE MUST DO ABOUT IT (2003) 163–8 (endorsing criticism of Israel's treatment of women, Arabs, and religious minorities while arguing that much anti-Zionism is also anti-Semitic); ABRAHAM FOXMAN, NEVER AGAIN? THE THREAT OF THE NEW ANTI-SEMITISM (2003) 195 (distinguishing anti-Semitism from "opposition to Israeli policies and actions" and asserting that "[p]rincipled, fair criticism of Israel and Israeli leaders is always permissible").

Bernard-Henri Lévy has characterized the denial of anti-Semitism as a reversal of what he calls the "love of victimhood." This denial of anti-Semitism accomplishes two simultaneous functions. First, it denies Jews and Israel the post-Holocaust mantle of victimhood. This reduces the sensitivity that conscientious people otherwise would have to a reawakening of socially stigmatized bigotry. Second, and more important, it recasts Jewish advocates as fraudulent pleaders of special interests. This feeds easily into long-established stereotypes of Jewish exploitation. As recast, the gist of this stereotype is that the "Jews are no longer exploiting the wealth of nations but monopolizing that much rarer good ... human compassion."[8] This putative hoarding of victimhood capital is "the first reason to start resenting them again and, in clear conscience, in the name of the sacred concern due to all the world's dead, to start hating them again."[9]

Nevertheless, it must be acknowledged that overplaying the "anti-Semitism card" must be avoided for several reasons. These are, generally speaking, a subset of the risks of playing "the race card" that Stanford Law Professor Richard Thompson Ford catalogued in his important recent book of that name.[10] First, it is dishonest (at least if it is done intentionally). "When people transgress or just screw up," Ford writes, "they should take their lumps – not try to wriggle out of them with tactics of distraction or blame shifting."[11] Ford almost certainly was not thinking of either Israelis or Palestinians when he wrote those lines, but each group likely would read his words as a fitting rebuke to the other. Second, it is shortsighted and dangerous in the way of the boy who cried wolf. It may be regretted if it is needed later, especially if others become wary of false or exaggerated claims. Third, it can be mean-spirited because it involves the use of charges that in some cases can have serious repercussions. In addition, there are two other dangers that Ford does not discuss. Even if true, an overplayed "anti-Semitism card" may distract socially concerned individuals and organizations from other pressing problems, including social injustices facing other groups. Finally, it may disrupt or retard outreach efforts to other groups, including Arab

[8] BERNARD-HENRI LÉVY, LEFT IN DARK TIMES: A STAND AGAINST THE NEW BARBARISM (2008) (Benjamin Moser, trans.) 155.
[9] *Id.*, at 156.
[10] RICHARD THOMPSON FORD, THE RACE CARD (2009) 18–22.
[11] *Id.*, at 18.

and Muslim groups, with whom partnership efforts may be jeopardized by insinuations that their members act in bad faith.

The question is whether, in light of present circumstances, these arguments counsel in favor of less vigorous opposition to existing anti-Semitism, a position that has been described as "quietism." The answer to this question might be "yes" if contemporary anti-Semitism were not widely and meticulously documented in the reports of such entities as the U.S. Department of State, the Stephen Roth Institute for the Study of Contemporary Anti-Semitism, the U.K. All-Party Parliamentary Group against Antisemitism, and the European Jewish Congress. The sad record of American Jewish organizations during the Holocaust demonstrates both the historical pressures to refrain from "playing the anti-Semitism card" and the dangers inherent in the decision to do so. Even if the resurgence of global anti-Semitism were not so widely documented, however, it also should be considered – in the spirit of the so-called broken windows theory – that to permit even minor infractions is to risk the recurrence of larger ones. In this respect, excessive vigilance must be considered preferable to a failure of resolve.

THE NEUMANN-BUTLER PARADOX

A more sophisticated argument, advanced by philosophers Judith Butler and Michael Neumann, posits that the opponents of the new anti-Semitism are engaged in a form of intellectual hypocrisy. On the one hand, as Butler explained in 2004, they argue that it is anti-Semitic to attribute collective responsibility for the actions of the State of Israel to individual Jews regardless of their personal involvement in Israel's affairs. In this argument, the equation of Israel with Jewry is viewed as an effect of anti-Semitism. On the other hand, they also argue that it is anti-Semitic to apply different standards to the State of Israel because Israel is the collective embodiment of the Jewish people. Here, by contrast, the equation of Israel with Jewry is an assumption on which the argument is based. The equation of Israel, Butler concludes, works both "in the service of an argument against anti-Semitism" and "as the effect of anti-Semitism itself."[12] To oversimplify somewhat, it is anti-Semitic either to claim that Israel collectively embodies the Jewish people to deny the claim.

[12] JUDITH BUTLER, PRECARIOUS LIFE: THE POWERS OF MOURNING AND VIOLENCE (2004) 125.

Michael Neumann more bluntly summarized the apparent contradiction: "'Anti-Zionism is anti-Semitism!' quickly alternates with 'Don't confuse Zionism with Judaism! How dare you, you anti-Semite!'"[13]

At first blush, this argument does have at least the superficial appearance of plausibility. Opponents of the new anti-Semitism do in fact argue simultaneously (1) that harms *to* Israel *are* harms *to* all individual Jews and (2) that harms *by* Israel *are not* harms *by* all individual Jews. These two claims are not, however, mutually exclusive, nor are they unique to the Jewish experience. They are closely analogous to the human rights advocate's belief that both (1) harms *to* humanity are harms *to* all individual human beings and (2) harms *by* humanity are not harms *by* all individual human beings. John Dunne's observation that "no man is an island" does not implicate every person individually in every murder, although it does imply that "any man's death diminishes" every other person and that his death bell "tolls for thee." In the same way, it is not inconsistent to insist both that anti-Israeli defamations can be hurtful to non-Israeli Jews and also that holding non-Israeli Jews collectively responsible for Israel's actions is inescapably racist.

Typically, it is not good form to question the motives for which scholars advance even unpersuasive arguments. In the case of Neumann, however, the question of motive may be unavoidable because he has raised it himself. "We should almost never take anti-Semitism seriously," he writes in a passionate indictment of Israeli politics, "and maybe we should have some fun with it."[14] Having "fun" with "anti-Semitism," then, is Neumann's self-described motive for developing this criticism. Indeed, Neumann reportedly described his methods even more candidly:

> If an effective strategy means that some truths about the Jews don't come to light, I don't care. If an effective strategy [of helping the Palestinians] means encouraging reasonable anti-Semitism, or reasonable hostility to Jews, I also don't care. If it means encouraging vicious, racist anti-Semitism, or the destruction of the state of Israel, I still don't care.[15]

Butler, a more serious thinker, professes concern for the phenomenon of anti-Semitism. Nevertheless, she has tethered her formidable reputation to an argument that had been developed in service of a rather questionable agenda.

[13] Michael Neumann, *What Is Anti-Semitism?* IN ALEXANDER COCKBURN AND JEFFREY ST. CLAIR, EDS., THE POLITICS OF ANTI-SEMITISM (2003) 1.

[14] *Id.*

[15] Jonathan Kay, *Trent University's Problem Professor*, NATIONAL POST, August 9, 2003; available at www.cjc.ca/template.php?action=itn&Story=379.

THE SUMMER-BUTLER DOUBLE-BIND

Another criticism is that the very notion of the new anti-Semitism has the tendency to suppress expression of legitimate political critique. Former Harvard University President Lawrence Summers once famously argued that anti-Israel boycotts "are anti-Semitic in their effect if not their intent." In response, Judith Butler has argued that Summers' argument amounted to an attack on academic freedom "in effect if not in intent."[16] Butler reasoned that "[i]f we think that to criticize Israeli violence, or to call for economic pressure to be put on the Israeli state to change its policies, is to be 'effectively anti-Semitic,' we will fail to voice our opposition for fear of being named as part of an anti-Semitic enterprise."[17] Summers and Butler each state a legitimate point, and the combined force of their arguments is to paired mirror-image ethical double-binds.

Summers is right to caution that some anti-Israeli activities may have an anti-Semitic effect even if they lack a demonstrable anti-Semitic intent. This is true for at least three reasons that have generally frustrated efforts to address racism and anti-Semitism in our putatively "postracial" society. First, intentional bias has become increasingly difficult to prove. As racial bigotry attained a social stigma during the late twentieth century, racial animus became more covert. Few bigots will admit to illicit forms of animus, which is why even intentional discrimination is often first identified in its effects. Second, biases against outgroups are frequently unconscious. This, too, may be a result of the social stigma that has lately attached to racial animus. Third, discriminatory effects sometimes can arise from actions that lack present conscious or unconscious bias. This is so because some practices, while pure of motivation, may exacerbate an environment that has already been polluted by the bigotry of others. Regardless of intent, actions that reinforce malignant racial stereotypes can be properly characterized as malignant.

Butler, however, is also correct in predicting that accusations of anti-Semitism may have the collateral effect of curbing speech. Indeed, that is the point of invoking the label: to discourage expressive conduct that manifests hostility toward Jews. But such accusations also may have the unintended effect of discouraging criticisms of Israel that are not

[16] Judith Butler, *The Charge of Anti-Semitism: Jews, Israel, and the Risks of Public Critique,* IN RON ROSENBAUM, ED., THOSE WHO FORGET THE PAST: THE QUESTION OF ANTI-SEMITISM (2004) 438.
[17] *Id.,* at 439–40. At times, it is unclear whether Butler's concern is for academic freedom or for freedom of political expression – two distinct ideals – but either way it is important.

motivated by animus. The hazard arises when the accusation is mistaken, and nonbiased speech is curtailed. An overzealous concern to limit anti-Semitic discourse can lead to inappropriate stigmatization of political expression that seeks to resist Israeli policies. The strength of this argument varies inversely with the weight of the anti-Semitism charge; that is to say, the less that conduct is tainted by anti-Semitic animus, the more attentive one may be to the prospect that it is unnecessarily discouraged. Thus there is strong reason for caution in playing the anti-Semitism card, especially against those who may be highly sensitive to the charge of bias (as Butler, for example, appears to be).

ANTI-SEMITISM CLAIMS AS A CYNICAL PLOY

Other commentators have been less delicate than Butler, bluntly charging that supporters of Israel "often make false accusations of anti-Semitism to silence Israel's critics."[18] For example, British-Pakistani intellectual Tariq Ali has claimed that "[t]he campaign against the supposed new 'anti-[S]emitism' in Europe today is basically a cynical ploy on the part of the Israeli Government to seal off the Zionist state from any criticism of its regular and consistent brutality against the Palestinians."[19]

An "Ad Hoc Committee to Defend the University" has circulated a petition, signed by over 650 university professors and others, denouncing efforts to "defame scholars and pressure administrators."[20] The petitioners argue that these "defenders of Israel" are threatening free speech, academic freedom, the "norms of academic life," and "the core mission of institutions of higher education in a democratic society."[21] Indeed, the petitioners warn that these efforts pose a "serious threat to institutions of higher education in the United States."[22] The methods that the ad

---

[18] *See, e.g.*, Scott Handleman, *Trivializing Jew-Hatred*, IN ALEXANDER COCKBURN AND JEFFREY ST. CLAIR, EDS., THE POLITICS OF ANTI-SEMITISM (2003) 13.

[19] Tariq Ali, *To Be Intimidated Is to Be an Accomplice: Notes on Anti-Semitism, Zionism and Palestine*, COUNTERPUNCH, March 4, 2004; available at www.counterpunch.org/ali03042004.html.

[20] http://sites.google.com/site/defenduniversity/adhoccommitteetodefendtheuniversitysigna. Signatories include academics from institutions such as Harvard, Yale, Princeton, Columbia, Brown, Cornell, Pennsylvania, MIT, Michigan, Northwestern, Berkeley, and many others. See Ad Hoc Committee to Defend the University, Petition, at http://defend.university.googlepages.com/home.

[21] *Id.*

[22] *Id.*

hoc committee specifically decries include "unfounded" allegations
of anti-Semitism, efforts to broaden the definition of anti-Semitism,
and certain lawsuits presumably brought under civil rights laws.[23]
In other words, the petitioners are broadly targeting a wide range of
efforts intended to protect Jewish university students from anti-Semitic
harassment.

This sort of charge appears to have rhetorical traction with many academics and is sometimes combined with stereotypical assertions about
Jewish conspiratorial power and Jewish control over the media.[24] Indeed,
Stephen Walt and John Mearsheimer recently called anti-Semitism allegations the "Great Silencer."[25] Interestingly, this Great Silencer has not stilled
Walt and Mearsheimer's presses, nor hampered their international tour,
nor quashed their audience before the United Kingdom's House of Lords,
nor prevented the reportedly healthy advances on sales of their book.[26]

The irony in this charge is that hostile campus environments serve
primarily to silence the victims of discrimination, and yet it is the discriminators and their allies who claim censorship. Specifically, anti-Semitic
incidents have had the affect of silencing some Jewish students and faculty on college campuses who are intimidated from expressing their
viewpoint publicly.[27] In reference to this problem, Natan Sharansky has
dubbed American Jewish college students the "new Jews of silence,"
a phrase resonant of the experience of Russian Jews in the old Soviet
Union.[28] In other words, the *failure* to enforce antidiscrimination law
may have a more chilling effect on campus free expression than the exercise of this power.

The silencing function of hate speech is well established in the literature. Henry Louis Gates, Jr., has suggested that "perhaps the most
powerful arguments of all for the regulation of hate speech come from
those who maintain that such regulation will really enhance the diversity and range of public discourse."[29] This is so because hate speech has

---

[23] *Id.*

[24] BERNARD HARRISON, ISRAEL, ANTI-SEMITISM, AND FREE SPEECH (2007) 32.

[25] JOHN J. MEARSHEIMER & STEPHEN WALT, THE ISRAEL LOBBY AND AMERICAN
FOREIGN POLICY (2007) 191–6.

[26] *See, e.g.,* THE ANNOTICO REPORT (October 3, 2007); available at www.annoticore-
port.com/2007/10/israel-lobby-to-be-translated-into.html.

[27] *See, e.g.,* TOBIN ET AL., UNCIVIL UNIVERSITY, at 107.

[28] Quoted in Sarah Stern, *Campus Anti-Semitism,* IN USCCR, CAMPUS ANTI-SEMITISM,
at 22.

[29] Henry Louis Gates, *War of Words: Critical Race Theory and the First Amendment,*
IN HENRY LOUIS GATES, JR., ET AL., SPEAKING OF RACE, SPEAKING OF SEX: HATE

the peculiar ability to silence the groups that it aims to diminish. As Charles Lawrence has explained, the visceral "fear, rage [and] shock" of hate speech systematically preempts response.[30] Some forms of campus anti-Semitism are more effective at silencing Jewish response than others. Given the sensitivity of many Jews to issues concerning the *Shoah*, Holocaust inversions have the power not only to shock but also to silence expression of Jewish viewpoints, including speech sympathetic to the State of Israel.[31] Moreover, the stereotype of Jewish conspiratorial power, combined with the use of Nazi motifs, has a peculiarly chilling effect. As activist Melanie Kaye/Kantrowitz explains, it "mutes our loud, proud Jewish energy, make us afraid of seeming too powerful, too ... well, Jewish. How can we fight injustice powerfully if we fear our power?"[32] Arguably, this was the function and perhaps also the intent of the Columbia professor who reportedly silenced an inquisitive Jewish student with the words, "You have no voice in this debate." This function of hostile speech is worth noting in light of the inevitable claims that those who oppose speech are the silencers.

The greatest irony is that some students are now silenced not only by the harassment itself but by faculty members who denounce efforts to eliminate anti-Semitism as a threat to academic freedom. As I have traveled to college campuses, students and faculty have expressed precisely this concern to me. That is, they are reluctant to speak out against hate and bias incidents for fear that they will be accused of trying to silence debate or suppress academic freedom. Recently, a self-styled "Ad Hoc Committee to Defend the University" circulated a petition condemning "defenders of Israel" for their putative "attacks on academic freedom."[33]

Increasingly, as a result of this type of on-campus bullying, many students have been warned not to use the word "anti-Semitism." This is

Speech, Civil Rights, and Civil Liberties (1994) 43–5. It should be noted that I am recommending only the enforcement of antidiscrimination law, not hate speech regulations. Nevertheless, some of the same arguments apply.

30 Charles R. Lawrence III, *If He Hollers, Let Him Go: Regulating Racist Speech on Campus*, Duke L. J. (1990) 431, 452.

31 The point is amplifed in Kenneth L. Marcus, *Higher Education, Harassment, and First Amendment Opportunism*, 16 Wm. & Mary B. Rts. J. (April 2008) 1025, 1050–2.

32 Melanie Kaye/Kantrowitz, *Some Notes on Anti-Semitism from a Progressive Jewish Perspective*, Jewish Currents, March 2007; available at www.jewishcurrents.org/2007-mar-kayekantrowiz.htm.

33 http://defend.university.googlepages.com/.

a particularly dangerous development. In the words of the Civil Rights Commission's Campus Anti-Semitism Public Education Campaign, "Silence is an Ally of Hate." According to pro-Israel professors, it is now adventurous, if not risky, to speak out against anti-Semitism in many of America's institutions of higher learning. On one campus it was even considered risky to openly discuss recorded acts of anti-Semitism; members of the faculty met in secret to discuss the rise of anti-Semitism and anti-Zionism on campus. The "Great Silencer" accusation is used by institutionally powerful voices to silence the voices of those who need to be heard.

5

First Amendment Issues

Literary critic and First Amendment scholar Stanley Fish has commented that crying "First Amendment" is the modern equivalent to crying "Wolf!"[1] This is particularly true, he argues, in the academy, where "the First Amendment ... is invoked ritually when there are no First Amendment issues in sight."[2] Interestingly, Fish observed that the First Amendment is misused most frequently on college campuses to defend anti-Jewish activities.[3] Fish gave several examples. At the University of Illinois at Champaign-Urbana, a student newspaper printed a letter arguing that Jews manipulate America and urging the president to terminate Jews from all government positions lest they "face another Holocaust." At Santa Rosa Junior College, a student published an article arguing that anti-Semitism is the result of Jewish behavior. At Harvard, the Education Department invited, disinvited, and then reinvited poet Tom Paulin to deliver a distinguished endowed lecture. Fish notes that Paulin, as we have seen in Chapter 3, had urged that Jewish settlers be shot dead and argued that Israeli police and military forces were the equivalent of the Nazi SS. In all these examples, Fish argues, campus figures have justified their role in anti-Semitic expression by insisting that it was mandated by the First Amendment. In fact, however, as Fish points out, anti-Semites have no constitutional right to receive such invitations and publications. Those who invite such Jew hatred do so out of their own discretion and bad judgment.[4]

---

[1] Stanley Fish, *The Free-Speech Follies*, CHRON. HIGHER EDUC. (June 13, 2003); available at http://chronicle.com/jobs/news/2003/06/2003061301c.
[2] *Id.*
[3] *Id.*
[4] *Id.*

In the *Irvine* case, the administration has consistently maintained that the alleged harassment of Jewish students is protected by the First Amendment.[5] Early on, administrators at the University of California at Irvine quoted to Department of Education's Office for Civil Rights' (OCR's) San Francisco investigators an OCR guidance letter that I had written for then-Assistant Secretary Gerald Reynolds. That letter clarified that OCR regulations "do not regulate the content of speech" and that "OCR does not require or prescribe speech, conduct or harassment codes that impair the exercise of rights protected under the First Amendment."[6] Nothing in my First Amendment letter, however, had suggested constitutional protections for the outrageous conduct that Susan Tuchman alleged. Oddly, Dean Erwin Chemerinsky, Irvine's widely respected constitutionalist, actually has argued that the allegations at Irvine involve only speech.[7] This is a rather remarkable (and clearly false) argument in light of the nonspeech elements alleged in that case: stone throwing, vandalism, and so on.

Nevertheless, *Irvine* argues that Tuchman and her clients are asking "that UC Irvine silence just one side of the [campus Middle East] dialogue: the Muslim side."[8] Indeed, it was Irvine's vice chancellor who reportedly claimed that "one person's hate speech is another person's education."[9] At Irvine, it appears, the administration refuses to distinguish between the two. The selective invocation and exaggerated posture of First Amendment absolutism can be somewhat trying when it is raised by those who have little concern for its application in other contexts. "What becomes interesting," as Catharine MacKinnon once observed, "is when the First Amendment frame is invoked and when it is not."[10] In many cases, the Free Speech Clause is invoked as cover for an agenda that at best is political, if not ethnic or racial, rather than jurisprudential.

---

[5] *See, e.g.,* H. G. Reza, *UC Irvine Chancellor Calls Harsh Speech Free Speech; Michael V. Drake Tells Concerned Jews that Muslims on Campus Have the Right to Vent,* LOS ANGELES TIMES, May 31, 2007, at B1.

[6] Letter of Diane Giocari to Gloria Guinto and Robert Scott, dated August 19, 2005, at 5.

[7] Erwin Chemerinsky, *Unpleasant Speech on Campus, Even Hate Speech, Is a First Amendment Issue,* 17 WM. & MARY B. RTS. J. (March 2009) 765.

[8] U.S. COMMISSION ON CIVIL RIGHTS, CAMPUS ANTI-SEMITISM (2006), at 65 (quoting UC Irvine counsel Diane Geocaris).

[9] *See* Reut Cohen, *Jewish Students Discuss Vandalism with Chancellor,* CAMPUS J., October 24, 2006; available at www.campusj.com/2006/10/24/jewish-students-discuss-vandalism-with-chancellor/.

[10] CATHARINE A. MACKINNON, ONLY WORDS (1993) 12.

The administration at Irvine has taken a far less absolutist position when other students' rights are at stake. For example, while Jewish students were claiming anti-Semitic harassment, a conservative campus organization staged what it called an "affirmative action bake sale." Protesting the use of racial preferences in college admissions, the students charged different prices for baked goods depending on the buyer's race. White and Asian students were charged the most in order to illustrate the burden, which conservative students argue is imposed by preferential policies. Interestingly, the Irvine administration did not hesitate to shut down the "bake sale," even though it was arguably a pure example of constitutionally protected free speech.

Unavoidably, antidiscrimination law will have the effect of silencing some discriminators, just as tort law silences some defrauders, securities law silences some con artists, and conspiracy law silences some conspirators. This will be true as long as lawbreakers use words to further their malfeasance. The serious First Amendment question here is not whether any speech is silenced but whether legitimate, protected speech is chilled in a manner that unacceptably hampers speech.[11] At the same time, it cannot be forgotten that to do nothing, and to permit harassment of Jewish students, is to permit a more insidious form of silence.

THE SCOPE OF FIRST AMENDMENT PROTECTIONS

To the extent that campus anti-Semitism raises First Amendment or academic freedom issues, they largely mirror those raised by racial, national origin, sexual, and disability harassment law.[12] In other words, university-based anti-Semitic harassment raises precisely the same speech issues that antifemale, antiblack, anti-Hispanic, or antidisability harassment raises under the same and comparable civil rights provisions, no more and no less. In all these cases, it is true that (1) the Supreme Court has not yet directly addressed the issue, (2) the Supreme Court has shown no inclination to address the issue, and (3) finding antiharassment law unconstitutional would overturn more than 20 years of legal development not only

---

[11] For a demonstration that the "charge of attempting to silence 'all critics of Israel' by smearing them as anti-Semites is absurd," see HARRISON, ISRAEL, ANTI-SEMITISM AND FREE SPEECH, at 35–7.

[12] See Eugene Volokh, *Freedom of Speech, Religious Harassment Law, and Religious Accommodation Law*, 33 LOY U. CHI. L. J. (2002) 57.

in education law but also in employment, housing, and other areas.[13] In fairness, it is also true that the opposite holding – that is, that there are no First Amendment limits whatsoever on campus speech and harassment codes – similarly would sweep away quite a bit of case law.[14]

These foundational issues, however, have been the subject of considerable litigation and scholarly interest. Harassment law imposes content-based (and arguably even viewpoint-based) restrictions on various forms of expression, and such restrictions are presumptively unconstitutional under current doctrine.[15] Harassment laws may be defended on several grounds, including that they are narrowly tailored means of achieving a compelling governmental interest. In other words, they meet the stringent standards of strict judicial scrutiny. Alternatively, to the extent that harassment laws are construed to reach no further than the "fighting words" doctrine under *Chaplinsky v. New Hampshire* or to curb imminent incitement to violence under *Brandenburg v. Ohio*, they may be defended under those precedents.[16]

In application, anti-Semitic harassment has various features in common with other forms of harassment, including its ability to yield easy cases. Few would argue that the rock allegedly thrown at a Jewish student at UC Irvine was constitutionally protected even if it was, as it appears, used moments before as a paperweight for anti-Israeli political literature. Similarly, the threats and intimidation alleged at several campuses are no more protected as a result of the anti-Zionist political discourse with which they are interspersed.

[13] See Richard H. Fallon, *Sexual Harassment, Content Neutrality, and the First Amendment Dog that Didn't Bark*, 1994 SUP. CT. REV. (1995) 1, 9–12; Andrea Meryl Kirshenbaum, *Hostile Environment Sexual Harassment sdaLaw and the First Amendment: Can the Two Peacefully Coexist?* 12 TEX. J. WOMEN & L. (2002) 67–9.

[14] *See, e.g.,* Iota XI Chapter of Sigma Chi Fraternity v. George Mason University, 993 F. 2d 386, 393 (4th Cir. 1993) (applying First Amendment protections to a fraternity's "ugly woman contest" and holding a university cannot selectively limit speech); Roberts v. Haragan, 346 F. Supp. 2d 853, 867–73 (N.D. Tex. 2004) (striking down portions of a campus speech code on First Amendment grounds); UWM Post, Inc. v. Board of Regents of the University of Wisconsin, 774 F. Supp. 1163 (E. D. Wis. 1991) (applying First Amendment doctrines of overbreadth, fighting words, and vagueness to a campus speech code); Doe v. University of Michigan, 721 F. Supp. 852, 861–67 (E. D. Michigan 1989) (applying vagueness and overbreadth doctrine to a campus speech code).

[15] *See* R.A.V. v. City of St. Paul, 505 U.S. 377, 382 (1992).

[16] *See* Chaplinsky v. New Hampshire, 315 U.S. 568, 572 (1942); Brandenburg v. Ohio, 395 U.S. 444, 448–49 (1969).

The hurling of cinder blocks through Hillel windows (University of California at Berkeley) and torching of campus *Sukkah* during the Jewish holiday of *Succoth* (San Jose State University) may be intended to express a political opinion, but they nevertheless also constitute a form of conduct prohibited by content-neutral laws of general applicability. Even the scrawling of swastikas, protected under some circumstances, is not protected when used to deface public property. This may be said, for example, of the swastikas carved into a residence hall bulletin board at the University of Colorado at Boulder, carved into freshly poured concrete at Atlantic Cape Community College, drawn on posters advertising Israeli events at the University of Chicago, and etched in acid on a campus café tabletop at the University of Oregon.

Given the detailed allegations of physical intimidation and assault that occur in the incendiary environment that now exists on some campuses, it is rather vacuous (if not untrue) to insist that the First Amendment may protect the purely political speech with which these incidents are interspersed. Those who would defend the recent outbreak of campus anti-Semitism on these grounds are rather like the man who shouts "First Amendment!" in a burning building.

6

Misunderstanding Jews and Jew Hatred

Beyond playing the First Amendment card, the University of California at Irvine publicly responded to the Zionist Organization of America's (ZOA's) complaint with a frontal assault on the 2004 Department of Education Office of Civil Rights (OCR) policy, flatly insisting that "Title VI does not apply to allegations of anti-Semitism."[1] UC-Irvine administrators reasoned that "religion is not a protected class for purposes of Title VI."[2] Additionally, the school argued that *Shaare Tefila* held that "Jewish" constitutes a "race" only for purposes of § 1982.[3] The Court "specifically rested its holding on the fact that when the Civil Rights Act of 1866, of which § 1982 is a part, was enacted, 'Jews ... were among the peoples then considered to be distinct races and hence within the protection of the statute.'"[4] By 1964, *Irvine* notes, "race theory had developed dramatically," and Jews were no longer considered a race.[5] Moreover, *Irvine* argued that Congress's inclusion of religion in Title VII of the 1964 Act "indicates that had Congress desired to also make religion a protected class under Title VI, it knew that it needed to do so specifically."[6] *Irvine* also denies that it has discriminated against any student.[7]

ZOA responded that Jews are a protected class under Title VI as both a religious minority and a national origin group. ZOA conceded that the

---

[1] U.S. COMMISSION ON CIVIL RIGHTS, CAMPUS ANTI-SEMITISM, at 16 (statement of Ms Geocaris).
[2] *Id.*
[3] *Id.*, at 16–7.
[4] *Id.*, at 17.
[5] *Id.*
[6] *Id.*
[7] *Id.*

term "religion" "is not expressly included in the language of Title VI" but nevertheless argued that "the legislative history of the statute suggests that Congress intended that religious discrimination be included."[8] In support of this counterintuitive theory, ZOA cited a substantial number of sources that include religious discrimination in a recitation of discriminatory grounds prohibited by Title VI ZOA also argued that Jews are protected under the broad interpretation that some lower courts have given to the term "national origin" (notwithstanding the narrow construction that the U.S. Supreme Court had established).[9]

After investigating the *Irvine* case for over three years, OCR dismissed the ZOA complaint in a way that demonstrates its inability to grasp the issues at stake. OCR dismissed the complaint without even addressing ZOA's ancestry claims because it no longer adheres to its policy of doing so. In a 13-page closure letter, OCR rejected ZOA's claims on the grounds of timeliness, sufficiency of Irvine's response, and failure to provide sufficient factual information to proceed. Astonishingly, OCR entirely ignored ZOA's claims that Irvine's Jewish students faced discrimination on the basis of their ethnic and ancestral heritage (*i.e.*, their "race" in the *Shaare Tefila* sense).

Moreover, OCR reviewed ZOA's national origin claims only to determine whether Jewish students of Israeli origin faced anti-Israeli national origin discrimination. OCR's opinion does not even consider whether anti-Jewish ethnic bias constitutes national origin discrimination in any other respect. OCR provides no explanation of its failure to address ZOA's allegations of anti-Jewish ethnic and ancestral discrimination. It simply ignores the allegations as if they had not been made.[10] In Paul Grossman's words, "the letter that was ultimately issued can only be interpreted as either the narrowest possible view of jurisdiction to protect Jewish students or as ducking the jurisdictional question altogether."[11]

In response to this closure, Irvine officials proclaimed that their institution had been fully exonerated. For example, Irvine's law school dean, Erwin Chemerinsky, insisted that "The Office for Civil Rights of the United States Department of Education did a through investigation and

---

[8] Transcript, of U.S. Commission on Civil Rights, apps. 70, 81 (letter from Susan B. Tuchman to Kenneth L. Marcus, Staff Director, U.S. Commission on Civil Rights (March 20, 2006)).

[9] *Id.*, apps. 82–3.

[10] *See, generally,* In re UC-Irvine (ignoring ancestry claims made by non-Israeli Jewish students); cf ZOA Complaint 10–1.

[11] Affidavit of Paul Grossman, February 20, 2008, p. 10.

concluded that there was no basis for finding that there was a hostile or intimidating environment for Jewish students on campus at the University of California, Irvine."[12] It should have been clear to Chemerinsky that he was, at the least, overstating his case because OCR had dismissed several of Tuchman's claims on technical grounds such as the statute of limitations. In fairness to Chemerinsky, however, he may not have understood just how misleading his characterization turns out to have been.

What Chemerinsky and his colleagues do not mention (and what the public does not know) is that career OCR officials had determined in 2005 that a hostile environment had developed at Irvine in violation of Title VI. The career officials were not inclined to proceed against Irvine because they believed in 2005 that Irvine had taken sufficient actions after the fact to avoid federal liability. On the other hand, the regional director who oversaw the investigation, Arthur Zeidman, also believes that subsequent developments at Irvine show that the administration had not responded adequately. If the OCR's regional office had not been overruled, it likely would have formed the basis for a finding of discrimination against Irvine in 2006, 2007, or 2008, when continuing problems revealed the depth of the problem there. Instead, OCR's political leadership reversed the regional office's determination and issued an opinion that did not find that a hostile environment had formed. Behind the scenes, the conflict between OCR's headquarters and its San Francisco office was both heated and ugly, ultimately resulting in bold allegations, harsh recriminations, widespread finger pointing, extraordinary disciplinary action, and still-pending internal litigation.

How did OCR come to its ultimate tortured resolution? As we have seen, Zeidman initially was skeptical when he received Tuchman's complaint on October 12, 2004. Grossman, also apprehensive, recalls that my senior staff and I firmly directed the regional office to open the *Irvine* case assuming OCR's jurisdiction to encompass most anti-Semitic harassment. Moreover, they recall that I directed them to construe time frames liberally on the grounds that they were, at least allegedly, part of a continuing pattern and practice of discriminatory conduct that continued up to the present. To the extent that jurisdictional questions would arise that my guidance letters had not resolved, I told regional staff to just get out there, find what the facts were, report back to me, and I would tell them how to proceed. This blunt micromanagement appears

---

[12] Erwin Chemerinsky, *Unpleasant Speech on Campus, Even Hate Speech, Is a First Amendment Issue*, 17 Wm. & Mary B. Rts. J. (March 2009) 765, 766.

to have stirred little resentment in contrast to the approaches that followed it. Staff understood that I was the one who would be personally accountable for the investigation and that they would be insulated from criticism to the extent that they followed clear, specific, and legally supportable directives.

After my departure, the agency's new leadership – first, Deputy Assistant Secretary David Black and, later, Assistant Secretary Stephanie Monroe – were less inclined to protect Jewish students from anti-Semitic harassment, but they also were reticent to make their position clear. From the regional staff perspective, headquarters placed them under great pressure but provided little policy direction. As Paul Grossman complained, "It was pathetic to try to reach a legally sound conclusion to the Irvine investigation without headquarters guidance on the scope of our national origin jurisdiction but that, originally, is what our office was told to do."[13] So they muddled through under Art Zeidman's command, trying to read what tea leaves Washington might provide. Absent clear alternative guidance from Monroe or Black, they continued to rely on the 2004 guidance. Where that guidance required interpretation, they relied in part on the analysis that I published in various law reviews after leaving OCR, much of which is integrated in this book. Given the paucity of guidance they had received from Washington, the San Francisco office was proud of its work on this case. Zeidman's top deputy, Charlie Love, comments that it was "probably one of the best investigations" that the office had conducted, "given that it was a novel area and something that required a degree of discipline and innovation and skill."[14]

In December 2005, Zeidman sent his final report to Washington.[15] The San Francisco office had determined that "the totality of the circumstances at UC-Irvine constituted a hostile environment based on national origin." In other words, regional staff concluded that Tuchman was right that Irvine students faced levels of discrimination that were so severe, pervasive, or objectively offensive as to limit their educational opportunities. Zeidman had gotten past his initial concerns about the timeliness of Tuchman's complaint because he saw that the pattern of anti-Jewish harassment continued well after the

[13] Aff., Grossman, at 10.
[14] Deposition of Charles Love, March 6, 2009, p. 56.
[15] Deposition of Arthur C. Zeidman, Vol. 2, February 25, 2009, p. 11; see also EDPAS – Supporting Narrative, Arthur Zeidman, Rating Period May 1–September 30, 2006, p. 2 (confirming Zeidman's characterization of his proposed closure letter).

complaint was filed into at least 2006 and 2007.[16] His jurisdictional
concerns evidently were satisfied to the extent that he believed that
OCR's policy had been fundamentally changed by the 2004 policy.
Indeed, San Francisco officials actually had drafted, revised, and prepared in final form a letter to Irvine informing campus leadership of
their findings. This was sure to send shock waves through the higher-education community: OCR's first investigation of systemic anti-
Semitism in higher education had resulted in a finding that a hostile
environment for Jewish students had formed on a major campus in the
University of California system.

San Francisco, however, was not prepared to find Irvine in violation
of Title VI at this point in time. Reviewing the actions that Irvine had
taken to address the campus climate, San Francisco determined that it
had done enough: "UC-Irvine took adequate steps to address the hostile
environment, and was therefore in compliance with Title VI."[17] In other
words, Zeidman had split the baby: The Irvine campus would be revealed
as a hotbed of anti-Semitism, but its senior administrators would be
acquitted for the actions that they had undertaken. As Zeidman looks
back on the case, he believes that this finding in 2005 would have led to
the opposite result in 2006 or 2007. In other words, if he had resolved
the case in this manner when it first arose, the recurrence of anti-
Semitism over the next two years at Irvine would have demonstrated that
the administration's response had not in fact been sufficient. If Tuchman
urged OCR to reopen the case at that time, Zeidman likely would have
had to concede that Irvine's response was not in fact sufficient and that
it was fully in violation.

Zeidman wanted to decide the case right away because he considered
it to be thoroughly investigated and ripe for decision.[18] Instead, Zeidman
got no response until the following summer. One reason for the delay,
according to Black, was my work at the commission. Zeidman had sent
his proposed resolution to Washington only one month after the commission held its November 2005 public briefing on campus anti-Semitism.
This gave the issue a heightened level of public attention, which some
media outlets had begun to attend to. Monroe saw the commission's
work as an effort to promote OCR's 2004 policy. Both Monroe and

[16] Zeidman, Zeidman Dep. v. Spellings, Vol. 2, at 12.
[17] EDPAS – Supporting Narrative, Arthur Zeidman, Rating Period May 1–September
30, 2006, p. 2.
[18] EEO Investigator, Summary of Interview with David Black, p. 5.

Black thought that the commission's attention had made the issue politically too hot to handle at that time – at least, too hot to handle if OCR's leadership intended to bury the case. As Black explained in an e-mail to Monroe, "This was a couple weeks after things started to heat up with the Commission and not a good time to close without violations, without interviewing all the [Z]OA witnesses."[19]

In July, David Black finally voiced his displeasure. Although he did not say so at the time, Black thought that the *Irvine* case never should have been opened in the first place.[20] His basic view was that anti-Semitism cases were religious matters that should be handled by another agency (or perhaps not at all).[21] Black's position on the *Irvine* case was quite simple: "The allegations in the UC Irvine case were religious discrimination" and "OCR doesn't have jurisdiction over religion.... "[22] He would have preferred to send the case to the Justice Department, if it would take it, for consideration under its discretionary jurisdiction.[23] Stephanie Monroe, however, indicated that she wanted OCR to handle the matter itself rather than shipping it off to another agency.[24]

Rather than giving Zeidman policy guidance, however, Black told him that the investigation was incomplete and sent him back to reinvestigate.[25] Black wanted more careful scrutiny of jurisdictional and timeliness issues, as well as more emphasis on unequal treatment and less on the question of hostile environment.[26] Black also insisted that Zeidman's staff "investigate whether Jewish students were Americans or of Israeli origin."[27] While Black maintained that he wanted further investigation, the San Francisco perspective was just that he wanted different investigation and that they never entirely understood the different direction in which he wanted them to move.[28] In retrospect, Zeidman

---

[19] Deposition of Stephanie Monroe, January 14, 2009, p. 61, quoting e-mail from David Black to Stephanie Monroe.

[20] Deposition of David F. Black, February 17, 2009, p. 18.

[21] *Id.*

[22] *Id.*, at 19; see also EEO Investigator, Summary of Interview with David Black, p. 5 ("Mr. Black viewed [*Irvine*] as religious discrimination as opposed to national origin. Mr. Black was also concerned with the facts and whether OCR had jurisdiction.")

[23] EEO Investigator, Summary of Interview with David Black, p. 5.

[24] *Id.*

[25] Zeidman Dep., Vol.2, at 12.

[26] Aff., Grossman at 10.

[27] Zeidman Dep., Vol.2, at 9.

[28] Deposition of Charles Love, March 6, 2009, pp. 56–7.

believes that from that point on, Black's efforts goal was mainly "to undermine the investigation," making it more difficult for Zeidman's staff to resolve.[29]

In August, Susan Tuchman complained in a letter to Stephanie Monroe that Zeidman's staff, in all the time that had passed, had not interviewed a single Irvine administrator. "This is deeply disturbing," Tuchman admonished, "and raises questions about how vigorously OCR is investigating the ZOA's complaint against UCI."[30] In light of Stephanie Monroe's letter to me presenting her interpretation of Title VI, Tuchman was nervous that the long delay suggested that OCR was looking for a way to dismiss the case. Certainly, she did not know that San Francisco's proposed resolution would have vindicated her position. Ironically, Tuchman did not imagine that the streamlined quality of the investigation reflected that San Francisco officials found the hostile environment at Irvine to be so *obvious* that it could be demonstrated through only a limited number of data requests and interviews. Even more ironically, she certainly did not imagine that the effect of her letter would be to tighten the noose around the one remaining OCR official who was most inclined to decide the case in her favor: San Francisco Regional Director Arthur Zeidman.

Senior OCR officials say they were very upset to read in Tuchman's letter about how cursory Zeidman's investigation had been.[31] David Black blasted Zeidman over the phone for not doing a more thorough job of investigating the case.[32] It is difficult to determine whether Black was angrier with Zeidman about the brevity of his investigation or about the conclusions that he had reached. For the record Black criticized Zeidman because his proposed closure letter "was based primarily on UC-Irvine's response to OCR's data request and records provided by ... [Tuchman] with practically no independent corroboration of this information."[33] Although Black knew that Zeidman's investigators had interviewed 16 Irvine students, Black was indignant that Zeidman had not interviewed Irvine's administrators, relying

---

[29] Zeidman Dep., Vol. 2, at 15.
[30] Letter of Mort Klein and Susan Tuchman to Stephanie Monroe, dated August 3, 2006, p. 2.
[31] Summary of Interview with Sandra Battle [official EEO record], June 21, 2007, p. 3.
[32] Summary of Interview with David F. Black [by EEO investigator], June 27, 2007, p. 6.
[33] EDPAS – Supporting Narrative, Arthur Zeidman, Rating Period May 1–September 30, 2006, p. 2.

instead on their answers to written requests.[34] Later, Black admonished Zeidman further in a meeting in Washington. "And he criticized the – the work on the U. C. Irvine case," Zeidman recalls. "He was very blunt with me and ever so critical."[35] Black expressed concern that there had been "no formal interviews of key UC-Irvine staff, administrators, or personnel involved in the events at issue, nor were Arab/Muslim pro-Palestinian students issued."[36] This led, Black argued, to "evidentiary deficiencies" and an "incomplete understanding of the events at issue."[37] In Zeidman's view, no further investigation was required because the facts the office had obtained spoke so clearly for themselves. Perhaps, he speculated, Black was simply delaying the process because he could think of no better way to avoid resolving the case in Tuchman's favor, given just how bad things had gotten at Irvine. When Zeidman defended his staff's handling of the *Irvine* case, Black "lost all confidence" in him and decided based solely on this case that he should rate Zeidman's performance for the annual rating period as "Minimally successful."[38] This was the first unsatisfactory rating that Arthur Zeidman had received in his long and distinguished career.[39]

Despite their concerns, headquarters staff prepared a letter for Assistant Secretary Stephanie Monroe's signature assuring Tuchman that its complaint "is being investigated in a rigorous and complete manner." Needless to say, Monroe did not inform Tuchman that the case had been dormant between December 2005 and July 2006, nor did she inform Tuchman that Black was expressing precisely the opposite view in his disparagement of Zeidman. Most important, Monroe gave Tuchman no inclination that her career staff had determined that Tuchman was right but that she and her political appointees were in the process of overruling them.[40]

Later in August, Black arranged separate meetings with Zeidman, Love, and Grossman during breaks in an agency-wide training session held in New Orleans. Although accounts of the New Orleans meetings

---

[34] *Id.*

[35] Zeidman Dep., February 19, 2009, at 72.

[36] EDPAS – Zeidman Narrative, at 2.

[37] *Id.*

[38] Summary of Interview with David F. Black [by EEO investigator], June 27, 2007, p. 6.

[39] Zeidman Dep., February 19, 2009, at 29.

[40] Monroe's recollection of San Francisco's position seems to differ from Zeidman's.

differ, Love recalls that on August 16, in front of several OCR managers at a New Orleans restaurant, Black told him that he was holding Zeidman responsible for making "bad decisions" on another case.[41] During this meeting, Love recalls, "Black made it very clear that he did not like" Art Zeidman.[42] Black told Love that the agency made a mistake in hiring Zeidman, that Zeidman could not do the job, and that Love should have gotten the job instead.[43] Love remembers that Black told him that he wanted to fire Zeidman and that he was going to start by formally disciplining him. Black later acknowledged that it was "unprofessional" and "a lapse in judgment" to badmouth Zeidman around the agency – especially to Zeidman's subordinate.[44] Although Black denies it, Love swears that Black warned him not to get in his way as he moved to terminate Zeidman.[45]

Black also demanded a close examination of the First Amendment issues that he believed were raised by the *Irvine* case.[46] The San Francisco regional office had already carefully examined this issue and determined that much of the alleged harassment at Irvine was not protected speech. Black, however, was not convinced.[47] If the incidents that Tuchman described had in fact been constitutionally protected, this would provide OCR with a clean way of dismissing the case, which had already become an acute headache for OCR's senior management. Black sent a young headquarters lawyer, Jill Seigelbaum, from Washington to San Francisco for a second opinion on the First Amendment question. As Zeidman recalls, this gambit failed because Seigelbaum concurred with San Francisco's analysis: "She helped confirm that we had a good case and a good letter."[48] Later, Black directed

---

[41] Affidavit of Charles R. Love, dated February 28, 2008, p. 5. OCR lawyer Sandra Battle, who was then Zeidman's immediate supervisor and Black's direct subordinate, was at this dinner and did not hear the remarks, although she believes that she would have heard the remarks if Black had made them. Love maintains that some of Black's statements were made at the table, whereas others were made "after dinner when we had returned to the hotel." *Id.*, at. 79.

[42] *Id.*, at 6. While defending himself against discrimination charges, Black subsequently denied saying this and, in fact, claimed that he told Love that he likes Zeidman because of their similar backgrounds. Summary of Interview with David F. Black [by EEO investigator], March 26, 2008, p. 8.

[43] Love Aff., at 6; Black Dep., at 47–49.

[44] Black Dep., at 43, 45.

[45] Love Aff., at 6. Summary of Interview of David F. Black [by EEO investigator], March 26, 2008, p. 8.

[46] EEO Investigator, Summary of Interview of David Black, p. 6.

[47] Zeidman Dep., at 73–74.

[48] *Id.*, at 75.

a Chicago-based First Amendment expert to question San Francisco further on this issue.[49]

Black delivered the formal reprimand that he had threatened, simultaneously disciplining both Zeidman and Grossman. Although Black based his criticisms on another of their high-profile cases, Zeidman is convinced that Black's actions were based on his disdain for the manner in which Zeidman was conducting the *Irvine* case.[50] Under intense Washington pressure, San Francisco then moved to investigate the *Irvine* case with great vigor, sending investigators to conduct a large number of interviews and to personally attend some of the events at which anti-Semitic invective was expected.

This was an odd by-product of a conflict in which Zeidman argues that Washington officials were attempting "to coerce me to find a way to close the investigation on a misinterpretation of the law or on an unjustified technicality."[51] If the San Francisco officials' perceptions were even partially accurate, there can be several reasons why Washington officials, desiring to *close* the case and dismiss the charges, would order an extensive and time-consuming investigation. Stephanie Monroe has admitted that she was reluctant, for political reasons, to conclude the case while the Civil Rights Commission was focusing public attention on the issue. Moreover, new data were needed because otherwise OCR would be in the awkward position of issuing a decision antithetical to the result that its own investigators had reached on the same record. Restarting the investigation would both delay the resolution and build a new record, and the resulting delays could be blamed on the San Francisco office.

As the San Francisco office returned to the investigation, it explored what Grossman called "an array of legally supportable outcomes."[52] Uncertain of Washington's preferred conceptual path (even though its preferred conclusions should have been increasingly obvious), Zeidman's team tried several approaches. The most extraordinary, perhaps, was the idea that it should ignore the question of hostile environment altogether, asking only whether Irvine treated Jewish students' discrimination claims any less diligently than it treated Islamophobia claims from Muslim students. OCR investigators actually went down this path

[49] *Id.*, at 74.

[50] Zeidman Dep., at 60.

[51] Arthur C. Zeidman, Narrative Attachment to Amended (11/03/07) EEO Complaint, Zeidman v. Spellings, Compl. No. (ED-2008–03-00) (U.S. Department of Education), p. 1 (November 13, 2007).

[52] Affidavit of Paul Grossman, February 20, 2008, p. 10.

only to find that Muslim students were unwilling to participate in an investigation that they knew was intended primarily to address anti-Semitism. At one point, thinking that Washington was enamored of this approach, Zeidman forwarded a proposed resolution that found that Irvine had not violated Title VI because it could not be shown that Irvine was treating Jewish complainants worse than Muslem complainants. As Zeidman observes, however, this was entirely unsatisfactory because Irvine is required to provide equal opportunities to both groups, and mistreatment of Muslim students would not justify harassment of Jews. When Zeidman dutifully presented a number of such proposed resolutions to Washington, his supervisors ultimately rejected every one of his attempted resolutions.[53]

In June 2007, under congressional pressure, Black sent four highly respected OCR lawyers – Randy Wills, John Fry, Tim Blanchard, and Wade Norman – to quickly wrap up the case.[54] Black's concerns were clear to these officials. The most senior of the four, Randy Wills, headed OCR's New York regional office and would later be appointed director of enforcement. Wills, an outstanding civil rights lawyer, does not recall Black expressing dissatisfaction with the thoroughness of San Francisco's investigation. Black made clear to Wills, however, that he was not pleased with the San Francisco office's conclusions.[55] Specifically, Wills recalls, Black "was not pleased with the determination that some of these incidents, anti-Semitic incidents, allegedly perpetrated against Jewish students who were born in America constituted national origin discrimination, such that they would be subject to our jurisdiction."[56] Clearly, then, this new legal team understood that it would need to reach different conclusions, one way or another, despite the findings of the investigators. The regional staff respected these lawyers and appreciated them for continuing to keep the regional office in the loop.[57] On the other hand, the use of these lawyers was an obvious slap in the face of the regional attorneys whom they displaced.

These four lawyers implemented the Washington view that, as Zeidman understood it, "OCR would protect only 'Israelis' and not

[53] *Id.*
[54] Arthur C. Zeidman, Narrative Attachment to Amended (11/03/07) EEO Complaint, Zeidman v. Spellings, Compl. No. (ED-2008-03-00) (U.S. Department of Education), p. 3 (November 13, 2007).
[55] Wills Dep., at 13.
[56] *Id.*, at 16-7.
[57] Grossman Aff., at 10; Zeidman Dep., Vol.2, at 14.

Jews."[58] Grossman realized that, in the end, David Black's view of OCR's jurisdiction was clear and simple: "[I]t was are you a citizen of Israel or not, and I frankly wish Mr. Black had just told that to me. It would have saved me a lot of grief."[59] If this theory was intended to provide a quick means of resolving the case against Irvine's Jewish students, however, Zeidman wryly noted that it could not do so. "Unfortunately for the theory, there actually were some native Israelis on this campus, so the quickly knocked-out letter" was delayed further.[60]

In August 2007, Black formally admonished both Zeidman and Grossman for their handling of the *Irvine* case.[61] At that time, Zeidman alleges, Black announced in front of several of Zeidman's subordinates that he intended to remove Zeidman from his position as regional director.[62] In October, Black blasted Zeidman in his annual review for his handling of the *Irvine* case. "In this case," Black wrote, "Mr. Zeidman did not complete a thorough investigation."[63] Black was irate when Zeidman, in turn, charged Black with "secret efforts to undermine my investigation...."[64]

Regional Counsel Paul Grossman has argued that OCR's difficulty with the *Irvine* case arose from the conflict between the unwillingness of OCR leadership to protect the rights of Jewish students and their determination to keep their position secret. On the one hand, Grossman explains, speaking of OCR's 2004 policy, "I strongly believe that Mr. Black either wished the 'dear colleague' letter had never been issued or that it be construed as narrowly as possible."[65] On the other hand, Black "did not want his 'fingerprints' on this decision."[66] In order to satisfy both interests, Grossman charges, OCR leadership "left Mr. Zeidman (and me) 'to spin in the wind' finding fault with everything we did in the case but giving us little or no real jurisdictional guidance as to what he desired."[67]

Love has a similar view of the way in which OCR headquarters managed the case. "In my entire ... 36 years with OCR," Love remarked,

---

[58] Zeidman, Narrative Attachment, at 1.
[59] Grossman Dep., at 53.
[60] Zeidman, Narrative Attachment, at 1.
[61] *Id.*, at 3. This formal admonition was subsequently replaced by a similar reprimand that Wills put in place after Black's departure.
[62] Arthur C. Zeidman, Rebuttal to Management Evidence, at 2.
[63] EDPAS – Zeidman Narrative, at 2.
[64] Zeidman, Narrative Attachment, at 1.
[65] Affidavit of Paul Grossman, February 20, 2008, p. 9.
[66] *Id.*
[67] *Id.*

"if headquarters thought something was important ..., it would tell you what it wanted to do, and unless you had a very good reason for doing something else which you were then responsible for explaining, you did it."[68] The *Irvine* case was different. "And the difficulty in this case was it was more like you guess what I want in this case. If you guess right, lucky you. If you guess wrong, you're gonna catch hell, and that's the way the game was played."[69] Grossman explained this problem in more detail:

> For example, we were instructed to get the national origin of every student we interviewed. Fine, that makes sense. But there was no guidance as to the significance of that information. Are only Israeli foreign national students covered? How about a first generation Egyptian Jew or a third generation Iranian Jew? How about the legal precedents under other civil rights laws treating all Jews as an "ethnic group?" How about a 15th generation American Jew who is harassed by Moslem students because the Jewish student has a "right of return" and can claim Israeli citizenship in a country Moslem student considers occupied land? Is this about a national origin imputed to the Jewish student by the Moslem students? Clearly, things can get very complicated. This is not the type of issue OCR normally leaves to case-by-case development in the regional offices.[70]

One cannot help wondering whether it was precisely this nuanced, sophisticated thinking that got Grossman and Zeidman into trouble in the first place. If their conclusions are correct, they would have avoided much trouble if they had realized earlier that headquarters' ultimate goal, as Zeidman came to understand, was to establish "some notion that Jewish Americans were not protected under Title [VI], but Jews of Israeli origin were."[71]

In the end, the OCR's final closure letter, signed by Charlie Love and affirmed by Arthur Zeidman, expressed precisely the opposite of the conclusions that these officials actually had reached. Instead of describing the hostile environment they had found, their letter actually denied it. Based on direct observation, OCR found that "during these events many speakers criticized Israel, its governmental policies, its treatment of the Palestinians, and Jews throughout the world who support Israel."[72] Moreover, they found that some speakers failed to distinguish between

---

[68] *Id.*, at 52.
[69] *Id.*
[70] *Id.*, at 9.
[71] Deposition of Zeidman, Vol. 2, p. 8.
[72] In re UC-Irvine, *supra*, note 3, at 7–8.

their opposition to Zionism and their opposition to Jews.[73] As if to miti-
gate this finding, however, they observed that "their criticism of Jews
was focused on their perceived support of Israel."[74] Love's closure letter
also found that some Irvine speakers during the course of the investigation "made broad generalizations *about Jews*, which were offensive
to Jewish students" (emphasis added).[75] Nevertheless, Love determined
that "although offensive to the Jewish students, the ... events at issue
were not based on the national origin of the Jewish students, but rather
based on opposition to the policies of Israel."[76] For this reason, Love
concluded, "These incidents, therefore, were not within OCR's subject
matter jurisdiction."[77] Given the severity of the situation at Irvine, this
letter made it clear that OCR would not protect Jewish students from
anti-Semitic harassment even in extreme cases.

OCR's political decision immediately provoked strong negative reactions from the organized Jewish community and from Congress. For
example, the Conference of Presidents of Major Jewish Organizations
announced that it was "troubled" by OCR's decision, which the conference explained "will affect Jewish students not only at UCI, but also
at other colleges and universities across the United States."[78] The conference complained that "when reports of anti-Semitic harassment and
intimidation on college campuses is [*sic*] increasing, [OCR] ... whose
mission is to redress racial and ethnic discrimination, should be seeking
to expand the protections of the law." The conference unquestionably
would have been more "troubled" if it had known just how the case had
proceeded. The decision also drew a response from U.S. Senate Judiciary
Committee members, who expressed concern that OCR's resolution
"is inconsistent with its prior policy statements."[79] Several members of

---

73   *Id.*, at 8.

74   *Id.*, at 8.

75   *Id.*, at 6. OCR acknowledged that some Irvine Jewish students felt deeply offended,
      intimidated, and harassed. *Id.* The task force's report went further, indicating that at
      least one Irvine gentile testified that "I am not even Jewish and I feel scared for Jewish
      students on campus." Task Force, at 9.

76   *Id.*

77   *Id.*

78   Letter of Conference Chairperson June Walker and Executive Vice Chairman Malcolm
      Hoenlein to Stephanie Monroe, Assistant Secretary of Education for Civil Rights, dated
      February 8, 2008; quoted in Zionist Organization of America, Press release, *ZOA
      Applauds Presidents' Conference for Criticizing Office for Civil Rights' Troubling
      Decision on Campus Anti-Semitism*, March 20, 2008; available at http://o2a4b8c.
      netsolhost.com/sitedocuments/pressrelease_view.asp?pressreleaseID=354.

79   Specter et al.

the U.S. House of Representatives also complained that Monroe and Black's handling of *Irvine* "reversed OCR policy, as clarified in 2004, of protecting Jews against anti-Semitism."[80] The congressmen are right. Zeidman has conceded that OCR's handling of the *Irvine* case under Black's directives "clearly undermined" OCR's 2004 policy.[81] OCR's decision in this highly publicized case not only disregards OCR's formal policy but also bespeaks a fundamental inability to grasp the two issues on which this case turns: the nature of Jewish identity and the character (and wrongfulness) of the new anti-Semitism.

OCR POLICY AND JEWISH IDENTITY

Beyond ignoring its own publicly stated policies and Supreme Court precedent – and aside from the questionable practices surrounding the entire investigation – OCR's *Irvine* approach fails to understand Jewish identity. OCR's current assumption that Jews are only a religion fails to appreciate that Jews share not only religion but also bonds of ancestry and ethnicity. Indeed, as we saw earlier, the U.S. Department of State has adopted *Merriam-Webster*'s long-standing definition of anti-Semitism as "hostility toward or discrimination against Jews as a religious, ethnic, or racial group."[82] The notion that Jews are only a religious group without ethnic or ancestral ancestry is a glaring error, although it is one that follows from OCR's understandable squeamishness about associating Judaism with either racial distinctness or national separateness.

The use of an antiracism provision to protect Jewish Americans from discrimination inevitably raises sensitivities about whether Jews can be considered a distinct "race." The very utterance of the words "Jews" and "race" in a single sentence evokes memories of Dr. Mengele and the pseudoscientific notion that Jews are members of a biologically inferior racial grouping.[83] On the other hand, it is little more credible to assert that "race" exists as a biologically or anthropologically meaningful category that simply does not include Jews.

---

[80] *Id.*, note 23.
[81] Zeidman Dep., Vol.2, at 8.
[82] USDS, at 6.
[83] *See* Bat-Ami Bar On and Lisa Tessman, *Race Studies and Jewish Studies: Toward a Critical Meeting Ground,* IN JEWISH LOCATIONS: TRAVERSING RACIALIZED LANDSCAPES (Bat-Ami Bar On and Lisa Tessman, eds.) (2001) 7 (citing Brodkin and Jacobson, describing the impact of the Shoah on the racial self-perception of American Jews).

Most commentators have long agreed that the weight of contemporary science rejects not only the notion that Jews are a racial group but also the entire racial concept, except as a means of describing social constructions.[84] Jews are, in this sense, neither more nor less racially distinct than other groups except to the extent that they have been perceived, portrayed, and constructed as such by racists. Using antiracism provisions to combat anti-Semitism both respects original statutory intent and also reflects that antiracism efforts by their nature target a prejudice that is founded on irrational or inaccurate group identifications. Moreover, the modern, post–*Shaare Tefila* understanding of antidiscrimination provisions asks only whether Jews are an ethnic or ancestral group – which Jews clearly are – not whether they are a biologically distinct race.

OCR POLICY AND ANTI-SEMITISM

If OCR's current practices misunderstand both Jewish identity and OCR's own policies, they also misconstrue contemporary anti-Semitism. Commendably, OCR investigators took the unusual step of attending several Irvine programs featuring speakers who were anticipated to present anti-Semitic content. Putting aside any First Amendment issues that might arise in this review, however, OCR clearly misunderstood the import of the events that it observed.

OCR's blithe dismissal misses the point of contemporary anti-Semitism, namely, that it frequently assumes the guise of anti-Zionism in order to evade social censure.[85] As the U.S. State Department recently observed, a distinguishing feature of the new anti-Semitism is "criticism of Zionism or Israeli policy that – whether intentionally or unintentionally – has the effect of promoting prejudice against all Jews by demonizing Israel and Israelis and attributing Israel's perceived faults to its Jewish character."[86] This fundamental tenet of contemporary anti-Semitism has been confirmed by many authorities, including the U.S. Commission on Civil Rights, the European Union Agency for

---

[84] The notion of biological racial distinctions was rejected, for example, in the UN Economic and Social Council's 1950 Statement of Race, drafted by Columbia University anthropologist Ashley Montagu, which announced that "scientists have reached general agreement that mankind is one: that all men belong to the same species, *Homo sapiens*." JON ENTINE, ABRAHAM'S CHILDREN: RACE, IDENTITY AND THE DNA OF THE CHOSEN PEOPLE (2007) 250–1.

[85] *See,* generally, Tobin, at 95.

[86] U.S. State Department, at 4.

Fundamental Rights, and the United Kingdom's All-Party Parliamentary Group Against Anti-Semitism.[87]

OCR's political leadership dismissed the evidence because it had failed to grasp that the anti-Zionist rhetoric at Irvine was not just anti-Israeli but more broadly anti-Jewish. To assume, as OCR did, that the anti-Zionist rhetoric does not violate Jewish students' civil rights is to misunderstand that anti-Zionist rhetoric is used to demonize both Israel and the Jewish people in a way that creates a hostile environment on the basis of Jewish ancestry. The hostility is not based on any narrowly conceived notion of Jewish nationality, of course, but rather on the mixed religious, ethnic, and ancestral characteristics of Jewish identity.

It is the complexity of Jewish identity – the mix of religious, ethnic, and ancestral characteristics – that still bedevils efforts to protect the rights of Jewish students. As we will see in the following chapters, the rights of Jewish students should depend only in part on the actual nature of Jewish identity. To the extent that a group is historically understood, socially perceived, or scientifically designated as a racial group, then antiracist provisions clearly should attach. However, if bigots misconceive them as being a distinct racial group, their actions also should be investigated as "racism" regardless of whether they form a "race" as that term has been understood historically, scientifically, or in common parlance. To the extent that prevailing legal standards require us to inquire as to the nature of Jewish identity, there are strong reasons to find that Jews, like other historically persecuted minorities, have precisely the characteristics that entitle them to civil rights protections even under antiracist statutes (such as Title VI) that do not address religion.

---

[87] *See* Marcus, *Anti-Zionism*, at 845–9 and sources cited therein.

7

Institutional Resistance

As we have seen, the federally enforceable civil rights of Jewish students largely turn on whether Jews are a "race" within the meaning of Title VI of the Civil Rights Act of 1964. But what does it mean to be a "race," given the extent to which traditional conceptions of race have been discredited in recent years. For our purposes, there are three alternative approaches to determining whether Jews are a "race" in this specific and technical sense: evaluating what Congress meant by the term "race" in 1964, determining the current scientific meaning of the term, or exploring its usage in contemporary common parlance. All three methods yield the same intuitive result, which is both emotionally compelling and entirely incorrect. After sustained reflection, they also have the same correct answer, which is as important as it is counterintuitive. The degree to which this conclusion has been resisted over the years, both by policy-makers and by members of the Jewish community, suggests the power of the preconceptions, illusions, ideological assumptions, and institutional baggage that stakeholders bring to the underlying question.

JEWISH RETICENCE

Many Jewish Americans have strongly felt emotions about this issue, complicated by the devastating consequences that wrong answers to this question have yielded. As with other predominantly light-skinned American ethnic groups, many Jews were discomforted by the notion of racial distinctiveness even before World War II. The Holocaust, however, immensely strengthened Jewish resistance to the notion of biological difference.[1] Since that catastrophe, Jews and others have

---

[1] Bat-Ami Bar On & Lisa Tessman, *Race Studies and Jewish Studies: Toward a Critical Meeting Ground*, IN JEWISH LOCATIONS: TRAVERSING RACIALIZED LANDSCAPES (Bat-Ami Bar On and Lisa Tessman, eds.) (2001).

undertaken great efforts to dismantle the idea of a distinct Jewish "race" and the belief that certain phenotypical qualities link the Jews of all nations.[2]

During the final quarter of the last century, the organized Jewish community slowly came to understand that this squeamishness over racial designations, if not overcome, could obstruct efforts to enforce Jewish civil rights. Eric Goldstein has described the process by which the organized Jewish community came to this view in his book THE PRICE OF WHITENESS. The *Shaare Tefila* case, Goldstein argues, may be legally important for its extension of federal civil rights protection to Jews, but it is more sociologically significant for the reversal in communal Jewish thought that it represents.[3] *Shaare Tefila* was an important Supreme Court case on which I relied in establishing the Department of Education's Office for Civil Rights's (OCR's) 2004 policy on anti-Semitism. It is a disturbing case in its own right, arising from vandalism in the Silver Spring, Maryland, Shaare Tefila synagogue. It may be worth considering the case in greater detail.

On November 2, 1982, vandals sprayed the synagogue's outside walls in red and black paint with large anti-Semitic slogans and symbols, including "Death to the Jude," "Take a Shower Jew," and "Dead Jew," swastikas, a skull and cross bones, and Ku Klux Klan symbols.[4] When the congregation identified the people whom they believed to be the perpetrators, they sued them in Maryland's Federal District Court under a federal civil rights law known as Section 1981. Based on legislation enacted just after the Civil War, Section 1981 provides for recovery of money damages against people who deprive one of certain constitutional rights on the basis of race.[5] The congregation did not claim that Jews actually are a biologically distinct race. Instead, it argued that the vandalism "was motivated by racial prejudice in that defendants perceive plaintiffs as racially distinct because they are Jews."[6]

[2] Tudor Parfitt & Yulia Egorova, *Genetics, History, and Identity: The Case of the Bene Israel and the Lemba*, 29 CULTURE, MEDICINE AND PSYCHIATRY (2005) 193, 197.
[3] Eric L. Goldstein explains this point in detail in ERIC L. GOLDSTEIN, THE PRICE OF WHITENESS: JEWS, RACE, AND AMERICAN IDENTITY (2006) 225–6.
[4] Shaare Tefila Congregation v. Cobb, 785 F. 2d 523, 524 (4th Cir. 1986), rev'd, 107 S. Ct. 2019 (1987).
[5] The Supreme Court had already held that Section 1981 applied to acts of racial discrimination but not to discrimination based on religion. *See* Runyon v. McCrary, 427 U.S. 160, 167–8, 96 S. Ct. 2586, 2593 (1976).
[6] Shaare Tefila, 785 F. 2d, at 525.

Reversing two lower court decisions, the U.S. Supreme Court unanimously held that Jews, like other ethnic groups, are protected from "racial discrimination" as prohibited under the Civil Rights Acts of 1866 and 1870.[7] On the same day, the Court also unanimously held in *St. Francis College v. Al-Khazraji* that Arabs receive the same protection under the same nineteenth-century statute.[8] The Court reached this result by examining the post–Civil War civil rights statutes to determine "what groups Congress intended to protect" in 1866 and 1870.[9] Reviewing the legislative history, the Court found that the congressional record was replete with references to Jews, Scandinavians, Germans, Gypsies, Chinese, Mexicans, and Mongolians as members of separate races.[10] In a nod to "public meaning," the Court noted that this dialogue conformed to the usage of the term "race" in countless contemporaneous dictionaries and reference books.[11] Based on this history, the Court concluded that "Congress intended to protect from discrimination identifiable classes of persons who are subjected to intentional discrimination solely because of their ancestry or ethnic characteristics."[12] Since Congress intended to protect these groups from discrimination based on their "ancestry or ethnic characteristics," the Court held that actions taken against these groups are "racial discrimination" prohibited under Section 1981 "whether or not it would be classified as racial in terms of modern scientific theory."[13]

When the *Shaare Tefila* case was first filed, Goldstein observes, the major Jewish advocacy organizations had been reluctant to support the congregation because they did not want to be associated with any effort to characterize the Jewish people in racial terms. As the National Jewish Community Relations Council explained, "there ought not to be the suggestion that the Jewish community in any way gives sanction to the notion that Jews constitute a race." Interestingly, however, the congregation increasingly gained support from the Jewish establishment as it wound its way through the courts. By the time the case reached the U.S. Supreme Court, the Anti-Defamation League and the American Jewish Committee submitted *amicus curiae* briefs arguing that Jews should be protected from "racial" discrimination.

---

[7] Shaare Tefila Congregation v. Cobb, 481 U.S. 615, 617–8 (1987).
[8] 481 U.S. 604 (1987).
[9] St. Francis College, 481 U.S., at 612–3.
[10] *Id.*
[11] *Id.*, at 610–1.
[12] *Id.*, at 613.
[13] *Id.*

A few years later, the major Jewish organizations supported this position even more strongly when the issue arose again in the wake of the 1991 Crown Heights Riot. As the world would soon learn, this Brooklyn neighborhood's Lubavitcher Hasidic minority had long experienced tensions with the majority black community. On August 19, a car riding in a Lubavitcher motorcade crashed into another car, jumped over a curb, and hit two black children on the sidewalk, killing one and seriously injuring the other.[14] Within several hours, rumors spread throughout the black community that the emergency medical crew called to the scene of the accident treated and evacuated the Lubavitcher driver of the car rather than the injured children pinned beneath it. Gathering to protest the neglect of the children, a large crowd of black residents formed. Shouting "Let's go to Kingston Avenue and get a Jew," 10 to 15 young black men walked a few blocks away to that predominantly Jewish area, throwing rocks at homes and vandalizing automobiles along the way. Near Kingston Avenue, they encountered 28-year-old Australian Lubavitcher named Yankel Rosenbaum. Shouting "There's a Jew, get the Jew," the group chased Rosenbaum across the street and then kicked, beat, and stabbed him.[15] Rosenbaum died early the next morning.

This time, the coalition of groups supporting Rosenbaum's case included the American Jewish Congress, the Anti-Defamation League, and the leaders of the Orthodox, Conservative, Reform, and Reconstructionist Movements. These groups all submitted briefs to the court to rebut the argument of the alleged perpetrator, Lemrick Nelson, that Rosenbaum, as a white person, was not afforded civil rights protection from racial discrimination under the applicable statute.[16] While none of the organizations believed that Jews actually constituted a "race" in any scientific sense, they agreed that Jews should be recognized and protected by law as a group like African Americans or Hispanics. Ultimately, they were willing to accept the terminology of "race" because

[14] The facts of this case are recited in the various opinions that it ultimately generated. See *United States v. Nelson*, 68 F. 3d 583, 585–6 (2d Cir. 1995); *United States v. Nelson*, 90 F. 3d 636, 637–8 (2d Cir. 1996), cert. denied, 117 S. Ct. 1259 (1997); *Rosenbaum v. City of New York*, No. 92–5414, 1997 U.S. Dist. WL 528584, at *1–4 (E.D.N.Y. August 22, 1997); *People v. Nelson*, 647 N.Y.S. 2d 438, 439–40 (N.Y. Crim. Ct. 1995). This recitation relies on the government's view of the case, which the circuit court characterized as largely uncontested.

[15] *United States v. Nelson*, 68 F. 3d 583, 585–6 (2d Cir. 1995).

[16] See AJC in the Court, 2001, pp. 27–9; available at www.policyarchive.org/bitstream/handle/10207/12307/AJC%20in%20the%20Courts%202001.pdf?sequence=1.

it was the only available language that could bring Jews under the protection of civil rights law.

Goldstein observes that "[f]or the first time in their history, American Jews were not trying to prevent the government from categorizing them as a 'race,' but were fighting to be recognized in the eyes of the government as a distinct group deserving protection from 'racial' discrimination."[17] Although Nelson's conviction later was overturned on a technicality, the court of appeals upheld the extension of another nineteenth-century civil rights law to cover Jews. Marc Stern, an attorney for the American Jewish Congress, called this result "a very big silver lining."[18] Together with *Shaare Tefila*, this case demonstrates that the Jewish community has overcome its initial reluctance to claim the protection of antiracism provisions in American law.

BUREAUCRATIC RESISTANCE

OCR officials also approach the question in light of their own historical and ideological baggage, but they have found it harder to overcome their misgivings than has the Jewish community. Career civil servants tend to be change resistant, and OCR's anti-Semitism policy represents a departure from prior practice. OCR's liberal careerists (not to mention Obama administration political appointees) also may be skeptical of Bush administration policies that seem to advance religious interests. From the careerist perspective, the Bush administration's religious freedom agenda had two dubious ramifications. On the one hand, the administration's Faith-Based and Community Organizations initiative threatened to abrade the traditional separation of church and state. On the other hand, the Bush Justice Department's emphasis on religious liberty litigation was seen as window dressing for efforts to reduce the enforcement of civil rights protections for African Americans and Hispanics.

During the Bush administration, some of OCR's conservative lawyers were, conversely, wary of statutory interpretations that appear to expand the scope of civil rights beyond what Congress authorized. This took the form, for example, of reticence over expansive "disparate impact" theories of discrimination. Conservatives tend to avoid overly expansive interpretations of civil rights laws, arguing that administrative

---

[17] GOLDSTEIN, PRICE OF WHITENESS, at 226 (citations omitted).
[18] *Id.*, at 225–6 (citations omitted).

agencies merely should apply the laws as Congress passes them rather than expanding them to fit a more robust social justice agenda.

More generally, OCR has tended to eschew aggressive interpretations of Title VI's racial provisions. This point is powerfully articulated in a recent account by Harvard anthropologist Mica Pollock based on her observations working in one of the agency's regional offices toward the end of the Clinton administration.[19] Pollock observes correctly that OCR had long since shifted the bulk of its efforts from protecting students of color from racial discrimination in favor of protecting white students from disability rights violations.

This is due in part to legal requirements that OCR establish, under exacting standards, that alleged mistreatments of minority students were undertaken "because of race." In the twenty-first century, this is typically very hard to show. By contrast, as Pollock points out, OCR is quick to find violations of disability laws because the legal standards are much less stringent. OCR's general historical approach to racial claims has influenced its approach to Jewish claims under Title VI. The bureaucrats who have resisted extending Title VI to Jews have not necessarily had a narrow view of what it means to be Jewish. In some cases, they simply have had a narrow view of what it means to apply Title VI. While the organized community has long since overcome its resistance to casting anti-Semitism as a form of racial discrimination, the OCR bureaucracy has not.

---

[19] *See* MICAH POLLOCK, BECAUSE OF RACE: HOW AMERICANS DEBATE HARM AND OPPORTUNITY IN OUR SCHOOLS (2008).

8

The Originalist Approach

The U.S. Supreme Court adopted an "originalist" approach in deciding, in *St. Francis College* and *Shaare Tefila*, respectively, that Congress
intended to treat Arabs and Jews as "races" within the meaning of an
earlier civil rights statute, the Civil Rights Act of 1866. That is to say, the
Court focused on the original intent of the framers of the Civil Rights
Act of 1866, as well as the public meaning of the statute at the time that
it was enacted, in order to determine how the statute's provisions should
be interpreted today. The Court reasoned that Congress and the public
considered groups such as Arabs and Jews to be racially distinct at the
time when the statute was passed, even though they are generally considered to be Caucasians today. Some jurists support this methodological
approach, known as "originalism," on the ground that it most faithfully
applies the terms to which the democratically elected branches agreed
when they passed the underlying statute.

Both cases instructed that Congress had "intended to protect from discrimination identifiable classes of persons who are subjected to intentional
discrimination solely because of their ancestry or ethnic characteristics."[1] It
was this holding that OCR extended in its 2004 policy, when it announced
that it would pursue cases of ethnic or ancestral discrimination targeting
groups such as Sikhs, Arabs, and Jews. The concept of "ethnic or ancestral discrimination" is somewhat vague, and it seems intuitively to vary
somewhat from the idea of "race." Judge Richard Posner explained the
Court's use of this concept with admirable lucidity:

> The awkward phrase, which appears in no statute, "ancestral discrimination"
> is an effort to convey in an inoffensive manner the dual character of

---

[1] St. Francis College, 481 U.S., at 613; *Shaare Tefila*, 481 U.S., at 616.

anti-Semitism. There is religious anti-Semitism, typified by the attitude of the medieval Roman Catholic Church, and racial anti-Semitism, typified by Hitler. The one objects to Jews because of their religion, the other objects to Jews because they are descended from Jews, even if they are converts to other faiths. Nowadays the use of the term "race" is pretty much limited to the three major racial divisions – Caucasoid, Negroid, and Mongoloid – but historically the term was used much more broadly, to denote groups having common ancestry or even a common culture (or, as often, both). And in this sense Jews are members of a distinct race. The civil rights statutes enacted in the period of Reconstruction, in guaranteeing all persons the rights of white citizens, have been held to protect all groups that are "races" in the traditional loose sense, such as Jews and Arabs.[2]

This approach, whatever its shortcomings, provided a clear statement of how the 1866 Act would apply to Jews. The more difficult question, however, is how the rationale of this decision would apply to subsequent legislation, such as the Civil Rights Act of 1964.

TWO ORIGINALIST APPROACHES TO THE CIVIL RIGHTS ACT OF 1964

A literal-minded court or agency applying these holdings today could ask whether Congress and the public still considered Jews to be members of a distinct race in 1964, when Title VI was passed. As Judge F. I. Parker argued in his dissent to the Crown Heights riot case, "the fact that Jews were considered a race in the mid-Nineteenth Century does not seem to me to support the enactment of a statute which provides religious protection in the mid-Twentieth Century when Judaism was considered a religion."[3] Moreover, the fact that Congress stripped the word "religion" from Title VI may suggest that it deliberately chose not to extend civil rights protections to Jews. In the *Irvine* case, the lawyers for the University of California at Irvine have been pushing hard on this line of argument, urging the federal government to *exclude* Jewish students from coverage under Title VI.[4] In other words, *Irvine* argues that

---

[2] Bachman v. St. Monica's Congregation, 902 F. 2d 1259, 1260–1 (7th Cir. 1990) (citations omitted) (Posner, J.).

[3] United States v. Nelson, 277 F. 3d 164, 214.

[4] U.S. COMM'N ON CIVIL RIGHTS, CAMPUS ANTI-SEMITISM (2006), available at http://www.usccr.gov/pubs/081506campusantibrief07.pdf, at 17 (statement of D. Geocaris).

since Jews were no longer considered to be members of a distinct racial group in 1964, they were not among the groups that Congress intended to shield from "discrimination because of ... race" under Title VI.

The problem with this argument is that it misconstrues the intent of Congress in passing the Civil Rights Act of 1964.[5] If the congressional intent (or original public meaning of Title VI) was to recognize a new set of rights against racial discrimination, then an originalist analysis appropriately could inquire as to the original meaning that Congress gave to those rights in 1964. In fact, that was not the intent of Congress in passing Title VI. Rather, supporters of Title VI explained very clearly that they were merely establishing an enforcement mechanism to protect rights that were already established in the Fourteenth Amendment to the U.S. Constitution.

Senator Hubert Humphrey, for example, explained that "the bill bestows no new rights" and seeks only "to protect the rights already guaranteed in the Constitution of the United States, but which have been abridged in certain areas of the country."[6] Senator Abraham Ribicoff was even more explicit: "Basically, there is a constitutional restriction against discrimination in the use of Federal funds; and [T]itle VI simply spells out the procedure to be used in enforcing that restriction."[7] This point must have been an important one because it was reiterated by numerous other congressmen during floor debate, including Senators Claiborne Pell, Gordon Allott, Joseph Clark, and John Pastore, as well as by the legislation's floor manager, Congressman Celler, in the House of Representatives.[8] For this reason, the Supreme Court has long recognized that Title VI effected what Justice Lewis Powell called the "incorporation of a constitutional standard" rather than the creation of a new statutory standard.[9]

Since Title VI merely incorporates the Fourteenth Amendment's prohibition on racial discrimination, rather than creating a new right against such mistreatment, an originalist analysis must ask whether Jews were

---

5   This point is explained in greater length in Kenneth L. Marcus, *Anti-Zionism as Racism: Campus Anti-Semitism and the Civil Rights Act of 1964*, 15 WM. & MARY BILL RTS. J. 837, 866–67 (2007).

6   110 CONG. REC. 5252 (statement of Senator Humphrey).

7   *Id.*, at 13,333.

8   *See id.*, at 7064 (Pell), 12,677 (Allott), 5243 (Clark), 7057 (Pastore), and 1519 (Celler); *see generally* Marcus, *Anti-Zionism as Racism*, at 866–7 (providing extensive quotations).

9   *Regents of the University of California v. Bakke*, 438 U.S. 265, 286 (1978) (Powell, J., opposed).

among the groups that Congress intended to protect at the time that it enacted that amendment. The heavy lifting for this analysis was done by the Supreme Court in *St. Francis College*. In that case, the Court recognized (albeit in *dicta*) that "discrimination ... on the basis of ancestry violates the Equal Protection Clause of the Fourteenth Amendment."[10] Indeed, it could not be otherwise. The Fourteenth Amendment was ratified July 9, 1868. This happened so quickly after the Civil Rights Act of 1866 that it is inconceivable that racial theory could have changed in the intervening months. Since Congress intended for the antiracism provision in the 1866 Act to protect Jews as well as blacks, the antiracism aspect of the Equal Protection Clause must have had the same meaning. Given the paucity of legislative history to explain the meaning of the Equal Protection Clause, legal historians consider the 1866 Act to be the best guide to the meaning of that clause.[11]

Moreover, there is an even stronger reason for interpreting the Equal Protection Clause consistently with the 1866 Act. One of the principal motivations of Congress in enacting the Equal Protection Clause was the urgent desire of many of its members to provide a stronger constitutional foundation for the 1866 legislation.[12] The Thirty-ninth Congress had passed the 1866 Act largely under the authority of the Thirteenth Amendment, which prohibited slavery. At the time, many people questioned whether the Thirteenth Amendment provided an adequate basis for supporting the act. Opponents vigorously argued that the 1866 Act was unconstitutional. Even some supporters of the goals of the 1866 Act, such as Congressman Bingham, believed that the statute was unconstitutional.[13] It was this doubt that led civil rights advocates to push for enactment of a constitutional amendment that would insulate the 1866 Act from legal challenge. This was the reason that Bingham played a central role in promulgating the Fourteenth Amendment.[14] Similarly, Representative Thomas D. Eliot explained that he would "gladly do what I may to incorporate into the Constitution provisions which will settle the doubt which some gentlemen entertain upon" the constitutionality of the 1866 Act.

---

[10] Saint Francis College v. Al-Khazraji, 481 U.S. 604, 613, note 5 (1987) (citations omitted). The Equal Protect Clause provides that "No state shall ... deny to any person within its jurisdiction the equal protection of the laws."

[11] *See, e.g.*, Rebecca E. Zietlow, *Juricentrism and the Original Meaning of Section Five*, 13 TEMP. POL. CIV. RTS. L. REV. (2004) 485, 505.

[12] See AKHIL REED AMAR, AMERICA'S CONSTITUTION: A BIOGRAPHY (2005) 362.

[13] See William J. Rich, *Taking "Privileges or Immunities" Seriously: A Call to Expand the Constitutional Cannon*, 87 MINN. L. REV. (2002) 153, 185.

[14] *Id.*, at 185.

Given that the Equal Protection Clause was promulgated in no small part in order to provide a constitutional foundation for the 1866 Act, it stands to reason that the protections that it affords can be no less broad than those provided under the act. For this further reason, it is clear that the groups that received protection against racial discrimination in 1866 also were protected by the Equal Protection Clause's equally broad protections in 1868. Since the purpose of Title VI was merely to enforce the rights established under the Equal Protection Clause, the scope of its protections are at least commensurate with those established in 1866. For this reason, when Congress determined that Jews are protected against racial discrimination under the 1866 Act, its holding applies in full measure to both the Equal Protection Clause and to Title VI of the Civil Rights Act of 1964. The Court's originalist approach in *Shaare Tefila* extends Jewish students the same degree of protection under all these provisions because they were all intended to protect the same set of rights.

The Court's approach draws tacit support from an unlikely source. Interestingly, the Court's approach is consistent with contemporary technical usage within at least one relevant scholarly community. "When theorists of modern racism speak of racism," Elizabeth Young-Bruehl has explained, "they mean both prejudice against people of color and anti-Semitism – they mean any prejudice against any group that was, in nineteenth and early twentieth century pseudo-scientific race theory, designated a 'race.'"[15] In other words, contemporary theorists often adopt the same antiquated understanding of "racism" that the Supreme Court has employed in *St. Francis College* and *Shaare Tefila*. These scholars are not endorsing statutory originalism. Rather, they are using a vocabulary that best explains the conceptions on which many racists are presumed to act. In other words, since bigots are presumed to act on notions of "racial" inferiority, some scholars of racism define the scope of their enterprise contiguously with the outdated concepts that underlie modern "racism."

PROBLEMS WITH THE ORIGINALIST APPROACH

There is, however, a drawback to the Supreme Court's decision to extend protections to Arabs and Jews by perpetuating nineteenth-century racial attitudes. Martha Minow has pointed out that the Court's "historical

---

[15] Elizabeth Young-Bruehl, *The Anatomy of Prejudices* (1996) 74.

test" for membership in a minority race under *Shaare Tefila* "effectively revitalized not just categorical thinking in general, but the specific categorical thinking about race prevailing in the 1860s."[16] As Minow observes (and as the *Shaare Tefila* opinion acknowledges), the Court's approach belies the considerable changes in scientific understandings of human difference.[17] One danger in this reliance on historical attitudes is that it may reinforce retrograde social thinking: "Whether the issue is gender, religion, or race, reviving old sources for defining group difference may reinvigorate older attitudes about the meanings of group traits."[18] One could argue, following on Minow's observation, that twenty-first-century jurists should not develop contemporary civil rights law on a foundation that perpetuates retrograde racial attitudes. While these "older attitudes" may lead to stronger protections in some areas, they also may lead to weaker protection in others.

THE LESSONS OF NATURALIZATION LAW

This can be seen in an analogous body of law that the Supreme Court chose not to rely on in *St. Francis College* and *Shaare Tefila*, although it certainly could have done so. Specifically, the Court could have acknowledged that it had followed similar reasoning more than half a century ago in important decisions that determined whether population groups share distinct racial characteristics in cases brought under the Naturalization Law of 1790.[19] That statute, which was effective until 1952, restricted the acquisition of citizenship to "white" persons and (after 1870) Africans.[20] Between 1878 and 1852, U.S. courts reported 52 cases, known as "racial prerequisite" cases, in which foreign-born applicants argued that they possessed the racial prerequisite to naturalization under the 1790 Act.[21] In other words, they argued that they met the definition of "whiteness."[22]

These cases were decided by courts all across the country, including two by the Supreme Court, and involved applicants from many

[16] Martha Minow, *The Supreme Court, 1986 Term: Foreword: Justice Engendered*, 101 HARV. L. REV. (November 1987) 10, 21.
[17] *Id.*, at 22.
[18] *Id.*, at 21–2.
[19] Act of March 26, 1790, Chap. 3, I Stat. 103.
[20] *See* IAN HANEY LÓPEZ, WHITE BY LAW: THE LEGAL CONSTRUCTION OF RACE (rev. ed. 2006) 1, 35.
[21] *See id.*, at 3, 35.
[22] *See id.*, at 35–6.

parts of the world, including Syria, India, Mexico, Japan, Canada, and the Philippines.[23] The common view of these cases is that they usually turned on two predominant rationales: social perception (or common knowledge) and scientific evidence.[24] In fact, however, original intent was an especially important rationale, although it was sometimes combined with the notion of "common knowledge." That is to say, some courts relied on the notion of "white people" that was widely shared by members of the public *when the naturalization act was passed.*

In these cases, the Supreme Court defined as "white," within the meaning of this statute, only those people who were so considered when the statute was first passed. These cases are known as the "racial prerequisite" cases because they determined whether applicants met the racial criteria that were prerequisites for naturalizations. In this manner, the Court denied citizenship to many population groups who might have been considered "white" under either then-current scientific standards or evolving popular racial understandings.

The two most important racial prerequisite cases, brought by Japanese applicant Takao Ozawa and Indian applicant Bhagat Singh Thindh, were decided by the Supreme Court in 1922 and 1923, respectively. These cases forced the Supreme Court to decide between the social perception and scientific evidence tests. While early cases had used the two tests together, by 1909, the courts had become divided between the two standards.[25] By this time, popular opinion had begun to diverge from scientific belief, particularly with respect to the status of dark-skinned peoples from southern and western Asia. While leading anthropologists classified these populations as Caucasians, they were popularly believed to be racially distinct. The extent of the schism was so great that in order to exclude Asians from citizenship, as popular sentiment supported, it was necessary to reject the evidence of science.[26]

In *Ozawa v. United States*, the Supreme Court denied Takao Ozawa's petition for naturalization.[27] The Court found that Ozawa's Japanese ancestry precluded his naturalization on the ground that he was not among the group "popularly known as the Caucasian race."[28] The following year, the Court denied Thindh's similar petition in an

[23] *See id.*, at 3, 35.
[24] *See, e.g., id.*, at 3.
[25] *See id.*, at 4–5.
[26] *See id.*, at 4–5.
[27] Ozawa v. United States, 260 U.S. 178, 198 (1922).
[28] *Id.*, at 198.

opinion that more decisively elevated social perception over scientific evidence.[29] Thind had relied on anthropological evidence to support his claim that Indians were eligible as whites for naturalization. The Court lambasted this "scientific manipulation" for defining as Caucasian "far more [groups] than the unscientific mind suspects," including even some people whom the Court perceived as ranging "in color ... from brown to black."[30] The Court rejected the scientific evidence test in favor of the prevailing public understanding of Asian population groups in the late eighteenth century.

For some 20 years, courts continued to emphasize original public understanding when determining racial group status.[31] As one district court explained in 1942, courts deciding petitions for naturalization must determine "whether the members of the group as a whole are white persons as Congress understood the term in 1790 when it first enacted the statute."[32] This historical approach eschews reliance on either scientific evidence or contemporary social perceptions: "[T]he test is not how the group in question would be classified by ethologists who have made study of racial origins, but, rather, what groups of peoples then living in 1790 with characteristics then existing were intended by Congress to be classified as 'white persons.'"[33]

Interestingly, the retrograde implications of adopting such antiquated racial notions lurked just beneath the surface of these judicial opinions. The *Thindh* Court insisted that its reliance on eighteenth-century racial opinions was not intended to reflect any notion of inherent inequality. "It is very far from our thought to suggest the slightest question of racial superiority or inferiority," the Court insisted.[34] In light of the exclusionist purposes to which it put these opinions, however, the Court has understandably been accused of disingenuousness.[35] Lower courts often were more candid about the supremacist cast of the racial perspectives on which they relied. For example, a Washington district court sympathetically noted that "the objection on the part of Congress is not due to color, as color, but only to color as an evidence of a type of civilization

[29] United States v. Thind, 261 U.S. 204, 215 (1923).
[30] Thindh, 261 U.S. at 211.
[31] JOHN TEHRANIAN, WHITEWASHED: AMERICA'S INVISIBLE MIDDLE EASTERN MINORITY (2009), at 43.
[32] In re Hassan, 48 F. Supp. 843, 846 (E.D. Mich. 1942).
[33] Id.
[34] Thindh, 261 U.S., at 215.
[35] TEHRANIAN, WHITEWASHED, at 42.

which it characterizes."[36] In that court's eyes, skin color was a mark of persons ill-suited to republican governance by virtue of their adjustment to foreign political arrangements that were perceived to be unfree. "The yellow or bronze racial color," the court succinctly explained, "is the hallmark of Oriental despotisms."[37]

The seamier side of racial originalism is starkly evident in the unusually candid South Carolina district court opinion *In re Dow*, which forthrightly described the form of white supremacy that originalism had entrenched.[38] In that case, the court denied the naturalization petition of a Syrian applicant, explaining that in 1790, the common white citizen was "firmly convinced of the superiority of his own white European race over the rest of the world, whether red, yellow, brown or black."[39] Rather than condemn the racism that the court imputed to eighteenth-century racial opinion, the court embraced it as a grounds for excluding people of Middle Eastern ancestry. Indeed, the court issued something to a paean to eighteenth-century white supremacy, bragging that white Americans "had enslaved many of the Indians on that ground" and that they "would have enslaved a Moor, a Bedouin, a Syrian, a Turk, or an East Indian of sufficiently dark complexion with equal readiness on the same plea if he could have caught him."[40] The Fourth Circuit later reversed this opinion on the ground that naturalization of Syrians was supported by congressional intent.[41] Nevertheless, the district court opinion remains a powerful reminder of the ugliness underlying the antiquated racial conceptions that originalist interpretations unavoidably perpetuate.

It is somewhat disquieting to recall that this is essentially the same reasoning that the Court used decades later in deciding analogous questions under the 1866 Civil Rights Act. The results, however, were quite different. While the *St. Francis College* and *Shaare Tefila* Courts relied on original intent (ignoring scientific evidence and popular perceptions) to include a broader range of groups within the protection of civil rights laws, the *Ozawa* and *Thindh* Courts used this approach to exclude groups from the benefits of naturalization law. The *St. Francis College*

---

[36] Terrace v. Thompson, 274 F. 841, 849 (W.D. Wash. 1921), *aff'd* 263 U.S. 197 (1923). *Terrace* addresses the ability under state law of someone excluded from citizenship to own land.
[37] *Id.*
[38] TEHRANIAN, WHITEWASHED, at 56.
[39] In re Dow, 213 F. 355, 365 (D.S.C. 914), reversed *sub nom* Dow. v. United States, 226 F. 145 (4th Cir. 1915).
[40] *Id.*
[41] *See* Dow, 226 F., at 145.

and *Shaare Tefila* Courts chose not to rely on this line of cases, even though their reasoning was similar. The reason may be that the Court was unaware of them at the time because it thought such historical discussions unnecessary to its short and unanimous opinions or because it chose not to remind the public of the rather unsavory exclusionist purposes to which the originalist approach had been put previously.[42]

The *Ozawa-Thindh* line of cases had been subjected to heavy criticism.[43] For example, one court had earlier ridiculed certain implications of this line of reasoning as "absurd." Because eighteenth-century immigration drew mainly from northern Europe, the Congress in 1790 may have considered only these groups to be "white." As early as 1910, the fifth circuit had argued that the "consequence of this argument, *viz.*, that Russians, Poles, Italians, Greeks, and others, who had not theretofore immigrated, are to be excluded, is … absurd."[44] The Court tried to avoid this problem in *Thindh* by arguing that eastern, southern, and middle European ethnic groups, including the "dark eyed, swarthy people," were "received as unquestionably akin to those already here and amalgamated with them" by the time that the naturalization test was reenacted in 1802.[45] This attempt to reconcile original statutory intent with the early-twentieth-century judicial view of European ethnic groups was, as others have observed, historically incorrect.[46] A faithful application of the originalist interpretive methodology would have excluded not only Asians but also most European ethnic groups from naturalization under the 1790 law.

IMPLICATIONS FOR ORIGINALISM

As long as the Supreme Court's unanimous *Shaare Tefila* opinion remains binding law, its ramifications for campus anti-Semitism will remain clear. Title VI demonstrably prohibits anti-Semitic discrimination because Jews are among the groups that the Equal Protection Clause and the Civil Rights Act of 1964 were intended to protect. To the

[42] Although the Ozawa-Thindh line of cases is now much analyzed, Ian Haney López described them as "now largely forgotten" in the influential monograph that he wrote a decade *after* the Supreme Court decided St. Francis College and Shaare Tefila cases. See IAN HANEY LÓPEZ, WHITE BY LAW: THE LEGAL CONSTRUCTION OF RACE (REV. ed. 2006) 2.

[43] TEHRANIAN, WHITEWASHED, at 44.

[44] United States v. Balsara, 180 F. 694 (5th Cir. 1910).

[45] Thind, 261 U.S., at 213–4.

[46] TEHRANIAN, WHITEWASHED, at 44.

extent that the Department of Education's Office for Civil rights (OCR) has failed to enforce Title VI against anti-Semitic discrimination, it has abdicated its mandate to apply the law. We could stop here because this is a full and complete answer to the question of civil rights coverage with which we began. The answer to the Sphinx is that Jews are a "race" in the very limited but legally dispositive sense that Congress intended to treat them that way when it passed the relevant civil rights law.

The reason to continue is that we have thus far answered the question only within one narrow conceptual framework. This framework is important because it is currently binding on U.S. courts and agencies. On the other hand, we have seen that there are other ways of approaching the problem. As the composition of the Supreme Court evolves over time, the Court at some point may abandon the originalist approach that underlies the *Shaare Tefila* and *St. Francis College* decisions. If those cases are one day revisited by a Court less prone to originalism, the drawbacks that originalism presents in cases of race may become more apparent. At some point, the Court may reject a methodology that requires continued adherence to nineteenth-century racial theories. While the use of those theories has had a beneficial impact in *Shaare Tefila* and *St. Francis College*, their less benign ramifications can be seen in the racial prerequisite cases.

9

Scientific Theories

What if a subsequent U.S. Supreme Court were to eschew the *Shaare Tefila* Court's originalism? Are Jews a "race" under other theories that the courts might adopt? Historically, as we have seen, there are two competing theories that courts have used to determine whether particular groups can be described as sharing common "racial" characteristics: the scientific evidence test and the social perception (or common-knowledge) test. The former approach to this question is to look to contemporary science for an answer. This method is appealing to those to whom it is important that governmental decision making rely on the best available knowledge. If contemporary science has already answered a question, according to this notion, it is folly to ignore its lessons and to rely instead on unscientific views (whether historical or contemporary) that may be ignorant, misinformed, prejudiced, or stereotypic.

Before the Supreme Court adopted an originalist methodology in *St. Francis College* and *Shaare Tefila*, the lower courts used these theories to determine whether Jews, Arabs, and other groups should be considered to be members of distinct "races" within the meaning of nineteenth-century civil rights laws. Earlier in the twentieth century, the lower courts also used more or less the same two approaches (in roughly equal proportion) to decide racial prerequisite cases during the years preceding the Supreme Court's decisions in *Ozawa* and *Thindh*.[1] Given changing understandings of "race," the more recent racial identity cases preceding *St. Francis College* and *Shaare Tefila* were less explicit in their reliance on science than were the older racial prerequisite cases preceding *Ozawa* and *Thindh*. Nevertheless, scientific

---

[1]   IAN HANEY LÓPEZ, WHITE BY LAW: THE LEGAL CONSTRUCTION OF RACE 5.

evidence remained an unavoidable issue for judicial considerations of race even into the present era.

How would the Court rule if it based its determination of Jewish "racial" character on the evidence of contemporary science? At first blush, the answer appears obvious. Few academic approaches are more discredited than the theory that characterized Jews as members of a distinct racial group. Indeed, three decades years ago, Patai and Wing set any remaining doubts to rest in *The Myth of the Jewish Race*. After all, as a column in *The Jewish Daily Forward* recently observed, "[T]here are no DNA sequences common to all Jews and absent from all non-Jews [and] [t]here is nothing in the human genome that makes or diagnoses a person as Jewish."[2] Even to ask the question is to raise suspicions of racist or pseudoscientific intent because the very idea of a "scientific" conception of the Jewish "race" has been so deeply discredited. Nevertheless, the judicial reliance on scientific evidence to determine racial identity is too deeply engrained to be ignored. Moreover, despite understandable contemporary squeamishness about this issue, the question of Jewish "racial" science is too complex to be dismissed preemptively.

The great evidence scholar John Wigmore developed a scientific evidence theory to argue, in an 1894 law review article, that Japanese immigrants were "white" for purposes of satisfying racial prerequisites. "In the scientific use of language and in the light of modern anthropology," he wrote, "the term 'white' may properly be applied to the ethnical composition of the Japanese race."[3] Interestingly, Wigmore's reliance on scientific methodology was the most progressive or inclusionist approach available in the context of the racial prerequisite cases. Between 1909 and 1923, every court that relied on scientific evidence to determine racial prerequisites concluded that the petitioner was a "white person," whereas nearly every case relying on common knowledge ruled to the contrary.[4] Since that era extended greater benefits to those deemed "white," its now outmoded racial science favored at least some population groups by conferring on them a sense of "whiteness" that popular opinion would have denied.

Even in the late nineteenth century, some jurists considered Jews to be clear examples of a white population. In his classic article, for example,

[2]   Robert Pollack, THE JEWISH DAILY FORWARD, June 10, 2005.
[3]   John Wigmore, *American Naturalization and the Japanese*, 28 AM. L. REV. (1894) 818.
[4]   LÓPEZ, WHITE BY LAW, *supra*, at 48.

Wigmore based his conclusion that Japanese petitioners should be natu-ralized on the similarity of their "claim to the color 'white'" with that of the "southern European and the Semitic peoples."[5] Like these groups, he argued, the Japanese have "greater affinities" with white American ethnic groups "in culture and progress and the facility of social amalga-mation than they have with any Asiatic people...."[6]

Indeed, to some nineteenth-century minds, questioning the racial status of the Jews could approach sacrilege. In *Dow*, the South Carolina District Court was anxious to demonstrate that its exclusion of a Syrian petitioner was not tantamount to impugning the race of Jesus Christ.[7] "Let it be claimed in the argument for the applicant," the court hypothesized, "that Christ appeared in the form of the Jew and spoke a Semitic language." The intent of the 1790 Congress could not have been to create a regime under which Jesus Christ would be denied the blessings of American citizenship. In other words, "He cannot be supposed to have clothed His Divinity in the body of one of a race that an American Congress would not admit to citizenship...." The court extricated itself from this theological difficulty only by arguing that the racial composition of the Middle East has changed in the interven-ing centuries: "The pertinent statement rather is that a dark complex-ioned present inhabitant of what formerly was ancient Phoenicia is not entitled to the inference that he must be of the race commonly known as the white race in 1790, merely because 2,000 years ago Judea, a country whose inhabitants have changed entirely, was the scene of the labor of one who proclaimed that He had come to save from spiritual destruction all mankind."[8] The appellate court, of course, resolved the problem more effectively by reversing the district court and admitting George Dow.

The reliance on scientific evidence is now outdated in light of the wide-spread rejection by modern anthropologists of biological conceptions of race. More than half a century ago, the UN Economic and Social Council convened a distinguished group of social scientists, led by Columbia anthropologist Ashley Montagu, to address the question of race. This group's manifesto, styled "The Statement of Race," announced that "[s]cientists have reached the general agreement that mankind is one: that

5   John Wigmore, *American Naturalization and the Japanese*, 28 AM. L. REV. (1894) 827.
6   *Id.*
7   *See, generally, id.*, at 52.
8   In re Dow, 213 F., at 364.

all men belong to the same species, *Homo sapiens*."[9] Montagu was even more explicit elsewhere, explaining that "so far as human beings and so far as society and social development are concerned, 'race' is not a biological problem at all; furthermore ... it does not even present any socially relevant biological problems."[10] Instead, "race" is "essentially a problem of social relations."[11]

For several decades now, anthropologists have largely agreed on the homogeneity of the human species, which has been bolstered through migrations and amalgamation. According to the American Anthropological Association, about 94 percent of human variation occurs within "racial" groups, whereas only approximately 6 percent of variation occurs between groups.[12] As Lord Simon acknowledged in the British case of *Mandla v. Dowell Lee*, "the briefest glance at the evidence ... is enough to show that, within the human race, there are very few, if any, distinctions which are scientifically recognized as racial."[13] Accordingly, it is now generally understood that Jews exhibit the full human range of phenotypes and that there is no phenotype that is exclusively Jewish. As Rabbi Dr. Tony Bayfield recently tutored the English government, "[A]ny visit to Israel will reveal Jews of different skin colours and appearance."[14] (Bayfield, who heads that country's Reform movement, concluded from this that "Jews are not a race within any accepted or acceptable definition of the word."[15])

The arbitrariness of the old racial thinking was nicely lampooned, as Alan Steinweis has observed, in the 1960 novel *Mendelssohn Is on the Roof*, by Jiří Weil.[16] In that story, as Steinweis retells it, an aspiring German SS officer in Nazi-occupied Prague is ordered to remove a statue of Felix Mendelssohn from among the composers represented atop the city's biggest concert hall. The officer and two assistants go to

---

9   Jon Entine, Abraham's Children: Race, Identity, and the DNA of the Chosen People (2007), at 250–1.
10 A. Montagu, Man's Most Dangerous Myth: The Fallacy of Race (1964), at 123.
11 *Id.*
12 *AAA Statement on Race*, May 17, 1998; available at www.aaanet.org/issues/policy-advocacy/AAA-Statement-on-Race.cfm.
13 [1983] 2 AC 548.
14 *JFS*, [2009] UKSC 15, slip op. at 15 (quoting T. Bayfield, *Background Information*, Response to Request for Information from the Treasury Solicitor).
15 *Id.*
16 *See* Alan E. Steinweis, Studying the Jew: Scholarly Antisemitism in Nazi Germany (2006), at 23, *quoting* Jiří Weil, Mendelssohn Is on the Roof (Marie Winn, trans.) (1988).

remove the statue. Unfortunately, the statues are not labeled, and they don't know what Mendelssohn looked like. The Nazi tells his assistant to examine all the statues closely and to remove the one with the biggest nose, since that must be the Jew. The assistants carefully examine all the statues, identify the one that seems most stereotypically Jewish, rope a noose around its neck, and start to yank it down. The Nazi officer panics when he realizes that the one with the largest nose is Richard Wagner. Weil's story deftly presents not only the absurdity of much racial thinking but also its tendency to rely on broad stereotypes and insupportable generalizations.

Anthropologist Melvin Konner recently explained that "[w]hat social and cultural anthropologists mean by it has little to do with biology."[17] Rather, anthropologists now perceive the human race as being essentially homogeneous: "They see, quite accurately, a unified species of six billion human hearts and minds artificially carved up by invidious distinctions – almost always visible ones, like skin color or the shapes of eyes or noses."[18] These distinctions are based not on biological evidence but on the "human weakness for dichotomizing the world."[19] This weakness "reflects night and day, pure and polluted, right and wrong, and of course black and white – each pair of contrasting opposites turns a natural continuum into a false dichotomy."[20] Similarly, race theorists (or at least critical race theorists) today tend to believe that "'race' is a fluctuating, decentered complex of social meanings that are formed and transformed under the constant pressures of political struggle."[21] Ian Haney López, for example, has defined "race" a "the historically contingent social systems of meaning that attach to elements of morphology and ancestry."[22]

Although scientific theories of race have been strongly discredited for many years, they have not entirely lost their grip on the law. For all its flirtation with the notion of social construction, the Supreme Court has never entirely abandoned the notion that "race" is at least in part associated with biological qualities. Even the Court's landmark decision

---

[17] MELVIN KONNER, THE JEWISH BODY (2009), at 228.
[18] *Id.*
[19] *Id.*
[20] *Id.*
[21] John Calmore, *Critical Race Theory, Archie Shepp, and Fire Music: Securing an Authentic Individual Life in a Multicultural World*, 65 So. CAL. L. REV. (1992), 2129, 2160.
[22] *See* IAN HANEY LÓPEZ, WHITE BY LAW: THE LEGAL CONSTRUCTION OF RACE (REV. ed. 2006), at 10.

in *St. Francis College* insisted that "at a minimum," the Civil Rights Act of 1866 reaches "discrimination directed against an individual because he or she is *genetically* part of an ethnically and *physiognomically* distinctive sub-grouping of *Homo sapiens*."[23]

THE RETURN OF JEWISH GENETICS

The scientific consensus on the social construction of race is less well settled today on this issue than it is among, say, social scientists or lawyers, whose views on the subject may be lagging indicators. "Until *very* recently," as Melvin Konner noted in 2009, "we might have ignored the question that the enemies of the Jews thought they had the answer to: Is there – truly – anything genetically distinctive about the Jews?"[24] A decade or two ago, one might have pointed to the enormous physical variety of Jews in different parts of the world and discussed the frequency of conversion to Judaism.[25] Today, as Konner points out, it is different. "The trouble with this answer today is that we are in the genomic era."[26] Given the enormous recent development of the field of "Jewish genomics," it is no longer possible to study the question of Jewish racial identity without taking account of new research suggesting that members of Jewish population groups may indeed exhibit a family of genetically related attributes. Indeed, some have heralded the dawn of a "golden age of Jewish population genetics," much to the chagrin of social scientists who are committed to the ideology of antiessentialism.[27]

Recent genomic advances have led some scholars to renew the question of race, inquiring as to whether scientists were too quick to dismiss the reality of phenotypic difference. Some of this research examines the incidence among Ashkenazic Jews of genetic markers of certain diseases (*e.g.*, Tay-Sachs, Gaucher's disease, Huntington's, etc.) or of particular mutations correlated with other diseases (*e.g.*, the breast cancer *BRCA1* 185delAG mutation). Other studies have compared "Jewish" chromosomes with those of other population groups in order to trace migratory patterns

---

[23] *St. Francis College*, 481 U.S., at 607; quoting *Al-Khazraji v. St. Francis College*, 784 F. 2d 505, 517 (7th Cir. 1986) (emphasis added).
[24] MELVIN KONNER, THE JEWISH BODY (2009) 229 (emphasis omitted).
[25] *Id.*
[26] *Id.*
[27] Susan Martha Kahn, *The Multiple Meanings of Jewish Genes*, 29 CULTURE, MED. & PSYCHIATRY (2005) 179, 182.

over several centuries and even millennia – providing support, for example, for the view that Jewish population groups originated in the Middle East. Even more important have been studies examining the origins of the *Cohanim* (Jewish priestly caste), the Lemba people of sub-Saharan Africa, and the *Bene Israel* of western India. In recent years, for example, some geneticists have argued that numerous genetic characteristics are significantly more common among persons of Jewish ancestry than among gentiles.[28] Indeed, a research team at Duke University recently announced the discovery of a distinct Jewish genetic signature that has enabled them to accurately predict individuals claiming either full or partial Jewish ancestry on the basis of their genetic composition alone.[29]

Some scientists have noted genomic similarities among Ashkenazic Jews, which increasingly will have relevance for medical research and health delivery. Recent studies in population genetics have indicated a high degree of Y chromosome similarity – that is, similarity along the DNA source that determines male sex – among Jewish men from all over the world. At the same time, the studies have found a much lower degree of Y chromosomal similarity when the comparison is made between Jews and non-Jews from nearby geographic locations.[30] Interestingly, the only place where Jewish Y chromosomes reflect the native gentile populations as closely as they match other Jews is in the Middle East.[31] This is exactly what might expect of a genetically related population group originating in that region.

A team of researchers from Israel, Germany, and India has drawn an intriguing depiction of the genetic landscape of the Middle East.[32] This team studied chromosomes from members of 14 European and Middle Eastern population groups. The research showed that Middle Eastern populations are closely related and that their Y chromosome

---

[28] See Harry Ostrer, *A Genetic Profile of Contemporary Jewish Populations*, 2 NATURE (November 2001), 891, 893.

[29] Anna C Need, Dalia Kasperavičiūtė, Elizabeth T Cirulli, and David B Goldstein, *A Genome-Wide Genetic Signature of Jewish Ancestry Perfectly Separates Individuals with and Without Full Jewish Ancestry in a Large Random Sample of European Americans*, 10 GENOME BIOLOGY (January 22, 2009); available at http://genomebiology.com/2009/10/1/R7.

[30] See Hillel Halkin, *Jews and Their DNA*, COMMENTARY (September 2008), at 37.

[31] M. F. Hammer, A. J. Redd, E. T. Wood, et al. *Jewish and Middle Eastern Non-Jewish Populations Share a Common Pool of Y-Chromosome Biaellic Haplotypes*, 97 PNAS (June 6, 2000), 6769, 6774.

[32] See Almut Nebel, Dvora Filon, Bernd Brinkmann, Partha P. Majumder, Marina Faerman, and Ariella Oppenheim, *The Y Chromosome Pool of Jews as Part of the Genetic Landscape of the Middle East*, 69 AM. J. HUM. GENET (2001) 1095–1112.

pool is distinct from that of the European groups. The three major Jewish population groups (Ashkenazic, Sephardi, and Mishrahi) showed a "high degree of affinity" with one another, although they also exhibit the differences that one would expect after a period of several hundred years' separation. Neither the Ashkenazis nor the Sephardis clustered with their former host populations, respectively, in Eastern Europe, the Iberian peninsula, and North Africa. Instead, the Ashkenazi, Sephardic, and Mizrahi populations all shared genetic affinity with Turks and Muslim Kurds. The researchers concluded that the Jewish population groups' Y chromosome pools are integral to the genetic landscape of the Middle East. In particular, the researchers demonstrated that Jews exhibit a high degree of genetic affinity with populations living in the north of the Fertile Crescent, such as Turks and Kurds. Interestingly, most Jewish populations show very close genetic resemblance to Iraqis, and Iraqis, in turn, cluster very closely with Kurds.

Population geneticists also have shown remarkable similarities in the genetic makeup of Cohanim, or people who claim desendence from Judaism's ancient priestly class, among both Ashkenazi and Sephardic communities. More than half the Cohanim studied share a chromosomal type now known as the *Cohen modal haplotype*.[33] Significantly, this commonality is shared both by Cohanim of the Sephardic community (56 percent) and of the Ashkenazi community (46 percent).[34] Moreover, it turns out that Cohanim from both communities share not only one chromosome type but also a cluster of related chromosomal types or mutations. Specifically, 69 percent of the Ashkenazi and 61 percent of the Sephardi individuals who claim membership in the Cohanim share halotypes within the modal cluster.[35] This is particularly remarkable in light of the long period of time during which the two communities developed separately. Thus a Russian Cohen and a Moroccan Cohen tend to have more Y chromosome similarities than a Russian Christian and a Moroccan Muslim.[36] Genetic analysis suggests that a shared ancestor at the onset of the Jewish priestly line probably lived over 3,000 years ago, consistent with oral tradition that traces the Jewish priestly line of

[33] *See David B. Goldstein,* Jacob's Legacy: A Genetic View of Jewish History (2008) 31.
[34] *Id.*
[35] *Id.*, at 32 (2008).
[36] *See* Susan Martha Kahn, *The Multiple Meanings of Jewish Genes,* 29 Culture, Medicine and Psychiatry (2005) 179, 182.

descent back at least to the Temple period and perhaps to the time of the first Jewish priest, Moses' brother Aaron.[37]

Some of the most intriguing population genetic studies have examined the Lemba of sub-Saharan Africa. This tribe of 50,000 to 70,000 dark-skinned inhabitants of South Africa and Zimbabwe have a number of Semitic customs, have been tentatively described as Jews for about a century, and refer to themselves as "the white men of Sena."[38] Religiously, their predominant affiliation is Christian, although many are Muslim, and there is an emerging movement to reclaim what they believe to be their ancient Jewish spiritual identity.[39] Genetic testing appears to confirm that the Lemba did indeed originate largely outside of Africa and probably in the Middle East. Moreover, genetic testing has shown that the incidence of Cohen modal haplotype is roughly the same among the Lemba as in other Jewish populations. This suggests not only that the Lemba share consanguinity with Ashkenazic, Sephardic, and Mizrahi Jews but also that they had roughly the same degree of descent from the ancient Jewish priestly caste.[40]

The recent advances have led one prominent geneticist to announce that it would soon be possible "to predict accurately those individuals claiming Jewish ancestry on the basis of their genetic composition alone."[41] Indeed, in 2009, David B. Goldstein and his research team at Duke's Department of Molecular Genetics and Microbiology published a landmark study that found that "individuals with full Jewish ancestry formed a clearly distinct cluster from those individuals with no Jewish ancestry."[42] In the words with which they entitled their paper in the

---

[37] *See id.*

[38] Tudor Parfitt, *Constructing Black Jews: Genetic Tests and the Lemba – The "Black Jews" of South Africa*, 3 Developing World Bioethics (2003), 112, 113–4.

[39] Diane Tobin, Gary A. Tobin, & Scott Rubin, In Every Tongue: The Racial and Ethnic Diversity of the Jewish People (2005), at 83.

[40] Tudor Parfitt & Yulia Egorova, *Genetics, History, and Identity: The Case of the Bene Israel and the Lemba*, 29 Culture, Medicine and Psychiatry (2005) 193, 195.

[41] See David B. Goldstein, Jacob's Legacy: A Genetic View of Jewish History (2008), at 117. Goldstein characterizes this claim as "provisional" because, as of 2008, the underlying science had not been subjected to peer review. However, that review has been completed with respect to the Genome Biology article addressed below, and Goldstein's conclusions were published in 2009.

[42] Anna C. Need, Dalia Kasperavičiūtė, Elizabeth T Cirulli, & David B Goldstein, *A Genome-Wide Genetic Signature of Jewish Ancestry Perfectly Separates Individuals With and Without Full Jewish Ancestry in a Large Random Sample of European Americans*, 10 Genome Biology (January 22, 2009); available at http://genomebiology.com/2009/10/1/R7.

journal *Genome Biology*, "a genome-wide genetic signature of Jewish ancestry perfectly separates individuals with and without full Jewish ancestry in a large random sample of European Americans." That is to say, Goldstein has demonstrated a perfect genetic corollary of Jewish ancestry among American Jews of European descent that, he posits, should, in theory, enable nearly perfect genetic prediction of Ashkenazic Jewish ancestry. Even more impressively, Goldstein's research determines that even people with only a single Jewish grandparent can be distinguished statistically from people who do not have Jewish ancestry.

While the older scientific race theories will never be reclaimed, the social constructionist orthodoxy may have reached its peak. The new science of genetic population demography has increased our knowledge about frequent biological characteristics among Jewish groups and especially within the Ashkenazic genetic pool dramatically. Most surprising has been the identification of a "Jewish genetic signature" that can predict at least Ashkenazic Jewish descent with a high degree of certainty (and with perfect accuracy within the tested group). As with any scientific data, these research results are subject to multiple interpretations, contentions, and caveats. Katya Gibel Azoulay has argued that the effort to identify Jewish genetic commonalities "is not an innocent pursuit that can be interpreted outside the politics of identity."[43] This is true in the sense that identities become meaningful only in social contexts and that those contexts are never free of politics. The importance assigned to this research undoubtedly has been determined by various civil, religious, and political groups in a manner that relates to their respective theological and political agendas. These caveats do not, however, vitiate the extraordinary new light that the scientific data present.

While the concept of biological "race" is imbued with far too much pseudoscientific and malignantly political baggage ever to be resuscitated, it now appears that certain population groups have retained sufficient genomic commonalities – even against the background of predominant human homogeneity and against the odds posed by migratory patterns and admixtures – to suggest that the "racial" aspect of population groups is not a wholly social construct. This genomically informed reconstruction of the old notion of race may never provide a practicable means of understanding what is meant by the idea of "race," but it does

---

[43] Katya Gibel Azoulay, *Not an Innocent Pursuit: The Politics of a "Jewish" Genetic Signature*, 3 DEVELOPING WORLD BIOETHICS (2003) 119, 126.

provide a limitation on the explanatory ambitions of the antiessentialist notion of "race." Biology does matter, and it matters in ways that we still do not fully understand. For American Jews, the apparent genomic distinctness to which recent studies point is far less socially and politically significant than the cultural context in which Jewish identity has been formed. Nevertheless, to the extent that biological attributes have any significance in the legal determination as to the demarcation of genetically distinct population groups, the latest data suggest that Jews should be included if anyone is.

10

Social Perception

Given the difficulties facing either the historical or the scientific approach, it is not surprising that jurists have sought an alternative means of defining racial groups. The most important alternative is the social perception approach, which assigns racial identification by reference to common perceptions or beliefs about race. The Supreme Court gave authoritative expression to this approach in *Thindh*, when it held that the naturalization act encompassed "only persons of what is *popularly* known as the Caucasian race."[1] Applying the logic of this expression, the social perception test would ask whether Jews are popularly considered to be members of a distinct racial group.

As early as 1878, the first racial prerequisite case, *In re Yup*, turned on social perceptions as well as scientific evidence.[2] Denying citizenship to a Chinese applicant, a California district court rationalized that the "words 'white person' ... in this country, at least, have acquired a well settled meaning in common popular speech, and they are constantly used in the sense it acquired in the literature of the country, as well as in common parlance."[3]

Nearly half a century later, *Thindh* and *Ozawa*, while based on original intent, focused on the public perception of Asians at the time when the 1790 naturalization statute was passed. "It may be true that the blond Scandinavian and the brown Hindu have a common ancestor in the dim reaches of antiquity," the *Thindh* Court explained, "but the average man knows perfectly well that there are unmistakable and

---

[1]   Ozawa v. United States, 260 U.S. 178, 197 (1927) (emphasis original).
[2]   *See* IAN HANEY LÓPEZ, WHITE BY LAW: THE LEGAL CONSTRUCTION OF RACE (rev. ed. 2006), at 4.
[3]   Ah Yup, 1 F. Cas. 223 (C.C.D. Cal. 1878).

profound differences between them."[4] The Court relied heavily on this form of popular knowledge or social perception, arguing that the nationalization statute was "written in the words of common speech, for common understanding, by unscientific men."[5] In this respect, the Court's reasoning prefigures contemporary judicial approaches that reject scientific evidence in favor of the external perception of population groups by others within the broader society. As we have seen, in *Thindh*, the Court did not present the clear example of social perception theory as some of its language would suggest. In fact, it based its decision in *Thindh* not on what "*is* popularly known as the Caucasian race" but on what *was* known as the Caucasian race in 1790. Other courts, however, have applied the language of the *Thindh* opinion more faithfully, basing racial determinations on what the courts then considered to be prevailing social perceptions of the racial characteristics of whatever population group was at issue.

Indeed, this social perception approach was taken by several of the courts that needed to determine the scope of racial discrimination under the 1866 act during the years prior to the Supreme Court's disposition of *St. Francis College* and *Shaare Tefila*. One leading case of that era, the Tenth Circuit's opinion in *Manzanares v. Safeway Stores*, explained that the social perception approach is based on the realization that all racism is based on erroneous views of race: "Prejudice is as irrational as is the selection of groups against whom it is directed. It is thus a matter of practice or attitude in the community, it is usage or image based on all the mistaken concepts of 'race.'"[6] A Pennsylvania district court provided a useful discussion of the social perception approach in the case of *Budinsky v. Corning Glass Works*:

> The terms "race" and "racial discrimination" may be of such doubtful sociological validity as to be scientifically meaningless, but these terms nonetheless are subject to a commonly-accepted, albeit sometimes vague, understanding. Those courts which have extended the coverage of § 1981 have done so on a realistic basis, within the framework of this common meaning and understanding.[7]

Courts following this approach considered a wide range of relevant literature, including the dissemination of racist literature and the use

---

4 Thindh, 261 U.S. at 209.
5 *Id.*, at 210.
6 593 F. 2d 968 (10th Cir. 1979).
7 Budinsky v. Corning Glass Works, 425 F. Supp. 786, 787–99 (W.D. Pa. 1977).

of racial epithets to determine whether a particular group is generally, even if mistakenly, identified as being racially distinct or "non-white."[8] Significantly, these courts frequently focus on whether the group in question is considered to be racially distinct by the prejudiced segment of society.[9]

In other countries, social meanings also have been used to determine whether certain groups, including Jews, should be considered to form distinct "races." In a 1979 House of Lords case concerning the ethnic status of Polish nationals, Lord Simon of Glaisdale exclaimed with some frustration that the word "'racial' is not a term of art, either legal or, I surmise, scientific." Indeed, he pointed out, "I apprehend that anthropologists would dispute how far the word 'race' is biologically at all relevant to the species amusingly called *Homo sapiens*." In this state of "amusement," Lord Simon did not suggest rejecting the notion of race or looking to nonbiological conceptions of racial difference. Rather, he suggested that "race" should be considered in its popular meaning rather than as a scientific concept.

"This rubbery and elusive language," he fretted, is "understandabl[e] when the draftsman is dealing with so unprecise a concept as 'race' in its popular sense and endeavoring to leave no loophole for evasion."[10] A decade later, Lord Fraser seconded Simon's view, exclaiming in the House of Lords that it would be "absurd" to imagine that Parliament intended for membership in a particular racial group to depend on "scientific proof" that one possessed the "relevant distinctive biological characteristics (assuming that such characteristics exist)."[11]

Fraser argued that proving biological characteristics would be highly impracticable and concluded that Parliament must have intended that the word "race" be understood in a more "popular" or colloquial sense.[12] In short, then, a better way of interpreting racial groups would be to abandon the pretense of scientific theory and to rely instead on popular usage.

Lord Simon's challenge is to interpret the "rubbery ... language of race" in a manner that employs its "popular sense" while leaving "no loophole for evasion." This project should be understood as an example

---

[8] *See* Lisa Tudisco Evren, Note, *When Is a Race Not a Race? Contemporary Issues Under the Civil Rights Act of 1866*, 61 N.Y.U.L REV. (November 1986) 976, 998.
[9] *Id.*
[10] Ealing London Borough Council v. Race Relations Board [1972], AC 342.
[11] Mandla v. Dowell Lee [1983], 2 AC 548.
[12] *Id.*

of the jurisprudential approach that interprets ambiguous legal terms in
light of the meaning that evolving historical attitudes have breathed into
them. Laurence Tribe has influentially advocated this approach. As Tribe
recently described his view of the Constitution, "all of its text and structure must be understood with an eye to its unfolding history – to the
history of events and attitudes that might help explain the ends Congress
sought to achieve.... "[13] In the same way, many scholars approach statutory texts in light of the meaning that supervening events and developing attitudes bring to them. In this light, the question as to whether
anti-Semitism is "discrimination ... because of race" would be examined
under evolving understandings of what it means to be a "race," what it
means to be a Jew, and what it means to be an anti-Semite.

To assume that there exists a legitimate category of "racial" groups
that excludes Jews is not sustainable. It is not correct, for example, to
conclude as Rabbi Hayim Donim has, that "Jews obviously do not constitute a race (for race is a biological designation).... "[14] The reasons for
which Jews are said not to constitute a "race" apply equally to all other
groups, which is one reason why race is no longer considered to be a primarily "biological designation." The scientific community increasingly
has rejected the validity of the concept of race as it recognized that there
is more genetic variation with any population group (or "race") than
between two groups taken as a whole.[15] In other words, the vast majority
of genetic material shows no racial distinction.

Interestingly, however, the theory that "race" is merely a social construct does not foreclose inquiry into whether Jews constitute a distinct
"race." In light of contemporary racial theory, the question becomes
whether Jews have been socially constructed as a racially distinct group.
In other words, have Jews been perceived, described, and treated in a
manner that has set them apart from those who are socially dominant?
At first blush, this question may provoke various forms of skepticism. In
the United States, light-skinned Ashkenazic Jews are today almost invariably viewed as whites by all except perhaps for certain white supremacists. Moreover, as a group, Jews are perceived to enjoy those forms

[13] LAURENCE H. TRIBE, THE INVISIBLE CONSTITUTION (Oxford University Press, 2008)
65 (emphasis omitted).
[14] RABBI HAYIM DONIM, TO BE A JEW: A GUIDE TO JEWISH OBSERVANCE IN
CONTEMPORARY LIFE (1991) 9.
[15] Lisa Tessman, *Jewish Racializations: Revealing the Contingency of Whiteness*, IN
JEWISH LOCATIONS: TRAVERSING RACIALIZED LANDSCAPES (Bat-Ami Bar On and
Lisa Tessman, eds.) (2001) 134.

of social and economic success or privilege which are often thought to distinguish whites from other groups.

Indeed, before the Supreme Court decided *Shaare Tefila*, a Pennsylvania district court stated in the *Budinsky* case's *dicta* that Jews should be excluded from the 1866 act's protection on the grounds that Jews, unlike blacks, Hispanics, and Indians, have not been among the "traditional victims of group discrimination" that "however inaccurately or stupidly, are frequently and even commonly subject to a 'racial' identification as 'non-whites.'"[16] However, the court was rather emphatic in explaining that it would have reached a different result if those groups were not able to avail themselves of a comprehensive remedy for employment discrimination under Title VII of the Civil Rights Act of 1964.[17] Since Title VI (unlike Title VII) prohibits neither religious nor national origin discrimination, it appears that the court would have reached a different result if Budinsky's case had involved discrimination in education rather than in employment.

Moreover, when Jews are viewed through a broader lens that encompasses the global and historical experience of this people, a more complex and nuanced picture emerges. Many commentators, writing in the emerging field of "whiteness studies," have observed that Jews have been socially constructed as a racially distinct group at various times and in numerous places. The collective common perception of Jews in America today is complicated by this history.

CHANGING CONCEPTIONS OF RACE

For official purposes, "race" is typically defined as a means of distinguishing among whites, blacks, Asians, native Americans, and (sometimes) Hispanics. Under this typology, which underlies contemporary federal racial policy, Jews are attributed no racial status of their own. This is consistent with the notion that Jews share only a common religion. Anthropologist Melvin Konner has argued that this perspective is dominant among intellectuals: "Today's intellectuals deny that the Jews are a race, or even a people, insisting that Judaism, like Christianity and Islam, is not tied to any particular ethnic group. For almost all it is the only respectable opinion."[18] It should be noted that Konner himself does

[16] Budinsky v. Corning Glass Works, 788 (W.D. PA. 1976).
[17] *Id.*, at 787–99.
[18] MELVIN KONNER, THE JEWISH BODY (2009).

not seem to share this view, and we will see below that it is probably not held nearly as widely as Konner believes. What is important is that the view has been influential over the last few generations and that it has reinforced the notion that Jews do not share racial difference. In most cases, Jews are relegated to the category of "whiteness." Some argue that this has been a source of enormous social privilege, but it is also potentially a barrier to civil rights protection.

This notion of race, however, is almost entirely discredited. While government policy continues to adhere to this typology, it has been universally rejected by the scientific community and may be accepted by the public only as a shorthand for the more complex characteristics that define the various population groups. Many Hispanics, certainly, reject efforts to categorize them as a distinct racial group. The increasing numbers of multiracial persons also frequently reject the standard categories. Stephan Thernstrom, editor of the authoritative *Harvard Encyclopedia of American Ethnic Groups*, has characterized this typology as arbitrary, unscientific, and derivative of nineteenth-century white supremacist ideology.[19] Indeed, these categories have been criticized by so many groups and from so many perspectives that it may seem that they are accepted only by federal policymakers and by those who must conform to their work.

JEWISH ETHNIC IDENTITY

In some respects, "ethnicity" has taken the place of the largely discredited notion of "race." While few people still believe that Americans are divided into five biologically distinct racial groups, it is not uncommon to speak of ethnic divisions among population segments. Some have suggested that "ethnicity" is a separate form of categorization, distinct from the terms "race" and "ethnicity" as they appear in the Civil Rights Act. In fact, the sponsors of that legislation considered "ethnicity" to be encompassed within the terms "race," "color," and "national origin." It is for this reason that one congressional sponsor rejected the idea that "ethnicity" should be added to the legislation on the ground that it was already tacitly included. Arguably, the notion of "race" actually has expanded over time, just like the term "sex" or "gender," whereas the

---

[19] *See* Stephan Thernstrom, *The Demography of Racial and Ethnic Groups,* IN BEYOND THE COLOR LINE: NEW PERSPECTIVES ON RACE AND ETHNICITY IN AMERICA (Abigail Thernstrom and Stephan Thernstrom, eds.) (2002) 15–8.

old-fashioned biological conception of race is largely superseded, and newer conceptions of population groups are more inclusive.

Overwhelmingly, Jewish Americans consider Jews to be a distinct ethnic group. This understanding is confirmed by large-scale surveys of the American Jewish community. It is also confirmed by survey research of American college faculty recently conducted, although not previously published, by the Institute for Jewish & Community Research. That survey's data demonstrate that both Jewish and non-Jewish American college faculty overwhelmingly consider Jews to be either an ethnic group or both an ethnic group and a religion.

RACIALIZED UNDERSTANDINGS OF JEWISH IDENTITY

Indeed, even the notion of racialized Jewish identity, while commonly considered a taboo, is reflected in some common attitudes of the American Jewish community. Susan A. Glenn has argued that "blood logic" is central to contemporary Jewish-American identity narratives.[20] This can be seen, for example, in the "knee jerk reaction of most Jews" that former Secretary of State Madeleine Albright is certainly Jewish because her mother's mother was born to a Jewish mother, even though Albright was unaware of this descent and practiced another religion.[21]

Glenn borrows the term "Jewhooing" from a public Web site to describe the widespread and long-established communal assertions of "blood logic" to name and claim Jews on the basis of inherited characteristics. "Jewhooing" may reflect the anxiety of assimilation, but it also reflects the sense that the process of Jewish reracialization remains incomplete. Despite the well-entrenched position of Jewish Americans within the geography of white privilege, the Jewish community retains a strong sense that some racial distinctness remains and perhaps always will. A classic example of "Jewhooing" is Robert Reich's description of the process by which he mentally transformed the powerful central banker Alan Greenspan into a prosaically avuncular ethnic figure:

> We have never met before, but instantly I know him. One look, one phrase, and I know where he grew up, how he grew up, where he got his drive and his sense of humor. He is New York. He is Jewish. He looks

---

[20] Susan A. Glenn, *In the Blood? Conscent, Descent, and the Ironies of Jewish Identity*, 8 JEWISH SOCIAL STUDIES (Winter–Spring 2002) 139.

[21] *Id.*, at 140; quoting Lawrence Shiffman, *Is Madeleine Albright Jewish?* 22 MOMENT (April 1977).

like my uncle Louis, his voice is my uncle Sam. I feel we've been together at countless weddings, bar mitzvahs, and funerals. I know his genetic structure. I'm certain that within the last five hundred years – perhaps even more recently – we shared the same ancestor.[22]

Public reception of Jewish genomic research also suggests that racial conceptions of Jewish identity persist, if tacitly, in public understanding. As Susan Kahn has argued, "Jews seem to be finding the concept of the Jewish gene irresistible."[23] Regardless of the validity of the recent genomic studies, the intense media interest and Jewish communal fascination with this research suggest that both Jews and non-Jews continue to understand Jewish identity to be in part a matter of bloodlines.

For example, extraordinary media attention, including front-page coverage in the *New York Times*, was attracted by genetic research indicating that the African Lemba community is of Middle Eastern origin and that the incidence of the Cohen modal haplotype (CMH) is substantially similar to what can be found in other Jewish populations.[24] Tudor Parfitt has argued that no Jewish organization showed any great interest before the genetic research was done but that enormous interest from the Jewish community, including a number of Jewish missions to the Lemba, followed immediately on publication of the results of DNA testing.[25] Among the Lemba themselves, the DNA results combined with newfound interest from Western Jewish religious groups has fostered the recent renaissance of Jewish religious practices within Lemba communities that previously had been affiliated with Christianity.[26]

In light of Sander Gilman's work, Parfitt has inquired why the Lemba story has excited so much media interest: "Was it because everybody knows that Jews are not black or is it because at some level they are assumed to be so?"[27] An alternative interpretation is suggested by Laurie Zoloth, the Northwestern University bioethicist who, earlier in her career (and in this book), provided eye-witness testimony on the anti-Jewish riot at San Francisco State. The Lemba tribe, she argues, has come to symbolize the classic Jewish yearning for a return from exile

[22] *Id.*, at 141; quoting ROBERT B. REICH, LOCKED IN THE CABINET (1997), at 81.
[23] Susan Martha Kahn, *Are Genes Jewish? Conceptual Ambiguities in the New Genetic Age.* Unpublished manuscript.
[24] Tudor Parfitt and Yulia Egorova, *Genetics, History, and Identity: The Case of the Bene Israel and the Lemba*, 29 CULTURE, MED. & PSYCHIATRY (2005) 193, 195.
[25] Tudor Parfitt, *Constructing Black Jews: Genetic Tests and the Lemba – The "Black Jews" of South Africa*, 3 DEVELOPING WORLD BIOETHICS (2003), 112, 116–7.
[26] *Id.*, at 117.
[27] Parfitt and Egorova, at 193, 195.

and the post-Holocaust desire for continuity in part because of the incongruity of their "lost tribe" tale and in part because of its familiarity.[28] Either way – whether the truer insight is Parfitt's or Zoloth's – the intensely specific interest in the genetic continuities between the Lemba and worldwide Jewry demonstrates that a significant part of the contemporary narrative of Jewish identity can only be understood as racial in character.

It has been argued that, anthropologically, the social importance assigned to the new population genetic research is of greater significance than the science on which it is based.[29] The fact that many Jews and others believe that the study of genetics provides appropriate tools to explain their past and to define the perimeters of "the family of Israel" speaks volumes about the continuing lure of "blood narratives" and the biological conception of Jewish identity.[30] To some commentators, such as Harvard anthropologist Susan Martha Kahn, it is "problematic" that biological and cultural inherences appear to be conflated.[31] While Jewish religious authorities do not argue that specific DNA could resolve the question of who is a Jew, many Jewish groups have taken genetic research on the sub-Saharan Lemba people as an indication that their claims to Jewish identity are in fact correct.[32]

Indeed, Tudor Parfitt has argued that geneticists and journalists together effectively invented the Lemba as a Jewish community in a manner that has been largely accepted both by the outside world and, with encouragement from Lemba elites, by the Lemba community itself.[33] It may be that the evolving cultural self-identification of the Lemba people has had an element of material self-interest, particularly in South Africa's historically race-conscious society because it has fostered identification with the Jewish elite of the great South African cities.[34] At the same time, the identification of indisputably nonwhite Jewish communities also may

[28] Laurie Zoloth, *Yearning for the Long Lost Home: The Lemba and the Jewish Narrative of Genetic Return*, 3 DEVELOPING WORLD BIOETHICS (2003) 127–8.
[29] Susan Martha Kahn, *The Multiple Meanings of Jewish Genes*, 29 CULTURE, MED. & PSYCHIATRY (2005) 179, 184.
[30] Parfitt and Egorova, at 193.
[31] Susan Martha Kahn, *The Multiple Meanings of Jewish Jeans*, 29 CULTURE, MED. & PSYCHIATRY (2005) 179, 184.
[32] Parfitt and Egorova, at 193, 202.
[33] Parfitt, at 117.
[34] *Id.*, at 117–8. Based on my conversations with elders of the Lemba, however, I have observed only a wholesome desire for fraternify among this proud and independent people.

support the political interest of organized Jewry in counteracting the image of Israel and the Jewish people as colonizing white racial elites. Nevertheless, the fact that DNA testing among a group that largely practiced Christianity has been so widely heralded as a sign of the Lemba's Jewish identity suggests that the tacit public understanding of Jewish identity has a very significant genetic component.

This, in turn, has engendered "anthropological anxiety" among academics, who are concerned that public perceptions are "essentializing and reifying" Jewish genetic difference, as well as Halakhic resistance to defining Jewish identity in biological terms.[35] What is interesting in this respect is the public reception given the converse results of genetic tests applied to other groups such as Ethiopia's Beta Israel – who have been shown by DNA testing to descend *not* from the Middle East but from Ethiopia itself and thus lack "bloodlines" to non-African Jewish communities.[36] This has not made any significant impact on support for these groups within the broader global Jewish community.[37] Moreover, the Ayudaya Jews of Uganda have received strong support from American Jews, even though the Ayudaya do not claim ethnic or ancestral ties to the broader Jewish community.[38] Rather, their tribe turned to Judaism at the turn of the twentieth century, and many members were formally converted by a conservative *beit din* only in 2002.[39] This seems to indicate multiple conjunctive theories of Jewish identity: Genetic continuity may be a necessary but insufficient condition for Jewish ethnoracial assignment. In other words, contemporary Jewry appears to embrace two routes to Jewish identity: ancestral continuity and religious conversion. Interestingly, this implicit narrative of Jewish communal identity is broadly consistent with normative Judaism on this point.

Very few Jewish Americans and very few academics consider Jews to be only a religious group. The Institute for Jewish & Community Research's recent survey data are instructive. University professors were asked, "Do you think that Jews are primarily an ethnic/cultural group, primarily a religious group, or both?" A substantial three-quarters of

35 Kahn, at 184.
36 *See* Gerard Lucotte, *Origns of Falasha Jews Studied by Haplotypes of the Y Chromosome*, HUMAN BIOLOGY (December 1999), FindArticles.com, June 4, 2009; available at http://findarticles.com/p/articles/mi_qa3659/is_199912/ai_n8872400/.
37 Parfitt and Egorova, at 204.
38 They have received notable support from the Institute for Jewish & Community Research.
39 DIANE TOBIN, GARY A. TOBIN, & SCOTT RUBIN, IN EVERY TONGUE: THE RACIAL & ETHNIC DIVERSITY OF THE JEWISH PEOPLE (2005) 82–6.

respondents agreed that Jews share both an ethnicity and a religion. Only one-tenth think that Jews share only (or primarily) a religion – the view tacitly enshrined in the Department of Education's Office for Civil Rights' (OCR's) current enforcement practices – and approximately the same percent think that Jews primarily share only ethnicity.

What this research demonstrates is that scholars (like the general populace) overwhelmingly reject the view of Jewish identity that is implicit in OCR's approach, supporting in large numbers views that are more consonant with the extension of civil rights protections to Jewish students. In short, it suggests that if the "rubbery ... language of race" is to be interpreted in light of popular usage, while foreclosing any "loophole for evasion" – as Lord Simon admonished – then Jew must be understood as sharing both ethnic and religious characteristics in a manner that entitles Jewish students to the protections of civil rights law. In the *Sandla* case, Lord Fraser argued that the "real test" of racial identity is "whether the individuals or the group regard themselves and are regarded by others in the community as having a particular historical identity in terms of their colour or their racial, national or ethnic origins."[40] This could provide a better way of understanding the "ethnic or ancestral" standard that the U.S. Supreme Court established in *Shaare Tefilah* and *St. Francis College* because it does not require reification of nineteenth-century racial categories.

RACIAL PERCEPTION OF JEWS

Historically, Jews have been variously perceived as black, Asian, or white depending on the nature of the perceiver's bias. Sander Gilman has shown that for centuries in Europe, Jews were considered to be nonwhite.[41] Specifically, they were considered to be black because they were understood to have intermarried with Africans. In the 1780s, one writer expressed this perception: "There is no category of supposed human beings which comes closer to the Orang-Utan than does a Polish Jew.... Covered from foot to head in filth, dirt and rags ... the color of a Black."[42] Gilman concludes that "[b]eing black, being Jewish, being diseased, and being 'ugly' come to be inexorably linked."[43] In the United

[40] [1983] 2 AC 548.
[41] SANDER GILMAN, THE JEW'S BODY (1991) 172.
[42] *Id.*
[43] *Id.*, at 173.

States, by contrast, Jews historically were more likely to be perceived as members of an Asians group, as Robert Singerman's research confirms.[44] This perception is expressed, for example, in Oliver Wendell Holmes's *At the Pantomime* (1874): "Amidst the throng the pageant drew/Were gathered Hebrews, not a few/Black bearded, swarthy, – at their side/ Dark, jeweled women, orient-eyed."[45]

THE JEWISH RACIAL QUESTION

Here and now, in twenty-first-century America, are Jews white? The putative whiteness of American Jews is a highly contested question that has generated an astonishing range of mutually contradictory responses. Commentators variously argue, to provide just a few examples, that Jews are obviously white,[46] that they are definitely not white,[47] that they are "off-white,"[48] that they are sometimes off-white and sometimes white,[49] that they recently became white, that they have occupied many different locations on the whiteness scale,[50] that their shiftiness on the whiteness scale is a significant source of anxiety to others,[51] that they are still negotiating a costly process in which they have become mostly but perhaps incompletely white,[52] and that they should take ownership of their

---

[44] Robert Singerman, *The Jew as Racial Alien: The Genetic Component of American Anti-Semitism*, IN ANTI-SEMITISM IN AMERICAN HISTORY (David Gerber, ed.) (1986).

[45] *Quoted in Jacobson, Whiteness of a Different Color, at 5.*

[46] This position is usefully explored in Melanie Kaye/Kantrowitz, *Notes from the (Shifting) Middle: Some Ways of Looking at Jews*, IN JEWISH LOCATIONS: TRAVERSING RACIALIZED LANDSCAPES (Bat-Ami Bar On and Lisa Tessman, eds.) (2001) 115.

[47] *See, e.g.,* MICHAEL LERNER, THE SOCIALISM OF FOOLS: ANTI-SEMITISM ON THE LEFT (1992), at 123; Michael Lerner, *Jews Are Not White*, VILLAGE VOICE (May 18, 1993) 33; ALLAN GOULD, WHAT DID THEY THINK OF THE JEWS? (1991) (attributing this position to Ralph Ellison). Jews are also seen as nonwhite by white supremacists. *See, e.g.,* KAYE/KANTROWITZ, COLORS OF JEWS, at 8; quoting ANDREW MACDONALD, THE TURNER DIARIES: A NOVEL (1978).

[48] CHARLES MILLS, THE RACIAL CONTRACT (1997), at 78–80. Mills also interestingly employs the term "inferior whites." *Id.,* at 80.

[49] KAREN BRODKIN, HOW JEWS BECAME WHITE FOLKS & WHAT THAT SAYS ABOUT RACE IN AMERICA (1998) 1.

[50] Tessman, *Jewish Racializations*, at 131.

[51] Daniel Itzkowitz argues that the most salient characteristic of the "Are Jews white?" question is its indeterminacy and the resulting anxiety: In Europe, where Jews were systematically murdered for racial inferiority, part of the perniciousness was precisely that you couldn't tell – so sinister and yet passing. Daniel Itzkovitz, *Secret Temples*, IN JEWS AND OTHER DIFFERENCES (Jonathan Boyarin and Daniel Boyarin, eds.) (1997) 180ff.

[52] ERIC L. GOLDSTEIN, THE PRICE OF WHITENESS (2006) 5.

socially constructed status as whites because it is the only position plausibly available to them, but they should do so in solidarity with nonwhite people.[53] In general, the more sophisticated contemporary commentators agree that the whiteness and nonwhiteness of American Jews largely has been a social construct and that, however read, Jewish nonwhiteness has entailed both social power and social disadvantage in varying mixtures at different periods.

The question of Jewish racial construction may appear obvious to those who observe that many American Jews appear white, are perceived as white, and experience themselves as white.[54] As Melanie Kaye/Kantrowitz poignantly observes, many light-skinned Ashkenazic Jews do not face various forms of disadvantage frequently experienced in communities of color:

> Along the city streets and state highways, where black and brown people pass and are routinely stopped, harassed, sometimes tortured and killed, these Jews pass freely. In stores no one immediately pegs them as shoplifters. Encountering these Jews in apartment building lobbies or elevators, no one assumes they don't belong.

At the same time, Kaye/Kantrowitz acknowledges that this distinction cannot be pushed too far because some Jews do share in experiences of persecution, which a must also be explained. She does so by noting the specific locations and marks that separate those Jews who are most likely to suffer from contemporary bigotry: "Hate violence against these Jews manifests, almost always, in Jewish spaces – that's how they're identified – or to Jews who visibly mark themselves, meaning, usually, orthodox men."[55] Empirically, this observation is confirmed by the Stephen Roth Institute's finding that in 2007 most anti-Semitic physical attacks were perpetrated against "Jews on their way to or from Jewish facilities, and bore symbols of their religious identity."[56]

This observation categorically fails to address what Kaye/Kantrowitz calls "the other Jews, the ones who don't look white," such as some "Miszrachi Jews from the Middle East, Latino/as from Latin America, Beta Israel from Ethiopia, Cochins from India, Chinese Jews from China …

---

[53] Tessman, *supra*, at 141.
[54] Kaye/Kantrowitz, *Looking at Jews*, at 115.
[55] *Id.*
[56] *See* The Stephen Roth Institute for the Study of Contemporary Antisemitism and Racism, Tel Aviv University, Antisemitism Worldwide 2007 (Dina Porat & Esther Webman eds., 2008); available at www.tau.ac.il/Anti-Semitism/asw2007/gen-analysis-07.pdf 2–3

Jews by choice ... [and b]iracial and multiracial Jews."[57] These groups arguably are "[i]nvisible, marginalized, not even imagined" in the narrative of obvious Jewish whiteness.[58] In fact, however, these groups represent a much larger share of the American Jewish experience than is typically recognized. The Institute for Jewish & Community Research estimates that at least 20 percent of the American Jewish community consists of African, African-American, Hispanic, Asian, Native American, Sephardic, Mizrahi, biracial, and multiracial Jews.[59]

The shortcomings of the mainstream narrative about Jewish "whiteness" are not limited to the ambiguous position that it leaves for these categories of Jews. In fact, that narrative cannot entirely cover even those Jews who seem most obviously white. Kaye/Kantrowitz illustrates this point well:

> Even the Jew who looks white on New York City's Upper West or Lower East Side may look quite the opposite in Maine or Colorado. Besides, what happens when you speak your (Jewish-sounding) name, or when your (less-white-looking) parent or child or lover meets you at work? What happens to your whiteness when you enter a Jewish space: a synagogue, Judaica bookstore, klezmer performance, or Jewish community center?[60]

Kaye/Kantrowitz provides what she calls the "correct" answer to the question of Jewish whiteness: "Jews are a multiracial, multiethnic people, and, anyway, what's white."[61] Indeed, as the court asked in the 1913 racial prerequisite case, *Ex parte Shahid*, "Then, what is white?"[62] As Kaye/Kantrowitz acknowledges, however, this response seldom satisfies her interlocutors, who respond with an annoyed insistency: "Yeah, but white Jews: Are Jews white?"[63] By this, of course, the questioner refers to those light-skinned Ashkenazic Jews who look white. At this point, Kaye/Kantrowitz can only throw her hands up in despair, asking further correct but unsatisfying questions: "Isn't whiteness, like race itself, a

---

[57] Kaye/Kantrowitz, *Looking at Jews*, *supra* note 489, at 115. For a comprehensive discussion of these and other diverse elements within the Jewish community, *see* Tobin, Tobin, & Rubin, *In Every Tongue*, *supra*; see also Kaye/Kantrowitz, THE COLOR OF JEWS (2007).

[58] Kaye/Kantrowitz, *Looking at Jews*, at 115.

[59] TOBIN, TOBIN, & RUBIN, IN EVERY TONGUE, at 21.

[60] Kaye/Kantrowitz, *Looking at Jews*, at 115.

[61] *Id.* (emphasis omitted).

[62] 205 F. 812, 813 (E.D.S.C. 1913).

[63] Kaye/Kantrowitz, *Looking at Jews*, at 115.

historical invention? What does whiteness confer or deprive, ensure or endanger?"[64]

Katya Gibel Azoulay, who occupies a peculiar vantage point on this issue as a Black Jewish Israeli-American Africana studies scholar, has argued that "[a]nyone familiar with twentieth-century anti-Semitism, particularly in Europe and the United States, should question the presumption that Jewishness and whiteness are coterminous particularly when it is recalled that until recently Jews were identified as a race.... White-skinned Jews, perhaps; Caucasian and Jewish is an oxymoron."[65] Indeed, Azoulay maintains that "[t]he tendency of most – though not all – American Jews to refer to themselves alternatively as 'white' and as 'Jewish' witnesses a collective amnesia of the roots of the Jewish people in the East."[66] This, in turn, has facilitated the imagination of Palestinians as 'people of color,' whereas Ashkenazic Jews have been seen more as white Europeans than as one branch of a multicultural people whose diversity reflects diasporic migrations and admixtures. Politically, this has facilitated the "misrepresentation of Israel as a colonial intrusion into the brown Arab and Muslim Middle East."[67] Azoulay points out that a quick trip to Israel will "dispel the myth of white Jewish Israelis versus brown Muslim and Christian Palestinians – despite the persistence of social discrimination and cultural elitism that cuts across party lines."[68]

HISTORICAL PERCEPTIONS OF JEWISH RACE

During some periods, Jews have been considered the paradigmatic example of racial stability.[69] Johann Frederich Blumenbach's important 1775 treatise, *On the Natural Varieties of Mankind*, describes the Jewish "racial face" as the foremost example of "the unadulterated countenance of the nations."[70] Blumenbach argued, authoritatively for his time, that

[64] *Id.*, at 115.
[65] Katya Gibel Azoulay, *Jewish Identity and the Politics of a (Multi) Racial Category*, IN JEWISH LOCATIONS: TRAVERSING RACIALIZED LANDSCAPES (Bat-Ami Bar On and Lisa Tessman, eds.) (2001) 97.
[66] *Id.*, at 97.
[67] Katya Gibel Azoulay, *Not an Innocent Pursuit: The Politics of a "Jewish" Genetic Signature*, 3 DEVELOPING WORLD BIOETHICS (2003) 119, 121.
[68] Azoulay, *Jewish Identity*, at 97.
[69] Tessman, *Jewish Racializations*, at 133.
[70] *See* MATTHEW FRYE JACOBSON, WHITENESS OF A DIFFERENT COLOR: EUROPEAN IMMIGRANTS AND THE ALCHEMY OF RACE (1998) 171.

"Jews ... under every climate, remain the same as the fundamental configuration of face goes, remarkable for a racial character almost universal
which can be distinguished at the first glance even by those little skilled
in physiognomy."[71] Similarly, in 1669, Increase Mather contrasted Anglo-
American racial heterogeneity with the racial purity of the Jews. As with
other nations that "have their blood mixed much," the English exhibit "a
mixture of British, Roman, Saxon, Danish [and] Norman blood."[72] But,
as for the Jewish people, it is different: "Let an English family live in Spain
for five or six hundred years successively, and they will become Spaniards,"
Mather argued, but "though a Jewish family live in Spain a thousand
years, they do not generate into Spaniards (for the most part)."[73]

As far back as the Middle Ages and until as recently as World War
II, Jews were thought to be distinguished from others by heritable biological attributes that distinguished them as a distinct race – and usually
were viewed as an inferior race at that, often with strange and subhuman
traits. One odd example of the latter is the tradition in which Jews were
understood to exhibit male menstruation.[74] Jews have been variously perceived as black, Asian, or white depending on the nature of the perceiver's
bias. Jews have in some cases been seen as the paradigmatic case of pure
racial immutability.[75] Paradoxically, they have been seen in other cases as
the archetype of mongrelized racial mixture. According to Count Joseph
Arthur de Gobineau, for example, "the Semites were a white hybrid race
bastardized by a mixture with blacks."[76] For centuries in Europe, Jews
were considered to be nonwhite, even black, because they were understood
to have intermarried with Africans.[77] In the nineteenth century, some commentators still perceived "the African character of the Jew, his muzzle-
shaped mouth and face removing him from certain other races."[78]

W. E. B. Du Bois illustrated the perception of Jews as blacks in his autobiography.[79] Writing of his trip to Germany at the end of the nineteenth

---

[71] *Id.*
[72] *Id.*, at 177.
[73] *Id.*
[74] Tessman, *Jewish Racializations*, at 132–3.
[75] *See* Singerman, *The Jew as Racial Alien*, at 103; citing Josiah Clark Nott, *Physical History of the Jewish Race*, 1 SOUTHERN QUART. (1850) 436.
[76] *See* Singerman, *The Jew as Racial Alien*, at 103; *citing Hannah Arendt*, THE ORIGINS OF TOTALITARIANISM (1951), at 174.
[77] SANDER GILMAN, THE JEW'S BODY (1991) 172–3.
[78] *Id.*, at 173.
[79] W. E. B. DU BOIS, THE AUTOBIOGRAPHY OF W. E. B. DU BOIS: A SOLILOQUY ON VIEWING MY LIFE FROM THE LAST DECADE OF ITS FIRST CENTURY (Henry Louis Gates, Jr., ed.) (2007) 110.

century, Du Bois notes (with no evident surprise) that he was mistaken several times for a Jew. For example, consider Du Bois' description of his visit to Slovenia: "My dark face elicited none of the curiosity which it had in blonde north Germany, for there were too many dark Gypsies and other brunettes."⁸⁰ Frequently, Du Bois was mistaken for a brunette of a particular type: "I was several times mistaken for a Jew; arriving one night in a town of north Slovenia, the driver of a rickety cab whispered in my ear, "*Unter die Juden* [among Jews]?" I stared and then said yes. I stayed in a little Jewish inn."⁸¹ Needless to say, this perception of the Jew as black occurred in times and places where the conflation marked a sense of the inferiority of these two groups. Such misperceptions have been the gist of imaginative and documentary literature into modern times. Laurie Zoloth, for example, tells the true story of a Jewish jazz singer who passed as black to participate in an early twentieth-century black women's jazz band.⁸² Similarly, Philip Roth tells the fictional story (which Anthony Hopkins and Nicole Kidman have enacted in film) of an African American who passed as a "white" Jew throughout his twentieth-century professorial career.⁸³

In the United States, Jews were also sometimes viewed as Asian.⁸⁴ In this vein, critics attributed George Gershwin's talent for African-American-inspired music to the "common Oriental ancestry in both Negro and Jew."⁸⁵ Indeed, the perception of Jews' Mongol-Khazar blood was used early in the twentieth century in efforts to restrict Jewish immigration.⁸⁶ The fact that Jews were seen as blacks at some times and in some places and as Asians in others should not be over-read because Western eyes were not always able to distinguish among the variations of what were considered to be "nonwhite" populations. In the nineteenth century, as Ronald Takaki has shown, racial characteristics associated with African Americans were ascribed to Chinese immigrants as well.⁸⁷

What is remarkable here is the extent to which Jewish racial difference (or nonwhiteness), which is now largely dismissed as a cultural myth or pseudoscientific fallacy, was once perceived with certainty as

⁸⁰ *Id.*
⁸¹ *Id.*
⁸² *See, e.g.,* Laurie Zoloth, *Locations in Jazz and Gender,* IN JEWISH LOCATIONS (Lisa Tessman and Bat-Ami Bar On, eds.) (2001).
⁸³ THE HUMAN STAIN (2000).
⁸⁴ Singerman, *Jew as Racial Alien,* at 103.
⁸⁵ *Id.*
⁸⁶ *Id.* at 103.
⁸⁷ RONALD TAKAKI, IRON CAGES: RACE AND CULTURE IN 19TH CENTURY AMERICA (1990) 101.

a visibly obvious biological fact. In this sense, Sander Gilman observes that "[t]he Jews' disease is written on the skin. It is the appearance, the skin color, the external manifestation of the Jew which marks the Jew as different."[88] This culturally laden, historically situated form of perception has parallels with other groups but particular salience in the case of Jewish Americans: "[V]isible Jewishness in American culture between the mid-nineteenth and mid-twentieth centuries represented a complex process of social value *become* perception."[89] Specifically, the "social and political meanings attached to Jewishness generate a kind of physiognomical surveillance that renders Jewishness itself discernible as a particular pattern of physical traits (skin color, nose shape, hair color and texture, and the like) – what Blumenbach called 'the fundamental configuration of face.'"[90] This configuration registers in social perceptions as Jewish "difference" to the extent that it is keyed to the particular social and historical conditions of Jewish Americans over time.[91]

Jews, like other immigrants who entered the United States under the 1790 naturalization law, increasingly were seen as a distinct racial group during the nineteenth century.[92] In the case of Jews, this meant that they were perceived as Orientals, Semites, or Hebrews.[93] During the mid- to late nineteenth century, this perception became stronger as the demographics of new Jewish immigrants tilted from Germans and other Western Europeans to the Yiddish-speaking Jews of Poland, Russia, and Eastern Europe.[94] It was only during the course of the twentieth century that Jews, like other non-Anglo-Saxon immigrants, gradually were recognized as Caucasians.[95]

EARLY JEWISH-AMERICAN RACIAL FORMATION

It is now increasingly understood that light-skinned Ashkenazic Jews have been widely if not universally perceived as white only since World

---

[88] GILMAN, THE JEW'S BODY, at 172.
[89] Matthew Frye Jacobson, whiteness at 174.
[90] *Id.*
[91] *Id.* It is only in this way, for instance, that a nineteenth-century essayist could observe that "among cultured Jews the racial features are generally less strongly defined." *Id.*
[92] *Id.,* at 172.
[93] *Id.*
[94] *Id.*
[95] *Id.*

War II.[96] Ironically, Jewish Americans have been active participants in the development of this whiteness myth since World War II, grasping for the golden ring of whiteness as a means of escaping the racial identities that were so disastrous in Europe.[97] "Having been racialized with geno-cidal results," Bat-Ami Bar On and Lisa Tessman have explained, "post–Holocaust Jews have been striving to escape their own racialization." Bar On and Tessman concede that "Jews responded to their own racial-ization before the Holocaust, but the Holocaust gave a strong impetus to Jewish attempts at deracialization."[98]

While this transformation had peculiar importance for Jewish Americans, it generally fell within the pattern of assimilation that other ethnic groups pursued in the postwar period.[99] If Ashkenazic Jewish racial formation during the postwar years differed from that of other light-skinned ethnic groups, it was in the ambivalence with which Jews accepted this transformation; having long suffered from intense per-secution, Jews were more likely to identify with the plight of African Americans.[100] This ambivalence, however, has largely occurred at the margins of a community which enthusiastically embraced its entrance into the white American mainstream.

This mid-century racial reformation has had unforeseen conse-quences. For example, it has fueled various forms of anti-Semitism, including black anti-Semitism, for several decades. As James Baldwin once explained, "In the American context, the most ironical thing about Negro anti-Semitism is that the Negro is really condemning the Jew for having become an American white man – for having become, in effect, a Christian."[101] Baldwin meant that twentieth-century Jewish-American

---

[96]   Karen Bodkin, How Jews Became White Folks and What That Says about Race in America (1998).

[97]   Bat-Ami Bar On and Lisa Tessman, *Race Studies and Jewish Studies: Toward a Critical Meeting Ground*, in Jewish Locations *supra*, at 7; citing Brodkin and Jacobson.

[98]   *Id.*

[99]   Azoulay, *Jewish Identity*, at 7 ("The binary division characterizing the American racial structure facilitated the mobility and leverage of white-skinned ethnic groups, including Jews from Europe, on condition that they adapt to the norms set by the dominant group, white Anglo-Protestants. If they conformed to this model, indi-vidual Jews might aspire to and attain a successful assimilation"; citing Brodkin and Jacobson, at 102.)

[100] Eric L. Goldstein, The Price of Whiteness: Jews, Race, and American Identity (2006), at 145–6. Goldstein argues that during the 1920s and 1930s American Jews emphasized their distinctiveness in racial terms but attempted to do so in a way that would not "put their whiteness in question." *Id.*, at 166.

[101] James Baldwin, *Negroes Are Anti-Semitic Because They're Anti-White*, in Black Anti-Semitism and Jewish Racism (Nat Hentoff, ed.) (1968) 9.

racial privilege had become a source of resentment: "The Jew profits from his status in America, and he must expect Negroes to distrust him for it."[102] In this context, the historical experience of Jewish persecution not only fails to engender solidarity but in fact may exacerbate conflicts with other minority groups. "The Jew does not realize," Baldwin observed, "that the credential he offers, the fact that he has been despised and slaughtered, does not increase the Negro's understanding. It increases the Negro rage."[103]

These perceptions are no longer widely shared in the United States or anywhere in the world today because most Jews are widely considered to be "white." Some people may perceive light-skinned Jews as "white" because of visual perceptions or governmental designations (such as definitions used for census taking or affirmative action compliance purposes). Others may perceive Jews to be "white" based on social or political analyses. James Baldwin wrote that while the Jew has suffered abroad, in the United States, his "only relevance is that he is white."[104] In the new field of "whiteness studies," it is often maintained that Jews (and other non-Anglo-Saxon immigrant groups) became racialized as "white" during the middle period of the last century.[105] Indeed, one important volume is entitled, *How the Jews Became White and What This Says about the Rest of Us.*

The common assumption of Jewish "whiteness" has been challenged by various revisionists. Some have pointed out that the assumption of Jewish whiteness ignores the diversity of global Jewry, which includes converts, persons of mixed ancestry, and Jewish groups in non-Western areas such as Africa.[106]

Similarly, some commentators argue that the concept of Jewish "whiteness" is inherently a historical and parochial in the sense that a broader global and historical view would reveal a more complex picture. Michael Lerner has argued that "[t]he linguistic move of substituting 'people of color' for 'oppressed minorities,' coupled with the decision to refer to Jews as 'Whites,' becomes an anti-Semitic denial of Jewish

---

[102] *Id.*

[103] *Id.*, at 9.

[104] *Id.*, at 10.

[105] *See, e.g,* MATTHEW FRYE JACOBSON, WHITENESS OF A DIFFERENT COLOR (1998) 172.

[106] For a comprehensive discussion of these and other diverse elements within the Jewish community, see TOBIN, TOBIN, & RUBIN, IN EVERY TONGUE, *supra*; see also MELANIE KAYE/KANTROWITZ, THE COLOR OF JEWS (2007).

history."[107] Similarly, Ralph Ellison once commented that "[m]any Negroes, like myself, make a positive distinction between "Whites" and "Jews." Not to do so could be either offensive, embarrassing, unjust or even dangerous."[108] For this reason, Lerner has argued that "Jews must respond with [a] determined insistence that we are not white, and that those who claim we are and exclude our history and literature from the newly emerging multicultural canon are our oppressors."[109]

In response to Lerner, Bat-Ami Bar On and Lisa Tessman argue that this historical approach to Jewish racial construction raises certain political concerns. They concede that thinking historically and globally is "absolutely necessary for fully understanding present locations."[110] Nevertheless, they argue that it also can distract from the very real problems of discrimination that face other ethnic and racial groups. In their words, "thinking historically and globally" about Jewish racial construction can "become a mechanism for evading – for those of use who live and carry out our ethicopolitical engagements in the United States – the conditions of racism, primarily antiblack racism, that surround us."[111] In other words, Bar On and Tessman argue that political considerations may require social theorists to ignore, or at least to deemphasize, the conclusions to which they otherwise would be drawn if they view current Jewish conditions in historical and global context. Ironically, Bar On and Tessman concede that the political calculation may be more difficult than it appears. They acknowledge, for example, that Melanie Kaye/ Kantrowitz has reached conclusions similar to Lerner's (and Azoulay's) for reasons that are consistent with Bar On and Tessman's avowed political goals. Kaye/Katrowitz, for example, has argued that the "desire to identify with whiteness, as well as bigotry and fear, blocks solidarity."[112] Tessman responds that identification with whiteness need not reduce cross-racial solidarity if it comes as a result of "simply acknowledging that one cannot help but be white when any other way of identifying oneself racially would be publicly implausible."[113]

---

[107] Michael Lerner, The Socialism of Fools: Anti-Semitism on the Left (1992) 123.
[108] Quoted in Allan Gould, What Did They Think of the Jews? (1991).
[109] Michael Lerner, *Jews Are Not White*, Village Voice (May 18, 1993) 33.
[110] Bat-Ami Bar On and Lisa Tessman, *Race Studies and Jewish Studies: Toward a Critical Meeting Ground*, in Jewish Locations, at 5.
[111] *Id.*, at 5.
[112] Melanie Kaye/Kantrowitz, *Jews, Class, Color, and the Cost of Whiteness*, in The Issue is Power (1992) 145.
[113] Tessman, *Jewish Racializations* at 141.

Putting aside the respective political considerations that have some-times colored (or discolored) theories of Jewish racial construction, the critics of Jewish whiteness theory have identified a material weakness in the conventional narrative. The notion that Jews "became white" like other ethnic groups during the twentieth century ignores the relative ambivalence with which Jews have accepted and been accepted into the boundaries of cultural whiteness. Significantly, Eric Goldstein chose not to frame his recent book on Jewish racial construction in terms of how Jewish Americans became white, describing instead "how Jews negoti-ated their place in a complex racial world where Jewishness, whiteness, and blackness have all made significant claims on them."[114] Goldstein explains that the entrance of Jews into the white mainstream did not resolve the "persistent ... tensions between whiteness and Jewishness."[115] One such tension is what Karen Brodkin calls the "double vision" that has enabled many American Jews to occupy a marginalized "racial middleness" between "whiteness" and "nonwhiteness" within a broadly "white" ethnoracial assignment[116]

This can be seen in countless other cultural phenomena as well. To mention just a few examples, one sees the popularity of *Heeb* maga-zine (subtitled *The New Jew Review*), the obsession with determining Jewish descent or "Jewhooing" (famously satirized in Adam Sandler's "Hannukah Song"), and the ubiquitousness of personal adds with terms such as "SJF" or "SJM" distinguishing Jews from racially identifiable categories such as "SWF" or "SBM." (There is no "SPM" for "single Presbyterian male" or "SEF" for single Episcopalian female; the cat-egories are exclusively racial.) Most of all, it is present in the emotional debates over Jewish "blood narratives" that arise whenever it is revealed that a prominent American, such as a Madeleine Albright or a John Kerry, has a secret family history of Jewish lineage.[117] For all the "white privilege" that Jews have achieved, the veneer of whiteness has not estab-lished conclusively the racial construction of American Jews.

It may be that this unfinished and evolving racial state reflects a con-dition that other groups share, although to varying extents. The concept of race can be understood as what philosopher Michel Foucault called a "regulatory ideal." That is, it serves as a process that both generates

[114] Eric L. Goldstein, The Price of Whiteness (2006) 5.
[115] *Id.*, at 4.
[116] Karen Bodkin, How Jews Became White Folks and What That Says about Race in America (1998).
[117] Susan Glenn, *In the Blood? Consent, Descent, and the Ironies of Jewish Identity*, 8 Jewish Social Studies (Winter–Spring 2002) 139.

and regulates the (perception of) bodies within its jurisdiction. In this way, Jewish bodies have been, at various times and in various places, regulated as white, as black, or as Asian. The same can be said, however, of whites, blacks, and Asians – that is, of the population groups variously assigned to these or other labels. Given the highly advanced state of feminist theory, his point may be grasped most readily by considering analogous insights about sex.

Judith Butler has described sex as "a process whereby regulatory norms materialize 'sex' and achieve this materialization through a forceful reiteration of those norms."[118] In other words, repeated normative articulation of gender conceptions has the power to change what it is to be a man or a woman. Moreover, Butler argues that the need for reiteration indicates that the process never reaches a conclusion, "that bodies never quite comply with the norms by which their materialization is impelled."[119] In other words, the continual assertion of group identity (specifically gender roles) would not be necessary if those identities were not always somewhat up for grabs. The unruliness of the human body resists efforts to regulate it under norms associated with group identity.

What is the status of Jewish bodies vis-à-vis the norms by which their materialization is imperfectly impelled? What, in other words, is the contemporary racial construction of American Jews? Charles Mill, an influential racial theorist, attempts rather awkwardly to recognize this phenomenon by characterizing Jews as "off-white."[120] Regardless of the precise formulation, modern social theory supports the characterization of Jews as something racially other than purely white. The nature of this characterization is understandably imprecise in light of the still inchoate state of contemporary race theory and the relatively recent emergence of Jewish "whiteness." Despite these difficulties, contemporary social scientific theory nevertheless provides another potential basis for Jewish antiracist claims: if American Jews are not wholly racially other, they are not wholly not-other either.

As we will see later on, the continuing evolution of Jewish racial identity provides not only opportunities but also dangers. To the extent that Jews have not fully negotiated their entrance into white society, Jews remain subject to adverse racial constructions. At the same time, for those to whom white society is itself a source of postcolonial or neocolonial

---

[118] Judith Butler, Bodies That Matter: On the Discursive Limits of "Sex" (1993) 2.
[119] *Id.*, at 2.
[120] Charles Mills, The Racial Contract (1997).

racial umbrage, the perception of Jewish whiteness is itself a grounds for further disparagement. In other words, racists can have it both ways with Jews. Those who associate nonwhiteness with racial inferiority invariably classify Jews as nonwhite, whereas those who associate whiteness with inequitable privilege invariably classify Jews as white. In both cases, those who associate racial status with moral stature lump Jews in with whatever group is most disfavored. This categorization is based not on religious groups but on some form of ethnic or ancestral categorization. It depends for its legitimacy on the tacit belief that Jews are in some fashion recognizably different from others. The British Supreme Court addressed just this feature of what it calls "the Jewish ethnic group" when it observed that "[t]he man in the street would recognise a member of this group as a Jew, and discrimination on the ground of membership of the group as racial discrimination."[121]

PERFORMATIVITY AND THE LIMITS OF SOCIAL PERCEPTION

This social perception approach is not without problems, however. Critics have demonstrated that it is particularly difficult to apply because it is hard to establish guidelines for determining how groups are commonly perceived.[122] The skin-color test is a particular problem. Many Americans would intuitively classify racial groups by skin color. Ian Haney López has argued that "race turns on physical features and lines of descent, not because features or lineage themselves are a function of racial variation, but because society has invested these with racial meanings."[123] As we have seen, however, even the perception of skin color has evolved over time and varied from place to place. Moreover, while this test may be a central element of social perception, it has been rightly rejected by both commentators and courts.[124] For example, the U.S. Supreme Court observed in *Ozawa* that a skin-color test "is impracticable as that differs greatly among persons of the same race, even among Anglo-Saxons, ranging by imperceptible gradations from the fair blond to the swarthy brunette, the latter being darker than many of the lighter hued persons of the brown or yellow races."[125]

[121] *JFS* [2009], UKSC 15, slip op., at 12.
[122] JOHN TEHRANIAN, WHITEWASHED, at 43.
[123] *See* LÓPEZ, WHITE BY LAW, at 10.
[124] *See, e.g.,* TEHRANIAN, WHITEWASHED, at 44.
[125] *Ozawa*, 260 U.S., at 197.

Tehranian has proposed a useful thought experiment to explain why skin color cannot provide a workable means for defining "racial" groups. He asks us to imagine a creature from another planet who is asked to divide human beings into several discrete groups. Even if the creature adopts the common social prejudice to perceive and differentiate people according to the color of their skin, the creature would not devise the racial divisions that our society has developed. Rather, Tehranian speculates, the creature that applies a skin-color test likely would group sub-Sarahan Africans together with Dravidian as "black," grouping northern Europeans together with Japanese as "white," and grouping Middle Easterners with the Mediterraneans as "olive." From this experiment, Tehranian demonstrates that despite their chromatic appellations, our racial categories have surprisingly little to do with actual skin color.[126]

Lacking meaningful guidelines or workable standards, even those courts which purport to follow social perception have in fact had to deviate from its results. Tehranian argues that in many cases these courts have in fact used what might be called "performative" standards. Instead of relying only on how groups are perceived externally by members of other social groups, courts frequently have examined whether individual members comport themselves in a manner that is consistent with the dominant social norms of a predominantly white society. Interpreting these courts through the lens of Judith Butler's theory of performativity, Tehranian argues that groups "perform" whiteness to various extents in a public drama through which racial identity is constructed.[127] Butler had argued that "gender is always a doing, though not a doing by a subject who might be said to preexist the deed."[128] Butler's argument, in turn, had appropriated Friedrich Nietzche's theory that "there is no 'being' behind doing, effecting, becoming; 'the doer' is merely a fiction added to the deed – the deed is everything."[129] Writing as a corollary to Nietzche's principle, Butler theorized that there "is no gender identity behind the expressions of gender; that identity is performatively constituted by the very 'expressions' that are said to be its result."[130]

---

[126] TEHRANIAN, WHITEWASHED, at 45.
[127] *Id.*, at 46.
[128] JUDITH BUTLER, GENDER TROUBLE: FEMINISM AND THE SUBVERSION OF IDENTITY (1990) 25.
[129] FRIEDRICH NIETZCHE, ON THE GENEALOGY OF MORALS (Walter Kaufmann trans.) (1969) 45.
[130] BUTLER, GENDER TROUBLE, at 25.

Building on this analysis, Tehranian argues that racial identity is established in the "dramaturgical" process by which population groups express themselves in public. For example, the Court dwelled in an otherwise inexplicable manner on Ozawa's matriculation at Berkeley High School, his matriculation at the University of California, his family's attendance at American churches, and his use of the English language at home.[131] Similarly, the Court treated Thindh's caste status as a "high-class Hindu" as if it were a countervailing factor in its decision to exclude him from membership in the white race.[132] Such considerations are relevant only if the Court's determination of racial status is based in part on whether the group has sufficiently assimilated to middle-class American norms. At first blush, this would seem to have little to do with social perceptions of "race." They become relevant, however, when the Court is understood to embrace, albeit tacitly, a performative conception of race.

How would Jewish identity be construed under a performative legal approach? There is a plausible reading of the case law which suggests that Jewish racial identity is not only performed, but performed in a manner which brings certain campus political activity within its embrace. One could read the *LeBlanc-Sternberg* and *Singer* cases as vindicating Jewish rights under a tacit form of performative analysis. While the courts did not articulate their rationales in this manner, the Lubavitcher Hasidim in these cases had little claim to distinctive racial status except under this approach. Singer, we may recall, was an Hispanic convert to Judaism. As Lord Phillips recently observed in the *JFS* case, it is not illogical to speak of conversion to the Jewish ethnic group because Jewish converts are understood to enter both the Jewish community and the Jewish religion. Indeed, Phillips writes that "conversion unquestionably brings the convert within the *Mandla* definition of Jewish ethnicity."[133] Nevertheless, converts present the most difficult challenges for case-by-case adjudication. LeBlanc-Sternberg, we may also recall, was the rabbi whose congregation faced discrimination because of their religiously motivated behavior. Ethnic or ancestral heritage, as distinguished from religious observance, had little or nothing to do with either case. In both cases,

[131] Ozawa, 260 U.S., at 189.
[132] Thindh, 261 U.S., at 206.
[133] [2009] UKSC 15, slip op., at 14–5 (Phillips, Pres., opposing). This two-fold nature of Jewish conversion was normatively expressed in GENESIS by Ruth the Moabite, who proclaimed on her conversion that "your people shall be my people, and your God my God.'" THE JEWISH PUBLICATION SOCIETY, TANAKH: THE HOLY SCRIPTURES 1420 (Ruth 1:16–7).

however, the plaintiffs had faced discrimination based on the manner in which they performed their Jewish identity. It may not be coincidental that both cases involved ultra-Orthodox Jewish men because members of this group perform Jewish identity in a particularly observable manner and sometimes face persecution because of it.

Another Jewish group that performs Jewish identity in especially overt fashion, frequently facing adverse reactions, is pro-Israel activists. The Jewish pro-Israel advocate often must distance himself or herself from the dominant campus culture, marking himself or herself as "other." This is clearly a political act, but it is also more than political. It is also, in many contexts, a means of expressing or performing identification not only with an ideology but also with a people in all of its dimensions. In this sense, campus attacks on pro-Israel Jewish activists can be seen as an assault on performative Jewish identity in every respect including that of ethnoracial identification.

DEFICIENCIES OF CATEGORICAL APPROACHES

The social perception approach, however, also other shares deficiencies with the historical and scientific approaches. What these approaches have in common is that they all require the victims to demonstrate that their group identity is protected as a "suspect class." This burden, whether defined in historical, scientific, or sociological terms, is problematic not only because it tends to reify traditional social stratifications – the so-called dilemma of difference – but also because it exposes the victims to a second form of attack, a kind of "identity theft" that takes place within the court or administrative agency. The victim is required to defend, before a skeptical authority, their group identity in the face of an alleged perpetrator who is given a legal incentive to challenge the victim's claim to membership in the sort of "suspect class" to whom Congress has afforded protection. It is partly for this reason that Kenneth Karst has castigated the very concept of "suspect class" as an "abomination" that "should be eradicated from our constitutional lexicon."[134]

The potentially adverse affects of this reification are not limited to the immediate victims who appear before the government. As Haney López has argued, the "law does more than simply codify race in the limited sense of merely giving legal definition to pre-existing social

---

[134] Kenneth L. Karst, *Myths of Identity: Individual and Group Portraits of Race and Sexual Orientation*, 43 UCLA L. REV. (December 1995) 263, 325.

categories."[135] Rather, the "law constructs race," in the sense that it fixes the boundaries of racial identities and distributes corresponding forms of social privilege and disadvantage.[136] Cheryl Harris demonstrated in a famous article that "the law's construction of whiteness defined and affirmed critical aspects of identity (who is white); of privilege (what benefits accrue to that status); and of property (what legal entitlements arise from that status."[137] While there are clearly some group advantages that now inhere in governmental recognition of racial distinctiveness, there are also social disadvantages in that same recognition. For the Jewish community, the recognition of racial distinctiveness has been extremely dangerous in the past. It may justly be asked whether the courts and regulators should continue to adopt legal standards that require groups to accept, as a condition of protection, that they participate in the legal construction of potentially dangerous racial identities.

[135] *See* LÓPEZ, WHITE BY LAW, at 7.
[136] *Id.*
[137] Cheryl Harris, *Whiteness as Property*, 106 HARV. L. REV. (1993) 107, 1725.

11

The Subjective Approach

The trouble with all the approaches described in preceding chapters is that they put the onus on victims of discrimination to prove their racial *bona fides*. This not only perpetuates the concept of race but also forces the victim to claim a kind of racial otherness as a prerequisite to obtaining civil rights protection. Regardless of the means of determining racial status, this requirement is inappropriate and offensive to some people.

There is a solution to this problem, which is to focus on the perpetrator, asking whether the discriminator targeted Jewish victims based on racial biases or misperceptions. Under this subjectivist method, one who targets Jews based on notions of Jewish racial inferiority discriminates "because ... of race" even if history, scientific evidence, and common usage indicate that Jews do not form a race. The subjectivist approach also can be described as a theory of imputed group membership, similar to the doctrine used in refugee and asylum law, because it permits persons to claim those group traits which are imputed to them by their oppressors, whether their oppressors' perceptions are accurate or not. This approach has powerful advantages, but it also has a substantial drawback, as we will see.

Karst argues that focusing on the wrongdoers' (mis)understanding of race is appropriate in light of the illusory or "metaphoric" nature of racial distinctions. In his words, "[R]ecognition of the metaphoric quality of race is no impediment to a holding that an actor commits a constitutional or statutory wrong when he discriminates against someone because he assumes his target to be a member of some race – or, as some statutes say, he acts on 'account of' or 'because of' the victim's race."[1]

---

[1] Kenneth L. Karst, *Myths of Identity: Individual and Group Portraits of Race and Sexual Orientation*, 43 UCLA L. REV. (December 1995) 263, 326–7.

The perpetrator may have a conception of race that is inconsistent with both technical and popular usage, and he may misperceive his victim's actual characteristics, yet he still may deserve be punished for racial discrimination – if this is how he perceived his actions.

This approach was articulated prominently by Judge Harvey Wilkinson in a dissent to the Fourth Circuit's decision affirming the dismissal of the *Shaare Tefila* case. Wilkinson argued that federal civil rights statutes protect even against racial discrimination that is based only on the "subjective, irrational perceptions of defendants."[2] Wilkinson explained that to do otherwise would be to allow ignorance and misperception to provide their own defense.[3] Thus, he argued, the "erroneous but all too sincere view of defendants that Jews constitute a separate race worthy of humiliation and degradation" is sufficient to bring the claim with the applicable statues.[4] Wilkinson observed that this focus on the subjective intent of the discriminatory reflects the view that discrimination is grounded in erroneous perceptions. Thus, while Wilkinson agreed with his appellate colleagues, the district court, and counsel that "Jews are not, under any legitimate view, a distinct race," he nevertheless concluded that anti-Jewish discrimination may constitute a form of racism.

Wilkinson's approach is consistent with an important pre–*Shaare Tefilah* line of cases that also focused on the perception of the discriminator when determining liability under the 1866 Act.[5] These cases relied in part on earlier Supreme Court *dicta* that had indicated that the Act prohibits discrimination on the basis of the "racial character of the rights being protected" rather than discrimination against plaintiffs who can demonstrate certain racial characteristics.[6] Under this approach, plaintiffs could establish racial discrimination by demonstrating that the wrongdoer perceived them to be racially distinct even if those perceptions were incorrect. This has enabled Hispanics, for example, to claim that they have faced racial rather than national origin discrimination.[7]

---

[2]   Shaare Tefila, 785 F. 2d, at 528 (Wilkinson, J., dissenting).
[3]   *Id.*
[4]   *Id.*
[5]   *See* Lisa Tudisco Evren, Note, *When Is a Race Not a Race? Contemporary Issues Under the Civil Rights Act of 1866*, 61 N.Y.U. L. REV. (November 1986) 976, 994–7.
[6]   Georgia v. Rachel, 384 U.S. 780, 791 (1966).
[7]   *See, e.g.,* Pollard v. City of Hartford, 539 F. Supp. 1156, 1164–5 (D. Conn. 1982); Apodaca v. General Electric Co., 445 F. Supp. 821, 823 (D.N.M. 1978).

In fact, the Third Circuit's opinion in *St. Frances College* insisted that "where a plaintiff comes into federal court and claims that he has been discriminated against because of his race, we will not force him first to prove his pedigree."[8] The court was hardly consistent on this point, however, because it also argued that "[d]iscrimination based on race seems, at a minimum, to involve discrimination directed against an individual because he or she is genetically part of an ethnically and physiognomically distinct subgrouping of *Homo sapiens*."[9] In other words, the court appeared to assume a genetic definition of "race" even while explaining why such definitions are inappropriate. What is most significant in this case, however, is that the court concluded that the legislative history of the 1866 Act supported a subjectivist approach. In this view, "Congress did not intend to limit Section 1981 solely to those groups who could demonstrate that they had been discriminated against because they belonged to a particular group identified by anthropologists."[10]

Other courts also had focused on subjective motivations in the years before *Shaare Tefila*. As one federal district court explained in *Banker v. Time Chem., Inc.*, "The vicious anti-Semitism directed against the Jews of Nazi Germany, for example, was racially motivated" despite the fact that, anthropologically, Jews are described as Caucasians.[11] The district court relied on this point in the course of explaining why East Indians should receive the same protections sought in *Shaare Tefila*, even though, like Jews, they are classified as Caucasian and considered to be socioeconomically successful. In a number of cases, Hispanics claiming racial discrimination under the 1866 act were permitted the opportunity to demonstrate that the problems they faced were "racial in character."[12] These courts emphasized that rigid racial classifications had been rejected because of their doubtful scientific and anthropological support. "To be blunt," one judge explained, "the court should not be in the business of permanently classifying groups of people, not just because it is unpalatable – but because it is untrue."[13]

Wilkinson's approach is also consistent with the way in which the courts have addressed closely analogous questions of refugee and asylum

---

[8]   St. Francis College, 784 F. 2d at, 517.
[9]   *Id.*, at 517.
[10] *Id.*, at 516.
[11] Banker v. Time Chem., Inc., 579 F. Supp. 1183, 1186 (N.D. Ill. 1983).
[12] *See, e.g.*, Cubas v. Rapid Am. Corp., Inc., 420 F. Supp. 663 (E.D. Pa.1976), Maldonado v. Broadcast Plaza, Inc., 10 FEP Cases 839 (D. Conn. 1974).
[13] Ortiz v. Bank of America, 547 F. Supp. 550, 568. (E.D.CA. 1982).

law.[14] The Immigration and Nationality Act (INA) defines a "refugee" as a person who is unable to remain in or return to a home country or residence owing to "persecution or a well-founded fear of persecution on account of race, religion, nationality, membership in a particular social group, or political opinion."[15] The Supreme Court addressed the meaning of this provision in the case of *INS v. Elias-Zacarias*.[16] Jairo Jonathan Elias-Zacaras had entered the United States illegally from his native Guatemal. When the former Immigration and Naturalization Service (INS) tried to deport him, Elias-Zacarias sought refugee status, arguing that he would be endangered by antigovernment insurgents whom he had refused to join for fear of retaliation by the government. The Board of Immigration Appeals dismissed Elias-Zacarias' appeal, and the Supreme Court affirmed, on the ground that a guerrilla organization's attempt to force a person into performing military service does not necessarily constitute "persecution on account of ... political opinion" under the INA.

The significance of this Supreme Court decision is not so much the decision as its reasoning. Justice Antonin Scalia, writing for the majority, emphasized that the record did not show a political motive on Elias-Zacarias' part. "Nor is there any indication (assuming, *arguendo*, it would suffice)," Justice Scalia wrote, that the guerrillas erroneously believed that Elias-Zacarias' refusal was politically based."[17] In other words, the Court considered not only Elias-Zacarias' actual political opinions but also the prospect that he was persecuted based on political opinions that were mistakenly imputed to him. Admittedly, the Court assumed only for purposes of argument that such imputed opinions would suffice. Nevertheless, this conditional assumption has proven influential.

Since Elias-Zacarias, the lower courts have widely interpreted the INA to protect applicants who actually meet one of these five factors or who are merely "imputed" by the persecutor to do so.[18] For example, a federal appeals court instructively explicated the doctrine of imputed group membership in the challenge that Salvadoran dissident Adela

---

[14] Peter Schuck pointed out this useful analogy to me.

[15] INA § 101(a)(42) (2004), 8 U.S.C. § 1101(a)(42) (2004); 8 C.F.R. § 208.13(b)(1) (2004).

[16] 502 U.S. 478, 482 (1992).

[17] *Id.*, at 816.

[18] *See* Shayna S. Cook, Repairing the Legacy of INS v. Elias-Zacarias, 23 MICH. J. INTL L. (Winter 2002) 223, 229.

Hernandez-Ortiz brought against an action by the INS to deport her.[19] Hernandez-Ortiz was not a member of any political group, and she was not involved in the conflict that then divided her country, so the INS did not accept that she was persecuted because of "political opinion." On the other hand, she had opposed the reigning regime, and several family members had been murdered or threatened. The Ninth Circuit rejected the notion that only the applicant's actual "race, religion, nationality, membership in a particular social group, or political opinion" could be considered in determining whether persecution can be claimed under the INA.[20] In order to determine whether Hernandez-Ortiz had been persecuted on the basis of political opinion, the court determined that it was necessary to examine the persecutors' motivations to determine whether they were acting on political antagonism.[21]

In the same way, asylum adjudicators who must assess claims of racial persecution cannot rely simply on anthropological or genetic definitions of "race" to determine whether racial persecution has occurred. Instead, they must consider the motivations of the alleged persecutors.[22] In other words, they must determine whether the applicant has been persecuted because of the persecutors' perception that the applicant is a member of a disfavored race."[23] In T. Jeremy Gunn's useful example of an asylum claim under South African apartheid, it is easy to see that it would have been inappropriate for an adjudicator to rely on such issues as "(a) whether "race" can be defined, (b) whether an applicant truly considers himself to be "Negroid," or (c) whether all four of the applicant's grandparents were black."[24]

The INA is of more than passing interest to the question of Jewish identity because the international convention on which it modeled was written with the Jewish experience specifically in mind. Justice Harry Blackmun pointed out many years ago that both the INA and the Convention Relating to the Status of Refugees were enacted in response to the plight of European Jewish refugees in the aftermath of World War II.[25] The authors of the convention considered Holocaust survivors to present

[19] Hernandez-Ortiz v. INS, 777 F. 2d 509 (9th Cir. 1985).
[20] *See id.*, at 516.
[21] *See id.*
[22] T. Jeremy Gunn, *The Complexity of Religion and the Definition of "Religion" in International Law*, 16 HARV. HUM. RTS. J. (2003) 189, 198.
[23] *Id.*, at 197–8.
[24] *Id.*, at 198, note 29.
[25] See Sale v. Haitian Centers Council, Inc., 509 U.S. 155, 207 (1993) (Blackmun, J., dissenting).

the paradigmatic case of refugees in need of asylum.[26] For this reason, the persecution of Jews because of their "religion, perceived 'race,' and 'nationality'" presented the archetypical situation that the convention's framers intended to encompass.[27] Commentators have observed that the historical context demonstrates that the framers' intent was to protect Jewish Holocaust survivors who had been persecuted because of their ancestry, whether they practiced the Jewish religion or not.[28] The theory underlying the post-Holocaust asylum regime was that persecuted Jews could avail themselves under at least several, and perhaps even all, of the five enumerated grounds: religion, race, social group, nationality, and political opinion.[29]

ADVANTAGES OF THE SUBJECTIVE APPROACH

Wilkinson's reasoning was not adopted by the Supreme Court, although, as we have seen, the Court accepted his conclusions on other grounds. Nevertheless, permitting civil rights suits based on imputed or perceived group membership has many advantages. Unlike the originalist approach, it does not perpetuate outdated and potentially offensive views of racial identity. Unlike the scientific approach, it does not require the courts to sift through, and decide among, the various emerging and conflicting approaches to race theory, nor does it limit protection to groups (if any) that are considered scientifically to be "racial." Finally, unlike the public-meaning approach, it does not subject civil rights protections to the vicissitudes of public opinion.

In these ways, Wilkinson's approach – which provides that discrimination undertaken on the basis of a person's perceived racial traits can be prohibited as racism even if the racial perceptions are erroneous – resolves many of the problems created by the rule that the Supreme Court ultimately adopted in *St. Frances College* and *Shaare Tefila*. By shifting the onus from victim to perpetrator, Wilkinson's rule resolves the "dilemma of difference." That is to say, it protects persecuted groups from conflicts arising from human difference without reifying or exacerbating those

---

[26] Daniel J. Steinbock, *Interpreting the Refugee Definition*, 45 UCLA L. REV. (February 1998).

[27] *Id.*

[28] Hathaway, *supra*, at 141.

[29] Tuan N. Samahon, Note, *The Religion Clauses and Political Asylum: Religious Persecution Claims and the Religious Membership-Conversion Imposter Problem*, 88 GEO. L. J. (July 2000) 2211, 2214–5.

differences. Government is not forced to recognize "racial" difference and thereby to reinforce it. Instead, government only recognizes and responds to discrimination based on irrational perceptions.

THE PROBLEM WITH SUBJECTIVIST APPROACHES

The problem with this approach is that it is often difficult to discern a distinctly racial animus within the complex prejudice faced by Jews and other groups in the twenty-first century. The vandals who desecrated the *Shaare Tefila* synagogue were neo-Nazis who admitted under oath that they believed that Jews were a distinct and inferior race, and they were clearly motivated by that belief.[30] This made their case easier than most. In the contemporary West, racial motivations are seldom so explicit. As Pierre-André Taguieff explained, "Post-Nazi judeophobia is grounded not upon the vulgar racialist theories of the nineteenth century, with their myth of a 'race war' between two imaginary constructs, 'Semites' and 'Aryans,' but upon a set of cultural and political elements quite different from those characterizing the anti-Semitism of the Dreyfus Affair or the state racism of the National Socialists."[31] Moreover, given the peculiar social stigma that has been attached to explicit racism since World War II, racial motivations that do exist are typically concealed by even the most flagrant bigots – sometimes even from themselves.

This is a substantial challenge for civil rights law enforcement. Efforts to defeat both racism and anti-Semitism have suffered from what Stanford Law School Professor Richard Thompson Ford has called a "crisis of success." Ford characterizes this crisis as a problem of what he calls "post-racialism." In the wake of President Barack Obama's election, the term "post-racial" has been used, or overused, frequently by the mainstream media to describe a wide range of social phenomena and political viewpoints. The varying opinions grouped under this rubric differ widely in persuasiveness, and some have the appearance of straw man arguments rather than actual positions. "Post-racism," in Ford's intriguing conception, "has emerged because legal rules and social norms against overt prejudice have succeeded."[32] By "post-racism," Ford

---

[30] *See* Shaare Tefila, 785 F. 2d at 529 (Wilkinson, J., dissenting).
[31] Pierre-André Taguieff, Rising from the Muck: The New Anti-Semitism in Europe (P. Camiller, trans.) (2004) 11.
[32] Richard Thompson Ford, The Race Card: How Bluffing About Bias Makes Race Relations Worse (2008) 338.

intends not the absence of racism but the expansion of its peculiar attenuated presence in disguised form: "[P]ost-racist is not the same as 'not racist.' Just as postmodernism is not just the withered hull of high modernism but also its apotheosis, so post-racism is, in an important sense, the continuation of racism by other means."[33] In other words, the success of postwar antiracist norms has driven hate and bias to the margins of socially unacceptable conduct, to the subconscious, and to subtle guises that are harder to identify and define. As Irwin Cotler has observed, this development has made it more difficult to monitor and combat contemporary anti-Semitism because we lack even the indicators to identify and measure it.

As we have seen, the Department of Education's Office for Civil Rights (OCR) has disregarded brazen attacks on Jewish students because it perceived that they were based only on opposition to Israeli policies.[34] In this way, the agency adopted the canard that the new anti-Semitism is neither ethnic nor racist harassment but political criticism. (To paraphrase British sociologist David Hirsh, such conflations make one wonder whether OCR also would consider the *fatwa* calling for the execution of Salman Rushdie to be a form of literary criticism.[35]) Yet OCR's confusion is understandable. An all-party parliamentary inquiry recently acknowledged in the United Kingdom that "when left wing or pro-Palestinian discourse around the Middle East is manipulated and used as a vehicle for anti-Jewish language and themes, the anti-Semitism is harder to recognise and define and Jewish students can find themselves isolated and unsupported, or in conflict with large groups of their fellow students."[36]

THE NEW ANTI-SEMITISM AS A NEW RACISM

In theory, the subjectivist approach should work even for the new anti-Semitism, despite the fact that racial motivations are more difficult to discern. The new campus anti-Semitism, even when camouflaged in political dress, can be considered "racist" in several respects: where it

---

[33] *Id.*, at 337.
[34] *Id.*
[35] David Hirsh, *Anti-Zionism and Anti-Semitism: Cosmopolitan Reflections*, Working Paper No. 1, in The Yale Initiative for the Interdisciplinary Study of Antisemitism Working Paper Series, at 53; available at www.yale.edu/yiisa/workingpaper/hirsh/David%20Hirsh%20YIISA%20Working%20Paper1.pdf.
[36] All-Party Parliamentary Group against Antisemitism, Report of the All-Party Parliamentary Inquiry into Antisemitism (September 2006) 38; available at http://thepcaa.org/Report.pdf.

exhibits continuities with racist ideologies and practices, where it adopts explicitly racial stereotypes, and where it is motivated by unconscious racial bias. The incidents that transpire on American campuses are not discrete and isolated. They are connected in profound ways with an ancient, ubiquitous, and sometimes genocidal ideology. A sophisticated subjectivist approach would recognize these continuities, but doing so requires a more complex analysis than governmental decision-makers can be expected to conduct.

CONTINUITIES WITH RACIAL ANTI-SEMITISM

The new anti-Semitism is the coalescence of geographically and historically disparate strands in what has been characterized as the "globalization of anti-Semitism."[37] Under globalized conditions – what French sociologist Michel Wieviorka has called the "dual compression of space and time" – elements of ancient and medieval Christian and Muslim thought merge with German, Russian, and Arab contributions to form a volatile, continually changing mix.[38] This globalized feature of the new anti-Semitism has an important ramification for its proper study: Both the nature and severity of the new domestic anti-Semitism must be understood in a broader context. Moreover, the interconnection of the various global and historical elements means that it is not possible to separate the new anti-Semitism's racialist and religious precursors from its current instantiations: all are mixed together, whether covertly or overtly, in a prejudice that unavoidably has aspects of all of them.

Anti-Semitism has long been a protean phenomenon, mutating continually to adapt to changing social conditions: at some times religious, at others racial, and most recently political. These manifestations are not, however, mutually exclusive. As Bernard-Henri Lévy has observed, they overlap, combine, and mix.[39] Each form contains within it elements of its antecedents: older myths, stereotypes, and defamations survive even when the intellectual context in which they develop is superseded. In this sense, racialism may be identified even within avowedly antiracialist forms of the new anti-Semitism. Given the extent to which racial anti-Semitism has pervaded Western culture for many years, it is difficult, if not impossible, for contemporary anti-Semitism to avoid elements of racism.

---

[37] See Michel Wieviorka, *The Lure of Anti-Semitism: Hatred of Jews in Present Day France* (Kristin Couper Lobel and Anna Declerck trans.) (2007).

[38] *Id.*

[39] LÉVY, at 150–2.

From the onset of the Christian era, anti-Semitism was primarily religious in character. The racial conception of Jews derives from late-fifteenth-century Spain. At that time, popular antipathy ran high against persons of Jewish or Muslim origin who had converted to Christianity early in the Inquisition. Spanish statutes of "purity of the blood" established the first official racial discrimination against persons of Jewish (or Muslim) origin, reflecting an animosity that was no longer directed at current religious practices – since no one in Spain was openly practicing Judaism at this time.[40] This strand of anti-Jewish bias received its fullest expression in Germany from the late nineteenth century until its culmination in the middle of the twentieth century.[41] During the nineteenth century, anti-Semitism tended to shift from a religious bias to a racial prejudice, facilitated by the work of German journalist Wilhelm Marr.[42] Marr popularized the term "anti-Semitism" to refer to an anti-Jewish animus that was based on Jewish racial characteristics.[43] Since then, racial anti-Semitism has portrayed Jews as members of a distinct racial group with biologically based moral and intellectual deficiencies.

As we have seen, anti-Semitism mutated again during the last half-century, frequently manifesting as a political antagonism against the Jewish state and those connected to it through blood, faith, or conviction. Walter Lacqueur has argued that the postwar mutation of racial anti-Semitism into an anti-Jewish anti-Zionism likely occurred first in the Soviet Union, where Jews were frequently persecuted as "Zionists" by Stalin and his successors.[44] Soviet spokesman were consistently hostile to Zionism.[45] This use of the term "Zionism" was purely euphemistic or pretextual because most true Russian Zionists had emigrated to Palestine

---

[40] See LÉON POLIAKOV, II THE HISTORY OF ANTI-SEMITISM: FROM MOHAMMED TO THE MARRANOS (N. Gerardi, trans.) (1973) 222.

[41] Bernard LEWIS, SEMITES AND ANTI-SEMITES: AN INQUIRY INTO CONFLICT AND PREJUDICE (1999) 81–4.

[42] WALTER LAQUEUR, THE CHANGING FACE OF ANTI-SEMITISM: FROM ANCIENT TIMES TO THE PRESENT DAY (2006) 91.

[43] *Id.*, at 21.

[44] *Id.*, at 180. In Soviet political rhetoric, as in later Muslim polemical writing, the term "'Zionist' simply means 'Jew' and therefore anti-Zionist means anti-Jew." LEWIS, SEMITES AND ANTI-SEMITES, at 19.

[45] This does not necessarily imply, however, that Soviet anti-Zionism was always motivated by anti-Semitism because Russian authorities also were concerned about Zionism's antiassimilationist and national consciousness-raising characteristics. See Zvi Gittelman, *The Evolution of Soviet Anti-Zionism: From Principle to Pragmatism, in* WISTRICH, ANTI-ZIONISM AND ANTI-SEMITISM IN THE CONTEMPORARY WORLD (1991) 12.

by the end of the war.[46] This mutation in the rhetoric of anti-Semitism mirrors the parallel transition in nineteenth-century Germany, where racialist anti-Semitism developed as a self-conscious alternative to the purely religious Judaeophobic antipathies that were already considered backward.[47]

Soviet doctrine fused the Nazi concept of Jewish criminality and Nazi anti-Zionism with both traditional stereotypes of Jewish conspiracy (influenced by the *Protocols of the Elders of Zion*) and an attack on the Jewish conception of "chosenness":

> The chosen people: is that not racism? What is the difference between Zionism and fascism, if the essence of the ideology is racism, hatred towards other peoples? The chosen people. The people elected by God. Where in the second half of the twentieth century does one hear anyone advocating this criminally absurd theory of the superiority of one race and one people over others?[48]

Here we see German-inflected anti-Semitism merging most forcefully with an attack on the idea of Zionism from a purportedly antiracist position. In Soviet usage, terms such as "Judaism," "Zionism," "Israel," and "Jewish bourgeoisie" were used interchangeably.[49]

While the Soviets were developing a political anti-Semitism, a similar project was also under way in the Middle East.[50] During the Nazi period, German anti-Semitism was exported to Arab countries in a deliberate, coordinated fashion and grafted onto local political concerns in order to become more palatable to the local populations.[51] Thus, by the time the Third Reich collapsed, an offshoot had already been carefully planted in Muslim lands through which the mission could be continued. The Nazi influence includes "the technique with which the anti-Semitic material has been reworked, and the political purposed being pursued,"[52] the

---

[46] LACQUEUR, CHANGING FACE OF ANTI-SEMITISM, at 180. Indeed, the Soviets had long since broadened the term to include all kinds of people whom the regime considered to be politically hostile. See Gitelman, at 17.

[47] For a discussion of this earlier transition, see Wistrich, at xv.

[48] Soviet Ambassador Yakov Malik, quoted in WISTRICH, ANTISEMITISM: THE LONGEST HATRED (1991), at 180.

[49] WISTRICH, LONGEST HATRED, at 182.

[50] See MATTHIAS KÜNTZEL, JIHAD AND JEW-HATRED: ISLAMISM, NAZISM AND THE ROOTS OF 9/11 (Colin Meade, ed.) (2007).

[51] *Id.* The formative Nazi influence on Arab and Muslim anti-Semitism is also discussed in LEWIS, SEMITES AND ANTI-SEMITES, at 143–63.

[52] Bat Ye'or, *Modern Egyptian Jew Hatred: Indigenous Elements and Foreign Influences,* IN THE LEGACY OF ISLAMIC ANTISEMTISM (Andrew G. Bostom, ed.) (2008) 617.

idea of an international Jewish conspiracy,[53] and the concept of Jewish contamination.[54] This last Nazi legacy is the basis for the widespread Arab view that a Jewish cancer (or catastrophic disease) infests the world.[55] This metaphor was expressed, for example, in Iranian President Mahmoud Ahmadinajad's August 2006 comment that "[t]he world powers established the filthy bacteria, the Zionist regime which is lashing out at the nations in the region like a wild beast.... " Israeli Foreign Minister Abromovich asked, "Doesn't this remind us of similar words from the past?"[56] Ahmadinajad has also commented that "[v]ery soon this stain of disgrace will be purged from the centre of the Islamic world – and this is attainable."[57] Similarly, Hizbollah Secretary General Hassan Nasrallah has admonished that "[a]ll the major disasters which befell the region stem from the existence of the state called Israel."[58] Indeed, Nasrallah has warned that as "long as there is a state called Israel, disasters and suffering will continue. This is a cancerous body in the region.... When a cancer is discovered, it must be dealt with fearlessly; it must be uprooted...."[59] Similarly, in 2005, Palestinian Authority (PA) TV broadcast a sermon by PA employee Sheik Ibrahim Mudeiris that included the following assertion: "With the establishment of the state of Israel, the entire Islamic nation was lost, because Israel is a cancer spreading through the body of the Islamic nation, and because the Jews are a virus resembling AIDS, from which the entire world suffers."[60]

[53] Jeffrey Herf, *Convergence: The Classic Case Nazi Germany, Anti-Semitism and Anti-Zionism During World War II*, in ANTI-SEMITISM AND ANTI-ZIONISM IN HISTORICAL PERSPECTIVE (Herf, ed.) 65.

[54] Ye'or, at 616.

[55] *Id.*

[56] *See* Aaron Abramovich, Dir.-Gen., Isr. Foreign Ministry, Address to the International Conference of the Global Forum for Combating Antisemitism (Feb. 24, 2008) (transcript available at the Israel Ministry of Foreign Affairs Online News Archives).

[57] Mahmoud Ahmadinajad, quoted in Matthias Küntzel, *Hitler's Legacy: Islamic Antisemitism in the Middle East* (paper presented at the international seminar series "Antisemitism in Comparative Perspective" under the auspices of the Institution for Social and Policy Studies at Yale University, New Haven, CT, November 30, 2006); available at www.matthiaskuentzel.de/contents/hitlers-legacy-islamic-antisemitism-in-the-middle-east (citing Zitiert Nach: Memri, Special Dispatch, November 2, 2005).

[58] Hassan Nasrallah, Speech delivered April 9, 2000; available at www.mfa.gov.il/MFA/MFAArchive/2000_2009/2000/4/Excerpts%20from%20Speech%20by%20Hizbullah%20Secretary-Genera.

[59] *Id.*

[60] *See This Week's Palestinian Authority Sermon: We (Muslims) Will Rule America; Israel Is a Cancer; Jews Are a Virus Resembling AIDS; Muslims Will Finish Them Off*, 908 MEMRI SPECIAL DISPATCH SERIES (May 17, 2005); available at www.memri.org/bin/articles.cgi?Page=subjects&Area=antisemitism&ID=SP90805. To view the sermon, visit http://memritv.org/search.asp?ACT=S9&P1=669.

In this way, each successive form of anti-Semitism continues to carry within it the remnants of its predecessors. German racialist anti-Semitism continued to propagate long-standing religious stereotypes about the Jewish people. Similarly, contemporary political anti-Semitism continues to disseminate traditional religious and racialist anti-Semitic defamations. Thus, for example, protesters at anti-Zionist rallies routinely voice the same anti-Semitic canards that their precursors used. Given the interconnection of the various forms of anti-Semitism, it would be virtually impossible for a contemporary anti-Semite to be wholly innocent of racist anti-Semitic conceptions. In the twenty-first century, as before, those who engage in anti-Jewish conduct act on a complex compound of ethnic, religious, racial, and political hatred.

USE OF RACIAL STEREOTYPES

In May 2004, one University of California at Irvine speaker argued that "[t]his ideology of Zionism is so racist, so arrogant, based on so much ignorance."[61] Another argued, in terms closely tracking older forms of Soviet ideology, that "anti-Semitism" charges reflect Jewh arrogance and racism: "They have taken the concept of the chosen people and fused it with the concept of white supremacy."[62] In a peculiarly potent hybrid claim merging traditional anti-Semitic stereotypes with accusations of racism, he explained, "Once you take the concept of chosen people with white supremacy and fuse them together, you will get a people who are so arrogant that that will actually make a statement and imply that [they] are the only Semites. That's arrogance and it's the same arrogance they display every day and that's the same type of arrogance that's getting them into trouble today."[63] Such statements manifest a virulent form of anti-Jewish racism, with clear parallels to Middle Eastern, Soviet, and Nazi ideology.

As expressed on California university campuses, however, such aspersions do not usually replicate the same sort of racism that Jews previously faced in Europe or at the hands of American white supremacists. Here, Jews are most frequently viewed not as black, brown, yellow, or even off-white. On the contrary, they are viewed as embodying an intensely malevolent form of whiteness that fuses all the worst traits

[61] In re UC-Irvine, note 7.
[62] *Id.*, note 8.
[63] *Id.*

that many anti-Semites attribute to whites and Jews: colonial iniquity, diabolical arrogance, and consuming power-hunger. This is a racially charged conception of Jews, although it varies significantly from older forms of anti-Semitism. We will examine this development further in Chapter 12.

UNCONSCIOUS RACIAL BIAS

Those who condemn Zionist, Israeli, and even Jewish behavior frequently disclaim any form of racial animus. In some cases, their protestations may be accurate, but in other cases, they may not be. Their denials may be suspect for three reasons. First, the new anti-Semitism shares extensive common tropes with its precursors.[64] As we have seen, much of the invective aimed at the State of Israel has been laced with traditional anti-Semitic stereotypes and defamations. Second, recent research demonstrates a close correlation between anti-Israeli and anti-Semitic views.[65] Specifically, a survey of citizens from 10 European countries demonstrates that those who hold anti-Israeli views are significantly more likely to have negative attitudes toward Jews.[66] Third, in contemporary society, anti-Semitism and racism are commonly denied or repressed as an unconscious response to guilt associated with these phenomena.[67] Where the outward signs of anti-Semitism appear (*e.g.*, anti-Israelism, anti-Zionism), it is not surprising to find repressed forms of this animosity below the surface.

The classic treatment of unconscious discrimination remains Charles Lawrence's STANFORD LAW REVIEW article entitled, *The Id, The Ego, and Equal Protection: Reckoning with Unconscious Racism.*[68] Lawrence observes that racial decision-making is often unconscious in the sense that certain outcomes may not be consciously sought but are influenced

---

[64] *See* Taguieff, Rising From The Muck and accompanying text.
[65] *See* Edward H. Kaplan & Charles A. Small, *Anti-Israel Sentiment Predicts Anti-Semitism in Europe*, 50 J. Conf. Res. (2006) 548.
[66] *Id.*
[67] *See, e.g.*, Jovan Byford, Denial and Repression of Antisemitism: Post-communist Remembrance of the Serbian Bishop Nikolaj Velimirovic (2008).
[68] Stan. U. L. Rev. (1987) 39; reprinted in Kimberlé Crenshaw, Neil Gotanda, Gary Peller, and Kendall Thomas, Critical Race Theory: The Key Writings That Formed the Movement (1995), at 235. For a more recent treatment of this topic, see Melissa Hart, *Subjective Decisionmaking and Unconscious Discrimination*, 56 Ala. L. Rev. (Spring 2005) 741.

by the decision-maker's underlying system of beliefs and values.[69] The problem, Lawrence explains, is that a shared cultural and historical heritage has transmitted unconscious racial beliefs that routinely influence behavior.[70] In many cases, this takes the form of expressive conduct that has an unconsciously motivated harassing effect. English philosopher Bernard Harrison has described as "[o]ne of the glories of French literary theory over the past thirty years" precisely this insight (which he notes with charming chauvinism has been "apparent to English-speaking philosophy a great deal longer") that "what one's words, as uttered, imply or entail, and what one may have intended to assert or imply in uttering them, are two quite different things."[71]

Lawrence provides two explanations for this, building on both Freudian theory and cognitive psychology. First, Freudian theory instructs that the mind protects itself from the discomfort of guilt by denying or refusing to recognize ideas or beliefs that conflict with what it has learned is good or right.[72] As Lawrence notes, our society has recently rejected racism as immoral, but our historical experience has made racism integral to our culture.[73] Much the same can be said of anti-Semitism since World War II. Second, cognitive psychology teaches us that culture transmits certain beliefs and values that are so culturally ingrained that they may never be explicitly articulated or consciously understood.[74] These tacit norms may entail various forms of bias. Here again, Lawrence's observation about racism applies equally to anti-Semitism.

In many cases, examples of the new anti-Semitism can be found among people who maintain that they are strongly opposed to all forms of racism and bigotry, including anti-Semitism. To the extent that these people reliably report their conscious attitudes and beliefs, they provide examples of "disassociation," which may be defined as a discrepancy between implicit and explicit attitudes toward the same subject.[75] Such dissociations are observed commonly not only in anti-Semitic attitudes but also in attitudes toward a wide range of other

---

[69] Lawrence, "The Id, the Ego, and Equal Protection," 237.

[70] *Id.*

[71] Bernard Harrison, The Resurgence Of Anti-Semitism: Jews, Israel, And Liberal Opinion (2006) 6.

[72] Lawrence, at 237–8.

[73] *Id.*, at 238.

[74] *Id.*; see also Hart, *Subjective Decisionmaking, supra*, note at 746 (explaining cognitive psychology research that demonstrates that the formation of unconscious stereotypes is part of the normal developmental process).

[75] *See* Grunwald & Krieger, at 949 (explaining the concept of disassociation and describing its application to antidiscrimination law).

stigmatized groups, including groups defined by race, ethnicity, and sexual orientation.[76]

This phenomenon is explained by the theory of implicit bias or aversive racism, which demonstrates that "many people who explicitly support egalitarian principles and believe themselves to be nonprejudiced also unconsciously harbor negative feelings and beliefs about blacks and other historically disadvantaged groups."[77] As Colorado law professor Melissa Hart observes, research on "aversive racism" presents important insights for civil rights law by revealing the unconscious behavior of people for whom opposition to prejudice is a central part of their self-conception.[78] This research suggests that aversive racists do not discriminate in contexts where discrimination would be obvious but that "because aversive racists do possess negative feelings, often unconsciously, discrimination occurs when bias is not obvious or can be rationalized on the basis of some factor other than race."[79]

In light of the general social disapproval of discrimination in the postwar period, unconscious or implicit bias is now famously widespread and encompasses not only implicit anti-Semitism but also other forms of bias.[80] Implicit beliefs, attitudes, stereotypes, and biases are not consciously endorsed, although they may provide a basis for action. "Implicit bias" has been defined as a discriminatory bias based on implicit attitudes or implicit stereotypes.[81] "Implicit attitudes and stereotypes," respectively, are tendencies to like or dislike someone or something (or to act favorably or unfavorably toward it) and mental association between social groups or categories and a trait in a manner that is not consciously endorsed.[82] Implicit bias has been described as "an aspect of the new science of unconscious mental processes that has substantial bearing on discrimination law."[83] In many cases, those who exhibit implicit anti-Semitism express explicit antiracist attitudes and condemn the hatred of any group.[84] In contemporary psychological terms, it may be said that

[76] *Id.*

[77] John F. Dovidio & Samuel L. Gaertner, *Aversive Racism and Selection Decisions: 1989 and 1999*, 11 PSYCHOL. SCI. (2000) 315.

[78] Hart, *Subjective Decisionmaking*, at 747.

[79] Dovidio & Gaertner, at 315.

[80] See Anthony G. Greenwald & Linda Hamilton Krieger, *Implicit Bias: Scientific Foundations*, 94 CALIF. LAW REV. (2006) 945, 955–6.

[81] *Id.*, at 951.

[82] *Id.*, at 948.

[83] *Id.* at 945–6.

[84] This is true of other biases as well. *See, e.g.*, Anthony G. Greenwald, Debbie E. McGhee, & Jordan L. K. Schwartz, *Measuring Individual Differences in Implicit Cognition: The Implicit Association Test*, 74 J. PERSONALITY & SOC. PSYCHOL. (1998) 1464, 1474–5.

much of this bias inheres within "System I" cognition (the rapid, intuitive, and error-prone part of our learning processes) rather than within "System II" cognition (the deliberative, calculative processes that are more accessible to conscious reflection).[85]

Granting anti-Zionists the greatest possible charity, Bernard Harrison nevertheless concludes: "A man or woman may well not be an anti-Semite; the sentences he or she utters, on the other hand, in their implications, their entailments, their silences, their evasions, may well be anti-Semitic in character."[86] In Harrison's view, this phenomenon is due in large part to "the floating, impalpable anti-Semitism of a certain climate of opinion."[87]

These observations do not merely explain the apparent sincerity with which discriminators sometimes disclaim any form of animus. They also indicate a significant challenge facing any antidiscrimination policy that turns on the discriminators' intent. In most incidents of campus anti-Semitism, one form of intent may be apparent. The discriminator intended to do what he did: vandalize property, harass students, engage in various forms of intimidation, and so on. The more difficult question is whether that intent is racial in character. For example, why exactly did the culprit choose to assault Jewish persons or property? What is it about the Jews? Is it because of their religion, their ethnic characteristics, or some elusive set of traits that has been correctly or incorrectly characterized under the rubric of "race"? Few bigots are sufficiently self-aware to answer this question properly, and fewer investigators will be able to ferret out the information in the absence of a confession. If much of contemporary bias is concealed even to the conscious mind of the discriminator, one can hardly expect a federal investigator to discern it. This is a significant drawback to the subjective approach.

SUBJECTIVE VERSUS OBJECTIVE APPROACHES

What if every means of establishing discrimination should prove inadequate not only for anti-Semitism but for bias more generally? As we saw earlier, the categorical approaches require bias victims to define themselves in terms of prefabricated identities that may not only constrain but

---

[85] *See* Christine Jolls & Cass R. Sunstein, *The Law of Implicit Bias*, 94 CALIF. L. REV. (July 2006) 969, 974–5.

[86] Harrison, *supra*, note at 6.

[87] *Id.*

also reify social characteristics in dangerous ways. This is particularly true of the dominant originalist approach, which freezes nineteenth-century racial attitudes in place. It is no less true of social perception and scientific theories, whether biological or social, that add a healthy measure of unpredictibility to the problem of reification. It is now clear that the subjectivist approaches, while resolving these problems, present a much harder one: they seldom identify racial animus even where it is present. In short, none of the alternatives is fully satisfactory.

The best and most purposive method would be to combine all these approaches. In this way, one would hold a discriminator liable if the challenged conduct is discriminatory "because of ... race" in *any* of four respects: (1) the victim was targeted for membership in one of the groups that the 1964 Act was intended to protect, (2) a group that can be characterized as "racial" under our best current scientific understandings, and/or (3) a group that is commonly understood to be a distinct "race," *or* (4) the victim was targeted for reasons of racial animus, whether the victim belongs to a racially distinct group in any of these respects or not. If any of these elements is met, the discriminator can be said to have engaged in at least one illicit form of racial discrimination (even if there are other illicit forms that he did not engage in).

Admittedly, this interpretation is broad. This is not necessarily a disadvantage. After all, civil rights statutes are supposed to be broadly construed to effectuate their remedial purpose. Under this comprehensive approach, the discriminator who harbors racial intent should not evade liability because he misinterpreted the social characteristics of his chosen victim; this is invariably true in bias cases. Similarly, the victim who is demonstrably a member of a racial group, as that term is understood under extant scientific or popular usage, should not be excluded from protection merely because nineteenth-century racial understandings were less advanced. Finally, a victim whose group Congress actually intended to protect should not be excluded merely because the statutory terms, as currently understood, would no longer cover it. Racial discrimination is sufficiently odious that it should encompass bias that can be captured under any of these interpretive approaches.

We could stop here, having assessed all the significant legal approaches to Jewish identity and concluding that they make sense only when they are operated in tandem. This is indeed a complete answer to the Sphinx based not only on current binding constitutional law but also on the various strands in contemporary jurisprudence that have been insufficiently embraced in recent decisions. For the sake of completeness, however, it must be said that there is one other subtle, important, and complex manner of addressing our question of Jewish racial identity. It has not been adopted in any legal opinion, nor has it been the subject of prior scholarship. It is, however, a legitimate means of addressing the question. Moreover, it illuminates an aspect of anti-Semitism and Jewish identity that the other approaches fail to recognize. It concerns the nature of anti-Semitic injury. We turn to this issue in Chapter 12.

12

Anti-Semitism as Harm to Racial Identity

Anti-Semitic harassment can also been seen as racial discrimination because of the nature of the harm that it inflicts. Even the "new" anti-Semitism is "racial" (in other words, it is "discrimination because of ... race") in the sense that the nature of the *injury* that it inflicts is racial, regardless of the presence or absence of any particular motivating animus. Anti-Semitism harms the development of individual and group identity as perceived by both in-group and out-group members. This is to say, anti-Semitism adversely affects the development of Jewish racial identity, incorporating harmful stereotypes and defamations into the manner in which Jews are perceived and self-perceived.

In his famous formulation, philosopher Jean-Paul Sartre argued that "it is the anti-Semite who *makes* the Jew."[1] This argument has been controversial to those for whom it seems to deny the possibility of Jewish self-definition. With this caveat in mind, however, Sartre's argument rings true in at least two important respects. First, while the anti-Semite may *target* actual Jews, the true *object* of the anti-Semite's animus is a falsely constructed idea of Jewish identity that is only loosely related to Jewish reality. In other words, anti-Semites do not hate Jews for what Jews are but for what they are falsely believed to be. This observation led Brian Klug to reject the commonplace notion that anti-Semitism targets Jews *as* Jews. Instead, anti-Semitism is "hostility towards Jews as not Jews" because the "Jew" whom anti-Semites hate is not an actual Jew at all.[2] "Thinking that Jews are really 'Jews,'" Klug observes, "is precisely the core of anti-Semitism."[3]

[1]   JEAN-PAUL SARTRE, ANTI-SEMITE AND JEW (George C. Becker, trans.) (1995) 69 (emphasis original).
[2]   Brian Klug, *The Collective Jew: Israel and the New Antisemitism*, 37 PATTERNS OF PREJUDICE (2003) 123–4.
[3]   *Id.*

Sartre's formulation contains another important insight as well. While the anti-Semite's idea of the Jew may deviate initially from the reality of Jewish existence, the social reality of Jewish lives is influenced by the stereotypes, images, and associations that are created both internally and externally to the Jewish community, including the false constructions developed by anti-Semites. As Slavoj Žižek observed, "[O]ne single individual cannot distinguish in any simple way between real Jews and their anti-Semitic image: this image overdetermines the way I experience real Jews themselves, and furthermore it affects the way Jews experience themselves."[4] The profoundest danger of anti-Semitism is the risk that Jews will disappear and be replaced only by "Jews" – in other words, that anti-Semitic tropes ultimately will come to constitute the complete social meaning of Jewish existence, as occurred in Nazi Germany.

INJURIES TO PARTICULAR DIASPORIC JEWS

In order to understand the nature of this racial harm – in which Jews are injured in the construction or reconstruction of their collective racial identity – it may help to begin with an example. A student complains that she is unable to withstand the extent of anti-Jewish animus to which she was regularly subjected on her campus. After a spate of serious anti-Semitic incidents on her campus, she says something like the following: "Not only do I feel scared to walk around proudly as a Jewish person on ... campus, I am terrified for anyone to find out. Today I felt threatened that if students knew that I am Jewish and that I support a Jewish state, I would be attacked physically."[5] At first blush, her professed inability to obtain equal educational opportunity would appear to be a paradigmatic case of the harm or injury that she is required to demonstrate in an antidiscrimination case. Skeptics may reply, however, that her claims of injury are exaggerated or manufactured. They may argue, for example, that there was no harm, that any injury could have been avoided by the victim, or that the extent of the harm was exacerbated by the victim's excessive sensitivity. Let us assume that the precipitating factors for her departure include a lengthy pattern of anti-Zionist diatribes

---

4   SLAVOJ ŽIŽEK, VIOLENCE (2008) 67.
5   *See* Susan B. Tuchman, *Statement Submitted to the U.S. Commission on Civil Rights Briefing on Campus Anti-Semitism*, in U.S.C.C.R., CAMPUS ANTI-SEMITISM, at 15. The actual graduate student who expressed these fears in a letter to the Irvine Chancellor was reportedly advised by university administration to visit the university's counseling center to "work through her feelings." *Id.*, at 16.

at campus-sponsored events, destruction and vandalism of Jewish emblems (such a Holocaust memorial and posters for Jewish communal events), and numerous threats aimed at various students, which may or may not include her. Further, assume that the university's administration has long been on notice of these facts and has failed to address them, perhaps on the ground that it does not intervene in the exercise of student political expression. These are actual allegations heard on several American campuses, and all of them are alleged in the *University of California at Irvine* case.

How was this individual student – who likely is an American-born Jewish woman – harmed in a way that should be cognizable by the law? More specifically, in what sense has the university, by permitting this environment to develop on campus, violated the antidiscrimination principle contained in both the Equal Protection Clause of the Fourteenth Amendment to the U.S. Constitution or Title VI of the Civil Rights Act of 1964? The analytical tools of antidifferentiation theory, which focuses on the use of wrongful classifications, will enable us to see that the harms include loss of dignity, formation of social stigma, and exacerbation of social conflict. By contrast, the analytical tools of antisubordination theory, which focuses on the development and maintenance of social caste systems, enable us to see that the harms also include what one might call malignant forms of racial misconstruction – a distinctly racial harm that presents yet another reason to characterize anti-Semitic harassment as "racial."

ANTIDIFFERENTIATION THEORY

Under antidifferentiation theory, wrongful discrimination consists of unequal treatment based on suspect characteristics, such as race, religion, or national origin. Discrimination so construed may be understood as a failure of impartiality.[6] Antidifferentiation theory is the basis for the Supreme Court's repeated injunctions that judicial strict scrutiny should be applied to governmental actions that distribute benefits or burdens on the basis of individual racial or ethnic classifications.[7] This approach increasingly has been associated with conservative commentators in recent years and is apparent in recent Supreme Court decisions

---

[6] *See* David A. Strauss, *Discriminatory Intent and the Taming of Brown*, 56 U. CHI. L. REV. (1989) 935, 940–1.

[7] *See, e.g.*, Johnson v. California, 543 U.S. 499, 505–6; Adarand Constructors, Inc. v. Pena, 515 U.S. 200, 224 (1995).

addressing affirmative action.[8] In *Gratz v. Bollinger,* for example, antidifferentiationism was articulated in these terms: "[R]acial classifications are simply too pernicious to permit any but the most exact connection between justification and classification."[9] While it is most closely associated with different treatment analysis, antidifferentiation theory also supports some forms of hostile environment analysis, including the Court's consideration of teacher-on-student and student-on-student harassment in educational settings.[10] Arguably, it is now the "standard view" that American antidiscrimination law is based on antidifferentiation theory, although some commentators argue that this theory does not fully explain contemporary civil rights jurisprudence.[11]

In recent years, the Court has offered two rationales for the antidifferentiation theory: individual stigma and social conflict. Strict judicial scrutiny is afforded to classifications that have these impacts. First, use of prohibited classification (such as a racial distinction) "demeans the dignity and worth of a person to be judged by ancestry instead of his or her own merit and essential qualities."[12] This has been explained in terms of the tendency of racial classifications to reinforce stereotypes of racial inferiority.[13] The genesis of this notion is in the Court's finding in *Brown v. Board of Education*[14] that the segregation of black children "generates a feeling of inferiority as to their status in the community that may affect their hearts and minds in a way unlikely ever to be undone."[15] More broadly, it has been explained as the indignity arising from "reduction" of individual identity to ancestral group

[8] John Hasnas, *Equal Opportunity, Affirmative Action, and the Anti-Discrimination Principle: The Philosophical Basis for the Legal Prohibition of Discrimination,* 71 FORDHAM L. REV. (November 2002) 423, 431.

[9] 539 U.S. 244, 270 (2003), quoting Fullilove v. Klutznick, 448 U.S. 448, 537 (1980) (Stevens, J., dissenting).

[10] *See* Gebser v. Lago Vista Indep. Sch. Dist., 118 S. Ct. 1989 (1998) (teacher on student); Davis v. Monroe County Board of Education, 526 U.S. 629 (1999) (student on student). For an explanation of how antidifferentiation theory now provides a basis for sexual harassment law, see Jack M. Balkin and Reva B. Siegel, *The American Civil Rights Tradition: Anticlassification or Antisubordination: The Origins and Fate of Antisubordination Theory,* 2003 ISSUES IN LEGAL SCHOLARSHIP (2003) 13–4.

[11] *See* Balkin & Siegel, *The American Civil Rights Tradition,* 2003 ISSUES IN LEGAL SCHOLARSHIP at 16.

[12] Rice v. Cayetano, 528 U.S. 495, 517 (2000).

[13] Richmond v. J. A. Croson, 488 U.S. 469, 493 (1989).

[14] 347 U.S. 483 (1954).

[15] *Brown,* 347 US at 494. This emphasis on "status in the community" also could reflect an antisubordination approach. Straus, *Discriminatory Intent in the Taming of Brown,* at 942.

membership.[16] This may be construed as a form of "dehumanization" insofar as the concern is that the victim's common humanity and individual dignity are robbed by classifications that reduce the victim to a single immutable characteristic. Second, prohibited classifications lead to a politics of intergroup hostility.[17] The Court's concern here is that governmental endorsement of "race-based reasoning and the conception of a Nation divided into racial blocs" contributes to "an escalation of racial hostility and conflict."[18] Historically, the Court has emphasized this encouragement of prejudice as a feature of illicit discrimination.[19] The Court has struck down state statutes that operate as "a stimulant to that race prejudice which is an impediment to securing ... equal justice."[20] As David Straus has pointed out, this approach may also overlap with antisubordinationism.[21]

Chief Justice Roberts has argued that this antidifferentiation approach formed the basis for the Court's decision in *Brown*, which "held that segregation deprived black children of equal educational opportunities regardless of whether school facilities and other tangible factors were equal, because government classification and separation on grounds of race themselves denoted inferiority."[22] In other words, it "was not the inequality of the facilities but the fact of legally separating children on the basis of race on which the Court relied to find a constitutional violation in 1954."[23] Roberts concedes, however, that this hallowed ground is highly contested and that various parties claim *Brown* as the heritage of their approach.[24]

ANTISUBORDINATION THEORY

Under antisubordination theory, wrongful discrimination consists of any conduct that has the effect of subordinating or maintaining

---

[16] *See, e.g.,* Parents Involved in Community Schools v. Seattle School Dist. No. 1, 127 S. Ct. 2738, 2796 (2007) (Kennedy, J., concurring) ("Reduction of an individual to an assigned racial identity for differential treatment is among the most pernicious actions our government can undertake").

[17] *Croson*, 488 U.S., at 493.

[18] *Metro Broadcasting*, 497 U.S. 547, 603 (1990) (O'Connor, J., dissenting).

[19] See Straus, *Discriminatory Intent in the Taming of Brown*, at 944–5.

[20] *See, e.g., Strauder v. West Virginia*, 100 U.S. 303, 308 (1879) (striking down statute that barred blacks from serving on juries).

[21] See Strauss, *Discriminatory Intent in the Taming of Brown* at 945.

[22] *Parents Involved*, 127 S. Ct., at 2767.

[23] *Id.*

[24] *Id.*

the subordination of a minority group[25] or that demeans individuals by denying them the concern and respect that flows from their equal moral worth.[26] In Owen Fiss's influential formulation, "[W]hat is critical ... is that the state law or practice aggravates (or perpetuates?) the subordinate position of a specially disadvantaged group."[27] Under this approach – which is based on "effects" rather than "intent" – conduct that has the unintended effect of increasing or preserving a minority group's disadvantaged status is foreclosed even if not directed purposely toward that group.[28] For example, the Supreme Court struck down anti-miscegenation laws in *Loving v Virginia*[29] partly on the ground that they are "measures designed to maintain White Supremacy."[30] In recent years, antisubordination theory has been more influential among academic commentators than within the Supreme Court, although its academic influence is formidable.[31]

Antisubordination theory has been refined importantly within feminist jurisprudence, particularly among commentators concerned to explain "what's wrong with sexual harassment"; that is, why should sexual harassment be understood to constitute a form of sex discrimination.[32] Catharine MacKinnon argued that sexual harassment was wrong because it institutionalized the sexual subordination of women.[33] In MacKinnon's influential view, the wrongfulness of sexual harassment arises largely from its use as an instrument of sex-role stereotyping.[34] MacKinnon observes that "a sex stereotype is present in the male

[25] John Hasnas, *Equal Opportunity, Affirmative Action, and the Anti-Discrimination Principle: The Philosophical Basis for the Legal Prohibition of Discrimination*, 71 FORDHAM L. REV. 423, 436 (2002).

[26] This latter formulation is based on the theory presented in DEBORAH HELLMAN, WHEN IS DISCRIMINATION WRONG? (2008). Hellman's contemporary formulation is analogous to Kenneth Karst's concept of equal citizenship. *See, e.g.,* Kenneth L. Karst, *Why Equality Matters*, 17 GA. L. REV. (Winter 1983) 245.

[27] Owen M. Fiss, *Groups and the Equal Protection Clause*, 5 PHIL. & PUB. AFF. (1976) 107, 157.

[28] Hasnas, *Equal Opportunity, Affirmative Action, and the Anti-Discrimination Principle*, at 436.

[29] 388 U.S. 1 (1967).

[30] 388 U.S. 1, 11 (1967). See Strauss, *Discriminatory Intent in the Taming of Brown.*

[31] *See, e.g.,* Cass R. Sunstein, *The Anticaste Principle*, 92 MICH. L. REV. (1994) 2410; Ruth Colker, *Anti-Subordination Above All: Sex, Race, and Equal Protection*, 61 N.Y.U. LAW REV. (1986) 1003.

[32] Katherine M. Franke, *What's Wrong with Sexual Harassment?*, 49 STAN. L. REV. (1997) 691.

[33] CATHARINE A. MACKINNON, SEXUAL HARASSMENT OF WORKING WOMEN: A CASE OF SEX DISCRIMINATION (1979) 174.

[34] Franke, *What's Wrong*, at 715.

attitude, expressed through sexual harassment, that women are sexual beings whose privacy and integrity can be invaded at will, beings who exist for men's sexual stimulation or gratification."[35] Influenced by both Marxism and the civil rights movement, MacKinnon argued that sexual harassment dehumanizes women by relegating them to subservience by exploiting both their sexuality and their work, just as African Americans have suffered both personal and economic exploitation.[36]

In *What's Wrong with Sexual Harassment*, a critique of feminist antisubordination theory, Katharine Franke argued that "the anti-subordination view of sexual harassment, while providing the something more that is lacking in the anti-sex and 'but for' paradigms, seems to over determine the nature of the harm as something males do to females"[37] Franke argued that this approach failed to acknowledge the problem of same-sex sexual harassment.[38] In order to address this problem, Franke refined MacKinnon's antisubordination approach in "hetero-patriarchal terms," arguing that "sexual harassment is understood as a mechanism by which an orthodoxy regarding masculinity and femininity is enforced, policed, and perpetuated in the workplace."[39] Specifically, Franke situated sexual harassment within the "technology of sexism"[40] that constructs gender identity according to "fundamental gender stereotypes: men as sexual conquerors and women as sexually conquered."[41]

In an important response to Franke's work, Kathryn Abrams conceded that feminist sexual harassment theory needed refinement in order better to accommodate same-sex harassment issues but that it should retain its emphasis on sexual subordination. In *The New Jurisprudence of Sexual Harassment*, she argued that sexual harassment jurisprudence does not require Franke's "readjustment of the balance away from a theory of sub-ordination toward a theory of gendering" but should be refined, instead, by "a more contingent, multifaceted account of women's subordination through sexual harassment."[42] In terms arguably similar to Franke's,[43]

---

35   MacKinnon, at 179.
36   Franke, *What's Wrong*.
37   *Id.*
38   *Id.*
39   *Id.*, at 760.
40   *Id.*, at 693.
41   *Id.*
42   Kathryn Abrams, *The New Jurisprudence of Sexual Harassment*, 83 CORNELL L. REV. (July 1998) 1169, 1230.
43   Katherine M. Franke, *Gender, Sex, Agency and Discrimination: A Reply to Professor Abrams*, 83 CORNELL L. REV. (July 1998) 1245, 1246 (commenting on the similarities

Abrams theorized that the wrongfulness of sexual harassment inheres in its tendency to "preserve male control and entrench masculine norms in the workplace."[44]

THE NEW ANTI-SEMITISM AS WRONGFUL DIFFERENTIATION

The new anti-Semitism is a technology of dehumanization: a mechanism by which an old system of stereotypes and defamations – increasingly congealed in some circles into an orthodoxy – regarding the role of global Jewry is disseminated, policed, and perpetuated. If the wrongfulness of sexual harassment arises largely from its use as an instrument of sex-role stereotyping,[45] then the wrongfulness of the new anti-Semitism arises similarly from its use as an instrument in stereotyping the role that Jews play, individually and collectively, in their communities, Israel, and the world. Philosopher Pierre-Andre Taguieff has characterized that stereotyping role effectively:

> Like the old "anti-Semitism," in the strong sense of the term, it is characterized by an absolute hatred of Jews as representatives of a single, intrinsically negative entity or exemplars of an evil force – that is, a total hatred in which Jews are "considered in themselves as endowed with a malign essence." ... The charge that Jews have a will to dominate, or are involved in a "plot to conquer the world," is recycled in this fantasy, as is the long-stereotypical rumble of accusation: "The Jews are guilty," which for more than half a century has been repeatedly translated into "the Zionists are guilty," "Zionism is guilty," or "Israel is guilty."[46]

The new anti-Semitism is dehumanizing to Jews because, as it grafts ancient anti-Jewish motifs on the State of Israel, it not only perpetuates them into a new century but also seeks to silence any objections with its claims of censorship: those Jews who have the temerity to call these forms of anti-Zionism by their true name are accused, in terms often redolent of old-fashioned anti-Semitism, of controlling media, government, and financial power to extinguish opposition.[47]

---

between their respective formulations and suggesting that each had amplified on the other's work).

[44] Abrams, The New Jurisprudence, at 1172.

[45] Franke, *What's Wrong*, at 715.

[46] Taguieff, *Rising from the Muck*, at 4.

[47] *See* BERNARD HARRISON, ISRAEL, ANTI-SEMITISM AND FREE SPEECH (2008); available at www.ajc.org/atf/cf/%7B42d75369-d582-4380-8395-d25925b85eaf%7D/ISRAEL_ANTI-SEMITISM_AND_FREE_SPEECH.PDF. at 30–9.

This stereotyping harms individual diasporic Jews in two respects: by demeaning an element deeply constitutive of Jewish identity and by laying the groundwork for further anti-Jewish assault. Insofar as Zionism has, since antiquity, been a central part of Jewish identity, it is not coherent to suggest that anti-Zionism is not also anti-Jewish. As Ruth Wisse has commented, Judaism without Zionism would no more be Judaism than Israel without Jews would be Israel.[48] The assault on Zionism is, in this sense, an effort to destroy a central aspect of diasporic Jewish identity. Irwin Cotler has described the new anti-Semitism as an assault on the Jewish people's right to self-determination; the "religious, cultural, national and juridical sensibility" of the Jewish people; and third, on Jewish memory and experience.[49]

On numerous college campuses, swastikas are drawn, carved, or etched in highly visible locations or in locations closely associated with individual Jewish students or Jewish groups.[50] In some cases, the swastikas are coupled with Jewish stars or Israeli flags. The swastika, in whatever form, location, or medium, is culturally significant as an emblem of the destruction of European Jewry. Even where the swastika is coupled with symbols of the Israeli state, its potentially harassing effect on Jews is unmistakable. In this respect, anti-Zionist expression can be compared with pornography: in certain forms, it is constitutionally protected, yet its aggressive usage may have a predictable effect on the creation of a hostile environment.[51]

The New Jersey Supreme Court adopted this position in the important 2008 case of *Cutler v. Dorn*,[52] which establishes under the laws of that state that anti-Semitic harassment may be demonstrated under the same standard used in racial and sexual harassment cases.[53] In that police department workplace discrimination case, the New

[48] Ruth Wisse, *On Ignoring Anti-Semitism*, IN THOSE WHO FORGET THE PAST: THE QUESTION OF ANTI-SEMITISM (Ron Rosenbaum, ed., 2004) 192.
[49] *See* Irwin Cotler, *The New Antisemitism: An Assault on Human Rights*, in ANTISEMITISM: THE GENERIC HATRED 119 (Michael Fineberg et al. eds., 2007) 18.
[50] *See, e.g.*, Kenneth L. Marcus, *Anti-Zionism as Racism: Campus Anti-Semitism and the Civil Rights Act of 1964*, 15 WM. & MARY BILL RTS. J. 837, 890 (2007).
[51] This analogy between anti-Zionism and pornography is elaborated further in Marcus, Kenneth L. Marcus, *Higher Education, Harassment, and First Amendment Opportunism*, 16 WM. & MARY BILL RTS. J. 1025, 1045 (2008);.
[52] 955 A.2d 917 (N.J. 2008).
[53] *Id.* The appellate court's contrary holding, which relied on the decision in Monmouth County, 321 N.J. Super. 133 (1999), to reverse the denial of a motion for dismissal n.o.v., was reversed, and Heitzman was overturned to the extent that it held that religious harassment must be determined based on a more demanding standard than racial and sexual harassment.

Jersey Court unanimously upheld a jury verdict that determined that a hostile environment was created by a pattern of derogatory comments relating to Jews, the Holocaust, and a particular Jewish police officer.[54] In one notable incident, the officer found that a sticker of an Israeli flag had been affixed to his locker.[55] A few weeks thereafter, a sticker of a German flag was placed above the sticker of the Israeli flag.[56] The New Jersey Supreme Court, as an initial matter, dispensed with the objection that some of the anti-Semitic remarks were not specifically directed at the plaintiff, explaining that "[c]ircumstances can give rise to an actionable hostile work environment claim even where the plaintiff was not the 'target' of the offensive or harassing conduct."[57] The Court then held that the plaintiff had adequately proven his harassment case.[58] Chastising the appellate court, the *Cutler* Court then explicitly adopted the pornography analogy: "If the 'ribbing' [that the plaintiff received] had been sexual in nature and female police officers were made to 'go-along-with' ... bawdy pictures of nude women, we doubt that a female officer's sexually hostile workplace claim would have been dismissed or a jury's verdict overturned."[59]

THE NEW ANTI-SEMITISM AS SOCIALLY DISRUPTIVE

Just as political anti-Semitism is demeaning to Jews, whether intended as such or not, it also foments social division in the same manner as other racist or ethnic hate and bias. That is to say, anti-Semitic speechacts increase the likelihood of anti-Semitic hate and bias incidents. This is, at least in part, an application of research finding that the presence of

---

54 The then–chief of police commented on the plaintiff police officer's Jewish ancestry once or twice per month, including frequent comments involving various traditional Jewish stereotypes (about noses, money, business, etc.), referred to the officer as "the Jew" in his presence, and asked him not to wear a yarmulke, although another officer was permitted to wear a "Jesus First" pin on his lapel. In addition, another officer referred to "dirty Jews" in the officer's presence and was, in the officer's opinion, insufficiently reprimanded for it. The officer also heard his brethren repeatedly say, "Let's get rid of those dirty Jews." The Court noted that "the supervisors' comments perpetuated some of the odious and vicious stereotypes of Jews circulated during medieval times and the Nazi era." *Id.,*

55 *Id.*
56 *Id.*
57 *Id.*
58 *Id.*
59 *Id.*

stereotypical images of a particular group tends to increase the level of implicit bias.[60] The rhetoric of anti-Zionism has measurably increased not only verbal but physical attacks on individual Jews around the world, as the U.S. State Department has documented.[61] The extent of "intergroup hostility" occasioned by contemporary political anti-Semitism has been likened to extension of the Middle East conflict by other means. Moreover, the attribution of demonic characteristics to Israel has a clear historical connection to efforts to lay the groundwork for extermination.

The relationship between traditional anti-Semitic expression and anti-Jewish hate and bias incidents is well established.[62] As Alexander Tsesis has observed of the *Shoah*, "[p]ropagandists not only made anti-Semitism acceptable, they made it respectable."[63] This has, of course, been the principal cause of concern with verbal expressions of the new anti-Semitism. Anti-Semitic slogans did not pose an immediate danger to Jews as the Nazis rose to power.[64] Yet, as Tsesis has shown, years of indoctrination paved the way to the "Final Solution."[65] The Nazi experience demonstrates that the most dangerous speech may not pose an immediate threat of harm, taking years to develop "until it becomes culturally acceptable first to libel, then to discriminate, and finally to persecute outgroups."[66]

THE NEW ANTI-SEMITISM AS A SYSTEM OF SUBORDINATION

We have already examined some of the ways in which the new anti-Semitism demeans Jews and encourages anti-Semitic hate and bias incidents. This section will examine the function of the new anti-Semitism

[60] See Christine Jolls and Cass R. Sunstein, *The Law of Implicit Bias*, 94 CALIF. L. REV. (July 2006) 969, 982 (noting that this finding is supported both by social scientific evidence and common sense); Irene V. Blair, Jennifer E. Ma, and Alison P. Lenton, *Imagining Stereotypes Away: The Moderation of Implicit Stereotypes Through Mental Imagery*, 81 J. PERSONALITY & SOC. PSYCHOL. (2001) 828, 832–3.

[61] U.S. Department of State, *Contemporary Global Anti-Semitism: A Report to the United States Congress* (2008), available at http://www.state.gov/documents/organization/102301.pdf.

[62] ALEXANDER TSESIS, DESTRUCTIVE MESSAGES: HOW HATE SPEECH PAVES THE WAY FOR HARMFUL SOCIAL MOVEMENTS, (2002) at 11–27.

[63] *Id.*, at 23.

[64] *Id.*

[65] *Id.* at 26.

[66] *Id.*

as a racialized system of moral subordination, affixing Jews with racial attributions that are imbued with stereotypes and attributions of moral inferiority.[67] Unlike other subordination systems, the new anti-Semitism typically racializes Jews not primarily as biologically inferior nonwhites but as paragons of a perverse racial whiteness combining dysfunctional ethnic traits with an arrogant racial supremacism. This process is not merely demeaning to Jews, individually and collectively; rather, it functions to dehumanize by constructing Jewishness from racial attributes that are rejected as beneath common humanity. This attribution frames Jews as suitable, by reason of racial guilt, for dispossession or destruction.

CONTEMPORARY JEWISH RACIAL REFORMATION

Adapting to contemporary norms, the new anti-Semitism reframes Jews in antiracialist terms as neocolonizing supremacist whites. This new racial construction retains stereotypical racialized perceptions of the Jew as greedy, murderous, conspiratorial, power hungry, treacherous, and diabolical while infusing these characteristics with attributes of racialism, colonialism, and imperialism.[68] Opportunistically, this reformation continues the process of racial reformation that began, with much Jewish participation, in the mid-twentieth century. This process has a dehumanizing effect, projecting onto Jews the most despised evils of the world's racist, colonialist, and anti-Semitic past in order to justify any harms (dispossession, destruction, etc.) that might be visited on them.

---

[67] This reracialization illustrates the principle that racial formation can be externally imposed, such as, for example, when social and political phenomena are explained in terms of an out-group's defective cultural norms. MICHAEL OMI AND HOWARD WINANT, RACIAL FORMATION IN THE UNITED STATES: FROM THE 1960S TO THE 1980S (1986/1989) 66. Adverse racial attributions and racial myths similarly have been affixed to other American groups in recent years: African Americans, for example, as having defective cultural norms and dysfunctional families. Id. at 66.

[68] Indeed, the new racial construction incorporates all seven classic categories of Jewish racial stereotype: deceitfulness, artfulness, and crookedness; foreignness and differentness; irreconcilability, hostility, and agitation; commercial talent and greed; corruption and greed; powerful, power hungry, and conspiratorial; and deicidal and demonic. See EUMC, MANIFESTATIONS OF ANTISEMITISM IN THE EU (2002–2003), at 12–3; available at http://eumc.eu.int/fra/index.php?fuseaction=content.dsp_cat_c ontent&catid=3fb38ad3e22bb&contentid=4146a7b291fff; citing Alexander Pollak and Nina Eger, *Antisemitismus mit Anspielungscharakter in Anton Pelinka, Ruth Wodak (eds.)*, POLITIK DER AUSGRENZUNG (Vienna: Czernin, 2002), at 187–210 and MARVIN PERRY AND FREDERICK M. SCHWEITZER, ANTISEMITISM: MYTH AND HATE FROM ANTIQUITY TO THE PRESENT (New York: Palgrave Macmillan, 2003), at 2ff.

This new racial construction has been called the "Jewish cracker theory."[69] That term, used at Irvine by an adherent of the new anti-Semitism, expresses the effort to fuse traditional contempt for Jewish religious doctrine, anti-Jewish ethnic antagonism, and a contemporary "antiracist" view of white guilt. At Irvine, public speeches lambasting Jewish cultural arrogance participate in this racial formation by fusing misconceptions of Jewish chosenness with accusations of white supremacism.[70] This emphasis on Jewish arrogance plays on traditional stereotypes as recently expressed in textbook descriptions of a putative "aggressive [and] evil tendency that is rooted in the Jewish personality."[71]

The racializing quality of the new anti-Semitism can be seen in attributions of physical or biological difference to Israelis and Jews. For example, at Columbia, one professor has reportedly described the "deep marks" that misconduct has inscribed "on the faces of ... [Israeli Jews], the way they talk, walk and the way they greet each other," arguing that "[t]here is a vulgarity of character that is bone-deep and structural to the skeletal vertebrae of its culture.[72] Similarly, at the University of California at Los Angeles, one cleric announced, "Israel is as racist as apartheid could ever be.... you can take a Jew out of the ghetto, but you can't take the ghetto out of the Jew."[73]

In some cases, this new racial formation is combined with older attributions of Jewish racial difference. It is common in some countries to describe Jews as apes and pigs based on koranic scripture.[74] Additionally,

---

[69] Susan B. Tuchman, Statement Submitted to the U.S. Commission on Civil Rights Briefing on Campus Anti-Semitism, in U.S. Comm'n on Civil Rights, Campus Anti-Semitism (2006), available at http://www.usccr.gov/pubs/081506campusantibrief07.pdf at 15.

[70] For example, see In re UC-Irvine, note 8 ("They have taken the concept of the chosen people and fused it with the concept of white supremacy"); Tuchman, *Statement* at 15.

[71] GABRIEL SCHOENFELD, THE RETURN OF ANTI-SEMITISM at 19; quoting B'NAI B'RITH INTERNATIONAL, JIHAD, JEWS, AND ANTI-SEMITISM IN SYRIAN SCHOOL TEXTS 15–6.

[72] Quoted in Sarah Stern, *Campus Anti-Semitism*, in U.S.C.C.R., CAMPUS ANTI-SEMITISM. at 25 (brackets inserted). Columbia Professor Hamid Dabashi has sworn that this quotation does not correctly translate his statement, but he has not provided an alternative version.

[73] Marc Ballon, *Campus Turmoil: Jewish Students and Activists Call UC Irvine a Hotbed of Anti-Semitic Harassment*, JEWISH J., Mar. 10, 2005.

[74] For documentation of recent usage of the Jews-are-dogs-and-pigs insult in Muslim countries, see Menahem Milson, *Arab and Islamic Antisemitism*, 442 MEMRI INQUIRY & ANALYSIS SERIES (May 17, 2007); available at www.memri.org/bin/articles.cgi?Page=subjects&Area=antisemitism&ID=IA44208. The scriptural foundation may be found at KORAN, 2:65, 5:60, 7:166.

government-owned media in some countries have frequently run hybrid new-old anti-Semitic content, such as the notion that "trickery is in the nature of the Jews" as "venom is in the serpant's son."[75] The new anti-Semitism both builds on and enlarges each of the anti-Semitic projects that preceded it in both ideological and racial content: early Christian and medieval religious anti-Semitism, Nazi and mid-century racialist anti-Semitism, and so on. This integration of religious, racialist, and political anti-Semitism is intended to advance anti-Zionism by building on those of its antecedents that dehumanize and demean not only Israel but world Jewry.[76]

As the racial theater on a field of political contestation, it is doubly ironic. During earlier periods of white dominance, Jews were constructed as paragons of racial color; more recently, as whiteness has become associated with racial guilt, Jews are increasingly constructed as preeminently white.[77] At the same time, the new Jewish racial formation is imbued largely with precisely those forms of racial guilt which have historically marked Jewish victimization (racism, *dhimmitude*, colonialization, and genocide). This inversion is a projection onto the Jews as racialized other of the traits that contemporary in-groups deny or repress from within their own psyches.

This chapter began with the story of a Jewish student who felt traumatized by the experience of extreme anti-Zionism on her campus. To the extent that she reasonably fears physical attack, based on her Jewish identity, it is easy to comprehend at least one aspect of the injury which she suffers. Even without that fear, however, this student presents another distinct and important form of injury. The extreme anti-Zionism on her campus not only reawakens older, latent forms of anti-Semitism which have not fully been extinguished within Western culture. More palpably, it also propagates newer forms. In some cases, individual Jews like this student may be held collectively responsible for the alleged wrongs of the

---

[75] This is taken from a statement by Sheikh Mansour Al-Rifa'i 'Ubeid, Egypt's former under secretary for religious affairs in charge of mosques and the KORAN, who wrote the following in an article for AQIDATI, which is published by the official Egyptian daily AL-GUMHURIYA: *Egyptian Government Weekly: Treason and Deception Are in the Blood of the Jews*, 594 MEMRI SPECIAL DISPATCH SERIES (October 23, 2003); available at www.memri.org/bin/articles.cgi?Page=subjects&Area=antisemitism& ID=SP59403.

[76] ROBERT S. WISTRICH, MUSLIM ANTI-SEMITISM: A CLEAR AND PRESENT DANGER (2002); available at www.ajc.org/atf/cf/%7B42D75369-D582-4380-8395 D25925B85EAF%7D/WistrichAntisemitism.pdf.

[77] See MICHAEL LERNER, SOCIALISM OF FOOLS (1992) 123 (observing that "Jewish history, totally denied or obscured by whites, is now excluded as white").

Jewish state. Even when they are not held collectively responsible in this explicit manner, however, a deeper injury occurs. The wild defamations, stereotypes and canards injected into the campus climate infuse malignant bias into the racial identification of Jewish students. While each incident may have a negligible effect, the combined effect of repeated verbal assaults is to reconstruct the manner in which these students perceive themselves and are perceived by others. This is the precise manner by which racial demonization and dehumanization transpire. To call it by any other name than racism is to be guilty of evasion.

Conclusion

However the issue is framed, Jewish students have powerful claims to the antiracism protections contained in Title VI. That is to say, harassment of Jews is "discrimination because of ... race" within the meaning of that law. Despite initial misgivings, the organized Jewish community has now long since recognized that such provisions are important bulwarks against anti-Semitism. The community's early concerns were not irrational. Some approaches to this question do require Jews to choose between loss of basic rights or adherence to a dubious conceptual framework. It is an awkward choice, and it is understandable that the organized Jewish community was slow to embrace such measures to protect them. The resurgence of anti-Semitism in recent years has generated an equally understandable but opposite reaction. Recently, a Jewish leader in the fight against anti-Semitism participated as a guest in my graduate seminar on anti-Semitism and civil rights policy. Asked how he and his colleagues felt about this question, he responded pragmatically: "We want the protections. The legal arguments that we use to obtain them are secondary."

From a practitioner's standpoint, this civil rights advocate probably was right. The conclusion can come first. Currently, the Supreme Court addresses such questions under *Shaare Tefila*'s "originalist" approach. As we have seen, Jews are unquestionably among the groups protected under Title VI of the Civil Rights Act of 1964 because that measure was devised to enforce rights created under nineteenth-century legislation that (as the Supreme Court has unanimously held) clearly applies to Jews. To the extent that *Shaare Tefila* provides a complete and correct answer to the Sphinx's question and is compelled by controlling legal authority, the practitioner really need go no further. If we pursue the issue beyond this answer, it is because there are so many other ways in which the question can be reframed, and some of them are attractive in ways that the originalist approach is not – although each of them has its own downside as well.

Shaare Tefila's approach has been criticized, in part, on the ground that it ignores advances made by scientific theory. Paradoxically, Jews could be denied protection under a "scientific" approach on the ground that contemporary science rejects the notion of a biologically distinct Jewish race. This "scientific" challenge, however, misstates contemporary science. In recent years, many scientists have rejected the existence of human races that are meaningfully distinct biologically. For this reason, it is misleading to suggest that Jews lack scientifically meaningful claims to racial distinctiveness *that other groups can claim*. If Jews are not a race, it is because no one else is either. Yet we cannot interpret a civil rights statute in a manner that provides no one with protection. Contemporary anthropology sees the concept of "race" as a social construction. Multiculturalists often scoff at the notion that Jews have been socially constructed as "nonwhite" given the degree of privilege that Western Jews are perceived to enjoy. In fact, Jews historically and globally have been "racialized" as a group separate from Western European whites. In recent decades, this construction has been complicated, at least as applied to light-skinned Ashkenazic Jews, who have long negotiated a process of "becoming white." Contemporary social scientific research suggests, however, that the "reracialization" of American Jews is hardly complete or uncomplicated and that American Jews often present as something other than fully and normatively white. Moreover, recent advances in genomic science have led some population geneticists to conclude that the distinct characteristics among Jews may be greater than is often assumed. Jews have both racial continuities and discontinuities with members of other population groups. The discontinuities, whether socially constructed or not, have been the source of severe and repeated adverse treatment of the sort that civil rights acts are intended to remedy.

The historical and scientific understandings both downplay contemporary public (nonscientific) understandings of what it means to be a race. Regardless of legislative history or the resolution of scientific arguments, some argue that the concept of "race" now has a distinct public meaning that describes five separate groups: whites, blacks, Hispanics, Asians, and Native Americans. This understanding underlies much governmental policy. In fact, however, this five-tiered approach is now so widely rejected that it no longer can be considered a reflection of modern public understanding. Public conceptions of race and ethnicity are more nuanced and less definite. Today, Jews are mostly considered to be more than a religion. Most Americans, most Jews, and most academics consider Jews to be an ethnicity or both an ethnicity and a religion. To the extent that "race" is now understood to be a matter of shared ethnic or ancestral heritage, Jews are publicly understood to be members of such a group.

All these approaches – historical, scientific, and sociological – share one basic flaw: They require the victims of discrimination to show that they are members of a "suspect category" that Congress intended to protect. In this way, they tend to reify outdated social categories and to impugn the self-conceptions of the victims. The alternative approach examines the subjective approach of the discriminator rather than asking whether the victim historically, scientifically, or sociologically deserves protection.

Under a subjective intent standard, Jews receive antiracist protections to the extent that their antagonists are racially motivated. This approach has the advantage of resolving the dilemma of Jewish difference: Jews are extended civil rights protections in a manner that does not exacerbate the very perceptions of difference that gives rise to the underlying offense. The problem is that it is so hard to prove that racial incidents are motivated by racial considerations. The new anti-Semitism, like the new racism, typically is based on concealed racial intent. In fact, however, the nature of contemporary anti-Semitism has been to combine elements of its precursors. Just as racial anti-Semitism included elements of religious anti-Semitism, so does the new anti-Semitism include elements of both religious and racial animus.

The injuries about which Jewish students complain are not, however, illusory, nor are they unreasonable. The new anti-Semitism dehumanizes all Jews, not only those who possess Israeli citizenship. This dehumanization is achieved in part through racializing discourses that subordinate Jews or the Jewish state as a morally inferior group. These discourses frequently adopt traditional anti-Semitic rhetoric while incorporating modern permutations, including even putatively antiracist elements. Many Jewish students may avoid personal harm by covering their identity, whether intentionally or not, but the increasing need to do so in some communities is itself a wrongful harm. While the law may be a blunt instrument to address conduct that perpetuates itself through public discourse, it is no less available as a means of remedying those forms of assault which assume the guise of a politics.

Thus, however the question is framed, anti-Jewish discrimination is "discrimination because of ... race" as Title VI uses that phrase. Each approach that we have considered illuminates some aspects of this question while confusing or ignoring others. From the perspective of public policy, the best way to answer the question may be to ask it in each of its variations. Bias incidents are "discrimination because of ... race" if they satisfy any of the standards we have explored: original intent, scientific validity, popular understandings, subjective belief, or racial injury. This is an admittedly broad construction of the statute, but that is not necessarily a vice. Indeed, it is hard to argue that discrimination in federally funded educational institutions should be permitted if it is racial (or racist) in any of these senses of the term.

ASKING A DIFFERENT QUESTION

For the sake of completeness, we also must examine whether the same result would obtain if we consider potential liability for anti-Semitic campus discrimination from yet another angle. As we have seen, the Department of Education's Office for Civil Rights' (OCR's) 2004 guidance letter emphasizes national origin rather than race. This emphasis was largely cosmetic: it is more politically palatable to discuss national origin protections for Jewish Americans than to raise the question of racial difference. Conceptually, however, this policy is really about race. As OCR's reliance on *Shaare Tefila* suggests, OCR was extending the Supreme Court's racial jurisprudence rather than its national origin jurisprudence to cover Title VI. The reason for this was simple: the Supreme Court had been less expansive in its interpretation of national origin than it had in its interpretation of race. Even apart from this, however, the fact is that characterizing Jewish Americans as a nationally distinct group also has other problems. Like the conceptual problems facing the racial approach, however, these problems may be solvable.

Legally, the main obstacle facing the national origin approach is the U.S. Supreme Court's 1973 case of *Espinoza v. Farah Manufacturing Co.*[1] This is the sole Supreme Court case exploring the meaning of "national origin," and it is not encouraging. Espinoza, a Mexican national, had sued a manufacturing company that hired only citizens of the United States. Espinoza argued that this policy amounted to national origin employment discrimination in violation Title VII of the Civil Rights

[1]   414 U.S., at 86.

Act of 1964. The Supreme Court, observing the absence of any significant legislative history on this issue, decided against Espinoza, holding
that Title VII protected only U.S. citizens from discrimination.[2] More
important for our purposes, Justice Thurgood Marshall provided what
remains to this day the Court's most authoritative opinion on the meaning of national origin discrimination. In a statement of deceptive sim-
plicity, Marshall explained that national origin "on its face refers to the
country where a person was born, or, more broadly, the country from
which his or her ancestors came."[3]

This commonsense definition of national origin has the virtue of con-
sistency with our commonsense intuitions. After all, what do we typically mean by "national origin" than the nation that one comes from?
When taken literally, however, this standard creates innumerable problems. In fairness to Marshall, his commonsense definition comports with
what at least some members of Congress thought they were voting for.
For example, Representative Roosevelt explained during floor debate
that "'national origin' means national." Specifically, he announced, it
"means the country from which you or your forebears came ... Poland,
Czechoslovakia, England, France, or any other country."[4] This is indeed
what many people understand by the term "national origin." As a legal
matter, however, it cannot serve the purposes that any reasonable legis-
lator would expect.

When national origin discrimination is limited to this commonsense conception, a large but uncertain category of seemingly substantial claims would appear to be excluded, and a number of other claims
become questionable. To start with, this definition would appear to
exclude claims by ethnic groups who claim national status but who do
not have their own countries. This would include, for examples, Kurds,
Tamils, Basques, and Palestinians. Under Marshall's definition, it would
appear that one could commit national origin discrimination against a
person of Basque ancestry if one is biased against Spain but not if one is
biased against Basques.

Ironically, the definition also would seem to exclude discrimination
against Puerto Ricans – even though Puerto Ricans were the paradigmatic

[2]   *Id.*, at 88–9.
[3]   *Id.*, at 88.
[4]   Juan Perea, *Ethnicity and Prejudice: Reevaluating "National Origin" Discrimination
      Under Title VII*, 35 WM. & MARY LAW REV. (1984) 818; quoting U.S. Equal
      Employment Opportunity Commission, Legislative History of Titles VII and XI of
      Civil Rights Act of 1964 (1968), at 3179–80.

example of a group that Congress intended to cover. During floor debate on the Civil Rights Act of 1964, floor manager Emanuel Celler made this clear:

Mr.ABERNATHY:... Now what national origin – what group of that character have been discriminated against?
Mr.CELLER: There were discriminations mentioned concerning certain groups like Puerto Ricans.
Mr.ABERNATHY: They were not discriminated against then because of color?
Mr.CELLER: Well, they were discriminated against because of national origin.[5]

The discrimination that Puerto Ricans face, however, has nothing to do with the country in which they or their ancestors were born because that country is typically the United States. In some cases, Puerto Ricans may trace their ancestry to Spain, but discrimination against Puerto Ricans is not necessarily motivated by anti-Spanish animus.

The question becomes more complicated if an ethnic group gains or loses statehood. For example, since the Slovak people now have an independent state, it would appear that Marshall's definition would cover anti-Slovak discrimination today. But would the same bias have been legally permissible during periods when no such country existed, such as the period from 1945 to 1993? An even greater problem concerns groups that span multiple countries. For example, Marshall's definition would appear to exclude discrimination against Hispanics as a group, although it would include discrimination against members of particular Latin American countries. Given the historical context in the United States, it is hard to justify a conception of national origin discrimination that strips this large and important group of their civil rights. For all these reasons, Justice Marshall's commonsense definition of national origin discrimination, if taken literally, is unworkable, inequitable, and arguably absurd.

It is therefore welcome that some lower courts have taken a broader view of national origin than *Espinoza* appeared to allow. A couple of district courts have held that Jews are a national origin group, although at least one court has held that they are not.[6] Other lower courts have

---

5 110 CONG. REC. (1964) 1528. See, generally, Perea, *Ethnicity and Prejudice*, at 805.
6 Compare Weiss v. United States, 595 F. Supp. 1050 (E.D. Va. 1984); Compston v. Borden, Inc., 424 F. Supp. 157 (S.D. Ohio 1976) with Lapine v. Edward Marshall Boehm, Inc., No. 89-C-8420, 1990 U.S. Dist. LEXIS 3459 (N.D. Ill. March 28, 1990) (unpublished).

defined "national origin" broadly to include, for example, Roma, Serbs, Cajuns, and Ukrainians at times when these groups have not had independent states.⁷ Such courts have established "nationality" based on such group traits as physical characteristics, language, culture, surnames, and shared religion.⁸

These traits may or may not conform to the commonsense notion of national origins. Interestingly, they are more than a little similar to the characteristics associated with another related concept: ethnicity. The clearest criteria that any English-language court has produced for identifying a distinct ethnicity are the one that Lord Fraser of Tullybelton established in his influential *Mandla* opinion. Two criteria, Fraser wrote, are essential: a long shared history and a unique cultural tradition. Additionally, several other criteria are "relevant": common geographic origins, descent from a few shared ancestors, a common language, a common literature, a common religion, and being a minority within a larger community.⁹ Although Fraser offered these traits as criteria for identifying an ethnicity under English law, they are also generally consistent with both the post-*Espinoza* U.S. trend toward conceptualizing "national origin" in broad ethnic terms and the *Shaare Tefila* conception of "race" as encompassing ethnic or ancestral heritage. Historically, the Jewish people have met all these criteria; arguably, they are the paradigmatic example of a people that meets them, and it is likely that Fraser had Jews specifically in mind.

The week after the U.K. Supreme Court handed down the *JFS* case, the European Court of Human Rights decided another important case that treats Jewish identity in a similar manner.¹⁰ Jakob Finci, the ambassador of Bosnia and Herzegovina to Switzerland, sued his own country under the Convention for the Protection of Human Rights and Fundamental Freedoms for adopting constitutional provisions that preclude persons

---

⁷ See Janko v. Illinois State Toll Highway Authority, 704 F. Supp. 1531, 1532 (N.D. Ill. 1989) (Roma); Pejic v. Hughes Helicopter, Inc., 840 F. 2d 667 (9th Cir. 1988) (Serbs); Roach v. Dresser Industrial Valve & Instrument Division, 494 F. Supp. 215 (W.D. La. 1980) (Cajuns); Kovalevsky v. West Publishing Co., 674 F. Supp. 1379 (D. Minn. 1987) (Ukrainians).

⁸ See, e.g., United States v. Texas, 342 F. Supp. 24, 25 (E.D. Tex. 1971) (physical traits, culture, surnames, religion); Lau v. Nichols, 414 U.S. 563 (1974) (language); Roach, 494 U.S., at 217 (documented history of group's existence).

⁹ Mandla v. Dowell Lee [1983], 2 AC 548.

¹⁰ Sejdic & Finci v. Bosnia and Herzegonia, Euro. Ct. Hum. Rts. (December 22, 2009); available at http://cmiskp.echr.coe.int/tkp197/view.asp?item=1&portal=hbkm&action=html&highlight=jewish%20%7C%20roma%20%7C%20bosnia&sessionid=4101 2940&skin=hudoc-en.

of Jewish ancestry from serving in the Bosnian House of Peoples or from being elected to its presidency. Under the Constitution of Bosnia and Herzegovina, forged during a time of ethnic upheaval, key political positions are shared among the Bosniacs, Croats, and Serbs. Those who descend from other groups, such as Jews and Roma, are excluded.[11] The European Court of Human Rights struck down the disqualifying provision as a violation of the convention. Significantly, the court observed that discrimination against Jews is a form of prohibited racial discrimination because ethnic discrimination is a form of racial discrimination under European law.[12]

National origin, especially when understood broadly to include ethnic descent, supplies a legitimate alternative basis to the racial approach, albeit one that is at odds with the Supreme Court's leading precedent. The notion of Jewish nationality will not be entirely comfortable for all American Jews any more than the notion of racial separateness may be. Many Jews understand their Jewish identity at least partly in ethnic terms, but others do not. Moreover, ethnographers likely will object that Jews do not constitute one ethnicity but several. For example, Ashkenazi Jews may form a distinct ethnicity, but Sephardim are usually considered to be a different ethnic group altogether, whereas Mizrahi Jews may constitute a third group or a number of discrete groups. So the ethnic approach is not without its flaws, even if proponents have the better of the argument.

NONWHITENESS

We have now comprehensively assessed the question as to whether anti-Semitism is a form of "discrimination on the basis of ... race" (or national origin). After considering the question from every possible angle, one cannot help but return to Sara Horowitz's observation, which we considered at the beginning. After contemplating the various categories into which Jews may be sorted – religion, race, or ethnicity – she concluded that "none of these terms suffices, suggesting that the categories we use to sort knowledge may be off the mark, not only for things Jewish, but in general."[13] While contemporary civil rights jurisprudence requires

---

[11] Mr. Finci was joined by a plaintiff of the Roma people who brought similar claims.
[12] Sejdic & Finci v. Bosnia and Herzegonia, Euro. Ct. Hum. Rts..
[13] Sara R. Horowitz, *The Paradox of Jewish Studies in the New Academy*, IN INSIDER/ OUTSIDER: AMERICAN JEWS AND MULTICULTURALISM (D. Biale, M. Galchinsky, S. Heschel, eds.) (1998) 116, 124.

courts and governmental officials to choose among the existing categories, Horowitz may be right that these categories are off the mark. If so, is there a jurisprudential alternative that fits with our constitutional and statutory civil rights law? In other words, could the right answer be that we are asking the wrong question and that it should not matter whether, in a narrow and technical sense, any particular incident of hate or bias is "discrimination on the basis of ... race"?

Civil rights law does not need to treat such categories as "race, color or national origin" as separate holes into which our pegs must be made to fit. Indeed, Congress has not treated them that way in drafting legislation. Consider the rote frequency with which Congress and the president included, in virtually all civil rights statutes and executive orders during the civil rights period, what one might call the very same "usual suspect classifications": race, color, creed or religion, and national origin. With two exceptions, Congress and the president seldom deviated from these categories and seldom reflected on why some categories were included and others excluded.

These exceptions may prove the rule. The first exception, sex, was included in Title VII of the Civil Rights Act of 1964. We know, however, the ironic reason for this anomalous inclusion. Opponents of the Civil Rights Act thought that including "sex" among the prohibited classifications was so absurd that it would bring the entire legislation to a halt. We now know how wrong they were. The other exception, of course, was excluding "religion" from Title VI.

Aside from these exceptions, it is rarely, if ever, clear why, for example, Congress chose to include, say, "national origin" within any particular legislative provision. It was simply included in every provision. Indeed, Congress routinely included the "usual suspect classifications" in civil rights legislation even when doing so made little sense. For example, there is no rational explanation for the inclusion by Congress of religion in Title IV of the Civil Rights Act of 1964, which gives the attorney general certain powers to address segregation. Religious segregation was not a pressing issue in 1964. Congress included religion there because it was included everywhere.

There is, however, a reasonable explanation for why race, color, national origin, and religion should be included in all the Civil Rights Era legislation, even when some of these categories do not seem to make sense in some of the statutory provisions. The answer becomes clear when one considers "race, color, religion, and national origin" as a single undifferentiated totality rather than four discrete categories.

Collectively, they represent the categories of disadvantaged otherness as that phenomenon, however phrased, was understood during the Civil Rights Era. These terms are grouped together not because each one discretely applies in each instance but because they jointly circumscribe the notion of disfavored group identity as it was understood at the time.

Interestingly, this notion fits better than standard amounts with the structure of civil rights legislation. Recall that the Civil Rights Act of 1964 was intended to provide enforcement mechanisms to ensure compliance with rights established just after the Civil War. In particular, Title VI ensures that the federal government will not fund violations of the Equal Protection Clause and its immediate statutory antecedent, the Civil Rights Act of 1866. What is most interesting about these provisions is that neither one of them mentions race, color, religion, or national origin. It is famously difficult to discern the categories to which the Equal Protection Clause applies because it was written in such abstract language. It does not even mention "race," although we know that it was intended to apply to race.

It is also fascinatingly difficult to discern the groups to which the Civil Rights Act of 1866 applies. Nevertheless, the question is especially important. After all, it was in the 1866 Act that Congress established the rights that were later enforced both through the Equal Protection Clause and then, indirectly, through twentieth-century legislation such as the Civil Rights Act of 1964. Earlier, we saw how the Supreme Court has addressed the meaning of "race" within that statute in the *St. Francis* and *Shaare Tefila* cases. Strangely, however, the word "race" does not actually appear in that statute. Rather, the Court inferred that Congress *must have been* referring to race and then struggled to determine what it meant by that term.[14] This is like arguing about what is meant by the name of "G-d" in the biblical Book of Esther, which famously does not include it.

What, then, did Congress protect in its most important Reconstructionist Era legislation if it did not explicitly speak of "race"? Section 1981, deriving in pertinent par from the 1866 Act, provides everyone in the United States the same rights to contract, property, and participation in litigation "as is enjoyed by white citizens."[15] Its coverage, then, extends to all persons who are denied the privileges of white citizens. To say that this provision bans racial discrimination is not incorrect, but

---

[14] Runyon v. McCrary, 427 U.S. 160, 168 (1976).
[15] 42 U.S.C. § 1981 (2000).

it may understate the scope of coverage. As the Court observed in *St. Francis*, Congress clearly intended for the 1866 Act to coverage a host of ethnic groups that are now generally considered "white": not only Arabs and Jews but also Scandinavians, Roma, and even Germans.[16] In fact, the 1866 Act carves out a protected class that is both more flexible and more sophisticated than the discredited notion of "race." That class consists of people who are denied, in any given exchange, the privileges of whiteness. The key attribute is, in other words, "nonwhiteness."

The overriding priority of Congress, of course, was appropriately to restore the rights and privileges of African Americans. The 1866 Act does more, however, protecting the rights of other groups, including European ethnic groups, that have in some circumstances been denied rights or privileges that are extended to others. Significantly, the groups discussed in the legislative debates include racial, ethnic, national, and religious groups. The proper lesson to draw from this is that the boundaries between race, ethnicity, nationality, and religion are not material to the determination of coverage. The important question is whether an individual has been denied, on the basis of group identity, any significant form of social privilege. If so, then the individual has experienced precisely the form of "nonwhiteness" required to establish coverage under the act.

In cases such as *Irvine*, are Jewish-American college students denied the requisite forms of social privilege as a result of the harassment that Susan Tuchman so ably alleged? Have they, in the nineteenth-century congressional argot, been denied the privileges of white citizenship? The answer is yes, at least for some Jewish students, such as those who were forced to withdraw from the university or to apply to other universities or to avoid certain campus locations or activities because they otherwise would be subjected to objectively offensive behavior. The answer is also yes for students who chose to "cover" their Jewish identity, refraining from Jewishly identifiable clothing, jewelry, language, or political activity for fear of adverse repercussions in an environment that had become starkly uncongenial to those who define their identity in certain Jewishly defined ways.

THE ZEIDMAN CASE

The *Irvine* case continues to shape discussions and perceptions of campus anti-Semitism. The events there have had enormous impact on many of

---

[16]   St. Francis College, 481 U.S., at 612–3.

the students. Surprisingly, the person who has most vehemently decried anti-Semitism in that case is the man who was charged with investigating it: OCR Regional Director Arthur Zeidman. Zeidman believes, moreover, that a defining feature of that case was deeply entrenched anti-Semitism not only at Irvine but at OCR. In a shocking formal complaint, which has not been reported previously, Zeidman charges that the agency responsible for protecting students from bigotry is guilty of the very evil that it was established to combat. Moreover, he accuses OCR of managing the *Irvine* case in a manner that was colored by precisely the sort of anti-Semitic stereotypes that he found had occurred on that campus.

Zeidman has sued the Department of Education for employment discrimination, arguing that he was adversely treated *as a Jew* because of the manner in which he attempted to pursue the case. This is an extraordinary claim coming from the head of an OCR regional office. Although he has handled countless complaints in his career, Zeidman never himself filed a grievance against anyone, an employer or anyone else, prior to his experience.[17] Yet he contends in his case against OCR that "as a Jewish employee, pursuing an investigation on anti-Semitism, pursuant to Administration policy and with the specific guidance of Mr. Black's predecessor, Mr. Black subjected him to harassment, humiliation, and criticism."[18] Zeidman argues that Black criticized all Jewish personnel associated with the *Irvine* case while praising the non-Jewish staff.[19] As a result of his efforts to enforce the Title VI rights of Irvine's Jewish students, Zeidman says, "I have been berated, humiliated (both before superiors, colleagues and even my subordinates), disciplined and isolated."[20]

The senior OCR officials who worked most closely on the *Irvine* case can imagine no better explanation for OCR's handling of this case other than anti-Semitism within the agency itself (an accusation that Black understandably denies).[21] OCR Regional Counsel Paul Grossman levels the charge directly, testifying that OCR's erratic handling of the case appears to result from precisely the bias that it is responsible for eradicating:

> How does one explain these illogical events? They are explained by the fact that Mr. Zeidman is a Jew. As a Jew, based on stereotype, it was

[17] Deposition of Arthur Zeidman, February 19, 2009, at 31.
[18] EEO Complaint, Zeidman v. Spellings, Complaint No. ED-2008–03-00, at 5.
[19] *Id.*, at 4.
[20] Arthur C. Zeidman, Narrative Attachment to Amended (11/03/07) EEO Complaint, at 1.
[21] Declaration of David F. Black, March 31, 2008, 13, at 4–5.

assumed he was Mr. Marcus's "man" and would use passive aggression to maintain Mr. Marcus's agenda. Based on religious stereotype, it was assumed that Mr. Zeidman would not take clear direct orders to interpret the "dear colleague" letter narrowly. Based on a religious stereotype, it was assumed that Mr. Zeidman (and I) would not reach a fair, balanced, and objective conclusion to the Irvine matter. He was not to be trusted because he is a Jew.... Rather than acknowledge that much that displeased Mr. Black was merely the residue of prior directives, Mr. Zeidman was held accountable as if he, as a Jew, had a hidden agenda that motivated him to disrespect the guidance of Mr. Black.[22]

Grossman concludes that "the most likely reason" for Zeidman's troubles with his Washington superiors "is that Mr. Zeidman is Jewish."[23] Indeed, Grossman believes that Black's determination to displace San Francisco's Jewish leadership with four gentile attorneys from other offices was based on distrust for Jewish legal work on this issue. As Grossman concluded, "I think the reason that he brought in the other people is that he did not trust me and he did not trust Mr. Zeidman, and I think the reason he did not trust us is because he felt that somehow as Jews, we were too close to the issue."[24]

Love drew a similar conclusion, although his reasoning was somewhat different. Significantly, Love has no apparent incentive that would bias his testimony. Black had praised Love's work, confided in him, and apparently wanted to make him the most senior OCR official in San Francisco by removing Zeidman. For Love, Zeidman's Jewishness (and mine) was always "the 500 pound gorilla in the room."[25] The problem in his mind is that my successors among OCR's senior leadership were distrustful of an investigation that, in their mind, had become too closely associated with Jewish OCR officials: "The Dear Colleague letter was issued by a Jewish person. At the time, the Enforcement Director, Sue Bowers, was a Jewish person. The Office that accepted and investigated the first complaint filed by a Jewish organization was headed by a Jewish person."[26]

Black acknowledges that he was conscious of the fact that *Irvine* was being handled by a Jewish man, but he claims that his view of this was favorable – that Zeidman had been able to suppress his personal beliefs

[22] Affidavit of Paul Grossman, February 20, 2008, at 11.
[23] *Id.*, at 12.
[24] Deposition of Paul D. Grossman, March 13, 2009, at 63.
[25] Affidavit of Charles R. Love, February 28, 2008, at 9.
[26] *Id.*, at 7.

and to handle the case in an unbiased manner.[27] Black has defenders within the agency. For example, OCR's long-time Seattle director, Gary Jackson, who worked closely with both Zeidman and Black, swears that "I seriously doubt that religion was a factor."[28] Nevertheless, Love is emphatic on this point: He has testified that anyone who denies that Zeidman's Jewishness was a factor in the manner in which headquarters treated him "was lying."[29] This is an extraordinary accusation for a senior OCR official to make, especially since it appears to implicate Jackson, a man who is senior to him in OCR's Western Division career hierarchy.

The irony that Grossman finds in Zeidman's travails is not just the belief that bigotry is driving decision making by an agency that was formed to combat that very evil. Rather, Grossman insists, "The great irony of all this is that like Mr. Black, Mr. Zeidman comes from a military background."[30] "In my 36 years as an OCR employee, I have never met a Regional Director with a stronger desire to please his boss and carry out orders. Had these stereotypes not existed, Mr. Black could have had any legally supportable outcome he desired ... in *Irvine*."[31]

The deeper irony for both Stephanie Monroe and David Black is, if any of their regional staff's perceptions are correct, that they have achieved precisely the opposite of their goal. In trying to undermine OCR's policy without leaving "fingerprints," they instead left the equivalence of hard DNA evidence. First, by failing to provide clear directives to career staff, they put themselves in the position of receiving a proposed final resolution that was opposite of the direction in which they wanted to go. This forced them to overrule the career investigators' "final" decision and to order a resolution that was inconsistent with the investigation the regional staff had undertaken. Next, by delaying the case resolution to avoid public censure at a time when they thought that things were too hot, they created an additional source of congressional displeasure: the delay itself. Worse, by failing to give clear directives to career staff and then leaving regional staff (in their view) to "twist in the wind," Monroe and Black only managed to infuriate what would otherwise have been loyal subordinates. Indeed, Black managed to get himself sued. The result is a formal public record containing the sworn testimony

[27] Deposition of David Black, February 17, 2009, at 116.
[28] Affidavit of Gary Jackson, February 8, 2008, at 3.
[29] Affidavit of Charles R. Love, February 28, 2008, at 6–7.
[30] Affidavit of Paul Grossman, February 20, 2008, at 11.
[31] *Id.*

of agency officials who described precisely the conduct that they believe he wanted kept quiet. Without that record, the story of OCR's internal machinations might never have come to light.

Whatever one's view of Monroe and Black's substantive disposition of the *Irvine* case, it is hard to deny that they badly mismanaged it, producing unnecessary delays, internal dissension, staff demoralization, employment complaints, congressional displeasure, a poorly crafted final product, and policy confusion so great that OCR's own officials cannot seem to agree on what their policy is. This is, moreover, the strongest argument that can be made in their defense. When an erratic pattern of behavior can be described in terms of either plain incompetence or invidious discrimination, the safer and more generous course (absent the sort of evidence that only a full trial would provide) may be to assume that the former rather than the latter was at work. This assumption is bolstered when a project has unquestionably been mismanaged and where the only question is whether that mismanagement alone was sufficient to describe the associated problems. As this book was going to press, Zeidman lost his employment discrimination case and indicated that he is, for a variety of reasons, unlikely to appeal. Regardless of that resolution, however, the fact that San Francisco's top three OCR officials believe that headquarters was motivated by anti-Semitic animus in its handling of the *Irvine* case speaks volumes about OCR's continuing inability to handle allegations of anti-Semitism.

THE ROAD FORWARD

What can be done to rectify this problem? As an initial matter, the Institute for Jewish & Community Research and the Zionist Organization of America are now working to advance Title VI reform at the Education Department and in Congress. Recently, representatives of a number of major organizations, including the Anti-Defamation League, the American Jewish Committee, and Scholars for Peace in the Middle East, have joined this effort. For the short term, the goal is to convince the Department of Education to return to the 2004 OCR policy. This could be easy for the Obama administration to do and would not require congressional approval. On the other hand, the challenge facing Title VI reform was made clear recently. Eric Fingerhut, a reporter at the Jewish Telegraphic Agency, unearthed a letter from my successor in the Obama administration, Russlynn Ali, that appears to indicate that she plans to continue the policy of Stephanie Monroe. This would be a grave mistake that would leave Jewish students bereft of civil rights protections. This development underscores the need for interested citizens to advocate for change at the Education Department.

Over the longer term, the solution to this problem lies with Congress. Even if OCR were to firmly and finally establish Title VI protections for Jewish students, those protections necessarily would be limited to the scope provided in the Civil Rights Act. Since that statute does not cover religious discrimination, there are some forms of hate and bias that OCR will not be able to address absent further legislation. Only Congress can protect all students from religious discrimination in American educational institutions. The solution would be a Religious Freedom in Education Act, which would bar religious discrimination in educational programs and activities that receive federal financial assistance. This is a complex subject because it affects the rights and obligations of a wide group of people. Its advantages and disadvantages exceed the parameters of this book. They do merit further thought at a later date, however, because combating religious discrimination in schools and colleges may be the next important battle in the fight to ensure equal opportunity for all.

POSTSCRIPT

As this book was going to press, Russlym Ali and other Obama administration officials entered into the dialogue which several Jewish organizations (and this author) had invited over Title VI reform. While the outcome remains uncertain, it is a hopeful sign that they are now reconsidering the disastrous policy which had been applied in *Irvine*. In an interview with *The Chronicle of Higher Education*, Assistant Secretary Ali commented, "I lose sleep over this one." As well she should.

Index

Abrams, Kathryn, 180
Abromovich, Aaron, 165
Academic freedom, 7, 11, 19, 51, 71, 72,
    74, 78
Accrediting agencies, 9
Ad Hoc Committee to Defend the
    University, 72, 73, 74
Adorno, Theodor, 51
African Americans, 3, 7, 8, 11,
    102, 109, 139, 142, 144, 145, 146,
    176, 179, 198
Agism, 7, 9
Ahmadinajad, Mahmoud, 165
Air Force Academy, 55
Albright, Madeleine, 132, 147
Ali, Amir Abdul Malik, 18, 19
Ali, Russlynn, 202
Ali, Tariq, 72
Allott, Gordon, 106
All-Party Parliamentary Group against
    Anti-Semitism, 57, 58, 59
Allport, Gordon, 62
American Association of Physical
    Anthropologists, 14
American Jewish Committee, 48, 73,
    100, 202
Americans with Disabilities Act, 36
Ancestral discrimination, 82, 104
Anti-Americanism, 50, 57
Anti-Defamation League, 39, 41, 42, 48,
    101, 202
Antifascism, 57
Anti-Westernism, 50
Arabs, 7, 26, 27, 30, 31, 34, 39, 54, 57,
    62, 68, 88, 100, 104, 105, 108, 115,
    140, 162, 164, 165, 198

Arendt, Hannah, 66
Ashkenazic Jews, 121–125, 129, 139–141,
    143, 144, 189, 195
Atlantic Cape Community College, 80
Ayudaya, 135
Azoulay, Katya Gibel, 124, 140, 146

Baldwin, James, 144, 145
Bar On, Bat-Ami, 95, 144, 146
Baruch College, 34, 188
Basques, 192
Bayfield, Tony, 118
Bedouins, 112
Ben Gurion, David, 11
Bene Israel, 121
Beta Israel, 135, 138
Bin Laden, Obama, 26
Bingham, Henry H., 107
Black, David, 84–93, 95, 140, 142,
    199–203
Blackmun, Harry, 158
Blanchard, Timothy, 91
Blood libel, 18, 19, 38, 53, 61, 64
Blumenbach, Johann Friederich, 140, 143
Book of Esther (biblical), 197
Bowers, Susan, 200
Boy Scouts of America, 7, 9
Braceras, Jennifer, 36, 46, 48
Brandenburg v. Ohio, 79
Breast cancer, 120
Brenda Hale, Baroness Hale of
    Richmond, 28
Brinkley, Alan, 40
Brodkin, Karen, 147
Brown v. Board of Education, 176,
    177

University of Illinois at Champaign-
  Urbana, 76
University of Oregon, 80
U.S. Commission on Civil Rights, 5, 6,
  10, 36, 37, 38, 40, 42, 44, 45,
  48, 75, 85, 86, 90, 96

Voting Rights Act, 36

Wagner, Richard, 119
Walt, Stephen, 73
Weinberg, Aryeh, 41
White House, 35
White Supremacy, 178
Wieviorka, Michel, 162
Wigmore, John, 116, 117
Wilkinson, J. Harvey, 155, 157, 159, 160
Wills, Randolph, 91, 92

Wing, Jennifer P., 24, 25, 116
Wisse, Ruth, 181
Wistrich, Robert, 59

Yale University, 42, 72, 165
Yankel Rosenbaum, 3, 101
Y-chromosome, 121, 122
Young-Bruehl, Elizabeth, 108

Zeidman, Arthur, 20–21, 83–95,
  199–203
Zionist Organization of America, 17, 48,
  81, 82, 87, 94, 202
Žižek, Slovaj, 174
ZOA. *See* Zionist Organization of
  America
Zoloth, Laurie, 37, 133, 134,
  142

For EU product safety concerns, contact us at Calle de José Abascal, 56–1°,
28003 Madrid, Spain or eugpsr@cambridge.org.

www.ingramcontent.com/pod-product-compliance
Ingram Content Group UK Ltd.
Pitfield, Milton Keynes, MK11 3LW, UK
UKHW020327140625
459647UK00018B/2054